Sea Stories

The "Tin Can" Navy from Korea to the Cold War

Archie T. Miller

ATM Consulting

SEA STORIES - THE "TIN CAN" NAVY FROM KOREA TO THE COLD WAR
by Archie T. Miller

Front Cover - **U.S.S Wren DD-568 in Korean Waters** - *US Navy Photo*

ISBN-13: 978-1466377707

ISBN-10: 1466377704

Roger Reid

This book is dedicated to the memory of Roger H. Reid.   Roger and I were best friends during our high school and college years.   Roger was an open and friendly guy with a great sense of humor and a warm smile.   We lived within a few blocks of one another in Fairlington in Arlington, Virginia.   We often double-dated.   We were both Captains in the Jr. ROTC at Washington and Lee High School.   We both joined the Navy.   On September 4, 1954 Roger was flying in a P2V-5 Neptune Patrol Bomber of Patrol Squadron 19 out of the Naval Air Station Atsugi, Japan.   In international airspace 40 miles off the coast of Siberia two Soviet Mig-15 fighters attacked and shot down the P2V. With the end of a wing shot off and burning, the pilot successfully ditched the bomber in the sea.   Roger was inside the plane trying to get life rafts for the rest of the crew, who were out on the wing, when the plane sank.   He was the only one of the crew of 10 that was lost.

Acknowledgements

I first started writing this in 1993 after I retired from GE American Communications. Over the next 9 years I worked on it in fits and starts. I was doing consulting work after retiring and we lived in Hong Kong and Beijing. I kept a copy of this book in my Apple Powerbook and continued to write wherever we were. The main source for the book was my own memory reinforced by many photos I took while in the navy and much research on the Internet. I also took every opportunity I could to talk to Navy veterans of the Korean War

My wife Catherine provided a critical eye throughout the project and helped me keep the perspective of the reader. Catherine died at Christmas 2004.

Gordon Hipp graciously made me a copy of a diary that he kept during Wrens' world cruise. It was an enormous help not only for the information it contained but also for establishing dates for various events.

Long conversations with Wren sonarmen Al Dodge and Ed McDonald at the Wren reunion in Charleston filled in lots of gaps in many tales. George Cromer who was on the bridge the night of our near-collision with the Korean frigate provided details of that incident. Les Berry provided the boiler/engine room details of the "By A Thread" incident. Charles Arnason provided details for "Grand Theft At Sea".

I am indebted to Gordon Hipp, Al Dodge, Carroll Powell and Sten Taube for photographs.

The U.S.S. Wren Association was an absolutely invaluable aid to this project. The ship reunions provided an opportunity to yarn with old shipmates and fill in details of days long ago. All of us Wrens owe a great debt of gratitude to Jim and Jean Warner who have been the moving force behind the association and its newsletter "Bird Call". Bird Call has been a terrific source for individual reminiscences, photos and other information.

The staff of the Dorothy Henry Branch of the Sussex County Library were a great deal of help in retrieving data from their New York Times microfilm archives.

The staff of the National Archives II in College Park, Maryland was most helpful in enabling me to review the original 1953 and 1954 paper deck logs of USS Wren (DD-568).

The staffs of the Norfolk Virginia Pilot and the National Archives II Photographic Branch were most helpful in an unfortunately fruitless search for photos of Lind and English after their collision. Subsequent to the original limited publication Sten Taube came up with snapshots he had taken at the time.

The staff of the Key West Citizen and the Monroe County Library were very helpful in providing contemporaneous accounts of the SS Alfhem's unplanned visit to Key West.

Over the years I did a lot of reading for background on the people, events and ships that affected the times covered in this book. Particularly helpful were:

Alexander, James Edwin *Inchon to Wonsan.* Annapolis: U.S. Naval Institute Press
Blackman, Raymond V. B. *Janes Fighting Ships 1953-54.* New York:
        McGraw-Hill Book Company Inc.
Bonner, Kit and Carolyn *Cold War at Sea* Osceola, WI MBI Publishing
Butler, John A. *Strike Able Peter – The Stranding and Salvage of the U.S.S. Missouri.*
        Annapolis: U.S. Naval Institute Press
Cagle, Malcolm. *The Sea War In Korea.* Annapolis: U.S. Naval Institute Press
Catchpole, Brian *The Korean War.* New York: Carrol and Graf Publishers, Inc.
Field, James A. Jr. *A History of United States Naval Operations: Korea* Naval
        Historical Center
Halberstam, David *The Fifties.* Random House Inc.
Lehman, John *On Seas of Glory* New York The Free Press
Milford, Frederick J., *U.S. Navy Torpedoes.* The Submarine Review, January 1997.
Raven, Alan *Fletcher Class Destroyers.* Annapolis: U.S. Naval Institute Press
Reilly, Robin L. *Mighty Midgets At War.* Hellgate Press
Schlesinger, Stephen and Kinzer, Stephen, *Bitter Fruit.* Cambridge
        Harvard University Press
Srodes, James. *Allen Dulles, Master of Spies.* Washington,:Regnery Publishing Inc.

This book was written almost 60 years after the events described actually occurred. Some of the stories may have lost accuracy in the telling and retelling that is a characteristic of all old sailors' tales. The naturally decaying processes of recall and memory that affect us all as we move in time away from even the most important events of our lives also affect them. Although I tried to use other reference sources to confirm events, errors may have occurred. Be assured this narrative is as accurate as I could make it and if I misrepresented any events or individuals roles in them, I apologize. Prior to the CreateSpace publication in 2011, I reviewed the entire book and updated some sections and added some newly acquired photos.

Archie T. Miller

Manchester, NJ

Table of Contents

The author as a young man.
Sasebo, Japan December 1953

"Destroyer men have always been proud people. They have been the elite. They have to be proud people and they have to be specially selected, for destroyer life is a rugged one. It takes physical stamina to stand up under the rigors of a tossing DD. It takes even more spiritual stamina to keep going with enthusiasm when you are tired and feel that you and your ship are being used as a workhorse. It is true that many people take destroyers for granted and that is all the more reason why destroyer men can be proud of their accomplishments."

Admiral Arleigh A. Burke

"Men mean more than guns in the rating of a ship"

John Paul Jones

The Best Stanchion Welders In The Navy

The World War II, Fletcher class destroyer plunged gracefully through the long swells as she proceeded westward across a sun splattered ocean. The U.S.S Wren, DD-568, was returning to Norfolk, Virginia on a Friday afternoon in the fall of 1954. She had spent the week at sea engaged in training exercises in the Virginia Capes Operating Area. The crew often referred to these out-on-Monday, back-on-Friday operations as "Chesapeake Raider". A lookout on the flying bridge called landfall on the tower of the Cavalier Hotel in Virginia Beach. The old and slightly dowdy hotel is the first sight of a friendly shore for those homeward-bound for Tidewater Virginia. Wren passed through the gateway of Cape Charles on the north and Cape Henry on the south and on into Chesapeake Bay. Wren joined the usual Friday afternoon single file parade of gray navy ships in Thimble Shoals Channel returning to Norfolk for the weekend. Wren was the last of the four destroyers in Destroyer Division 61 headed for Naval Operating Base, Norfolk. Noa was immediately ahead of Wren with Stribling ahead of her and Cone in the lead.

U.S.S. Wren (DD-568) returning to port in Norfolk, 1954 (US Navy Photo).

I was standing on the starboard wing of the bridge observing Noa directly ahead of us in the line. My Special Sea Detail Station was to spot speed signals from the ship in front of us. There was a ripple of colored flags on Noa's yardarm. "Noa now showing 10 knots." I called out. "10 knots aye" the OD answered. Almost immediately I could hear the engine order bells as we slowed to 10 knots. I liked standing watches on the bridge. You not only see everything that was going but also hear the officer's discussions and the radio traffic. The only disadvantage was that my job required me to be on the open bridge no matter what the weather.

Shortly after joining the queue, we did a bit of line jumping. Captain Johnson told Mr. Davis, the OD, "The division is going outside the channel… follow Noa". Because destroyers drew less then 15 feet of water we could go into the shallower water north of the 40 foot deep ship channel and pass the long single file line of deep hulled capital ships. The Old Man was a real liberty hound and he was hot to get back to Norfolk. We had all noticed in the past that as soon as the ship was tied up we would hear "Wren departing" over the 1MC PA and the captain was gone. I never saw Mrs. Johnson but I always figured she must have been quite a woman. This Friday as usual we swung north of the Thimble Shoals Channel. There was another ripple of flags on Noa's yardarm. . "Noa now showing 15 knots." I called out. "15 knots aye" the OD answered. With a jangle of bells on the engine order telegraph we accelerated and started passing the line to head for CE Piers.

Every time we steamed into Hampton Roads outside the marked channel, I was reminded of the predicament of the U.S.S Missouri in these same waters. On January 17, 1950 the 45,000-ton battleship Missouri was outside of the marked channel heading for an acoustic test range near the Thimble Shoals Light. It was in the same north side area that we used to pass the larger ships in the channel when it ran hard aground. The battlewagon slid on to the sandy bottom at 15 knots and at high tide about 1.7 miles off Old Point Comfort. It plowed 1500 yards through the sand and was so hard aground when it stopped that its waterline was 7 feet above water. All initial efforts to get it off were unsuccessful. Eventually, 12,000 tons of fuel, ammunition, anchors, food and water were removed and eight submarine salvage pontoons were used to lift it. A new channel was dredged around the ship and out to deep water. Even so, it took 14 tugs, two salvage ships and a very high tide to get it off. The captain, navigator and operations officer were tried at general courts martial and found guilty. The moral to that story is that 2100-ton destroyers can get away with line jumping outside the channel – 45,000-ton battleships can't.

Wren came to the left as we passed Thimble Shoals Light and slowed as we went through the antisubmarine nets at Fort Wool. We proceeded past Sewalls Point and into the Elizabeth River off of the Naval Base. As we maneuvered a little left to avoid the Newport News ferry I started thinking about weekend liberty. At the rate we were going we would probably be secured from Sea Detail by 3 PM and with a little luck Everly and I could be on the road by 4. Everly was a radarman, who lived in Alexandria, Virginia only a few miles from my home in Arlington. He had a 1941 Ford that he had "souped up" and we always had a fast trip home. A little cloud of concern about his driving flashed through my mind but I quickly dismissed it. I probably would not have dismissed it as lightly if I had known that Everly would die in the wreckage of his Ford in less than two years.

The 376-foot, ship was now in a slow left turn in toward Pier 21 at the Convoy Escort Piers. These piers were added to the naval base during World War II to berth the destroyers escorting Atlantic convoys to Europe. The other three ships in Destroyer Division 61, Cone, Stribling and Noa were already tied up in a nest of three alongside the pier. Wren was assigned to tie up starboard side to Noa. A yellow signal flag with a black ball in its center (Item) was hoisted close up on Wren's starboard yardarm and Noa's port yardarm. This indicated that both ships agreed that Wren would moor her starboard side to Noa's port. Both ships had heavy manila fenders hanging over the side to cushion the expected gentle contact between the ships. The deck force on both ships was standing by to handle mooring lines.

On the Wren's bridge, Lt.(jg) Davis had the conn. A Navy Yard Tug (YTB) was standing by off Wren's port quarter ready to assist if required. Mr. Davis gave a series of rudder and engine commands to the helmsmen to bring the ship roughly parallel to Noa. At this slow speed, Wren did not have much steerageway and was responding rather sluggishly to rudder. As we approached Noa it became apparent that we were pointed more toward the other ship and going a little faster then was desirable. Captain Johnson shifted nervously from foot to foot and finally suggested to Davis that he might want to reverse the port engine to slow our approach and try to swing Wren more parallel to Noa. Although we slowed some, it was apparent that our bow, and not the soft fenders, was going to contact Noa first. The tug was summoned to try to push our stern over but it was too late. I put out a hand to steady myself waiting for the bump when we hit.

Destroyers have lifeline stanchions made of two-inch pipe at about six foot intervals around the main deck. These three and half-foot tall stanchions supported the top, middle and lower steel lifeline cables. As Wren approached Noa the tip of Wren's anchor hit one of Noa's lifeline stanchions rather gently. "PING" went the stanchion as it was torn from the deck. As Wren proceeded forward there was a series of PINGS as stanchions flew loose from the deck and lifelines collapsed. Line handlers on Noa's foc'sle backed across the deck away from the path of destruction. Davis ordered "Port Back Full". Down on Wren's main deck, Lt.(jg) George Cromer, whose men would have to repair the damage, was surveying the mess. The look on his face conveyed not so much his distaste of the task at hand as much as the prospect of having to deal with Noa's Repair Officer, a feisty young Annapolis grad named E. Ross Perot. As you probably recall, Mr. Perot more recently became famous for his feisty approach to national politics and everything else.

On the bridge, Captain Johnson's mouth was in a tight straight line and he avoided looking at Noa's captain who was right at eye level on the port wing of his bridge. The captain of the Noa was getting red from the neck up as his lifelines came cascading down. Davis ordered "All Stop". Finally as Wren stopped moving and the mooring lines went over, Johnson looked at the captain of the Noa and yelled, "Our welders will be over as soon as we get doubled up". So they were. Noa's lifelines were restored to some semblance of their previous state in short order. The Wrens chipped off the old welds, straightened and replaced pipe, welded on new clips and welded each to the deck with a coat of zinc chromate paint to finish. The reason for this expeditious repair was that our welders got a lot of practice. In a perverse sort of pride we would proclaim that Wren had "the best stanchion welders in the Navy."

I always figured that the facility of the stanchion welders was a reciprocal function of the skill of Wren's shiphandlers. I don't suppose our shiphandlers were that much worse than those in most other ships of that time but they certainly weren't any better. In their defense, it must be said that handling a one of these destroyers is a little like driving a Camaro in the snow -- its all engine and the back slides around a lot. The executive officer, Lcdr. Baker, was probably one of the better ship handlers of the officers qualified as OD's. He had been an enlisted pilot in World War II, was later commissioned and then grounded when his eyes went bad. He seemed to be able to picture the whole evolution and knew what to do to get it accomplished. Most of the junior officers were very inexperienced, very nervous and had a hard time getting the pointy end of the ship in the right place. Most of the time, as long as the approach was simple, with little or no wind or current, they did OK. Other then that -- watch out!

We didn't always knock down other ships stanchions. Very often we knocked down our own. On a really big arrival we could knock them down on two ships -- theirs and ours. "Away the stanchion welders, away." Coming alongside the smooth side of a large ship such as a destroyer tender you would guess that the stanchion welders could stand easy. Guess again. Along the high smooth side of the destroyer tender Grand Canyon there was only one major protuberance, the curved steel attachment point for the boat boom. We found it. Ping, ping, ping went the stanchions.

Actually, the captain wasn't a bad ship handler but his caution often got him in trouble. He would be super careful in making an approach when a little boldness was called for. He had gotten his own share of stanchions. When forced by circumstances to act quickly and decisively, he did very well. When the Suez Canal pilot cast off from the buoys at the Port Said fueling station and then got us going sideward toward the shore was one of those times. As he exclaimed "What is this son of a bitch doing to me?" Captain

Johnson took the conn and skillfully threaded the Wren between the buoys and back out into the channel to the Mediterranean.

All of the Wren ship handlers spoke in awe of the British pilot that came aboard to moor us between buoys in Colombo, Ceylon (now Sri Lanka). Colombo was a very small, crowded harbor with ships moored to buoys bow to stern in long lines. The pilot resplendent in his white shorts, shirt, high socks, shoes and hat, and undoubtedly retired from the Royal Navy, took the conn and snappily made a 180 degree turn in the turning basin. Then he backed down between the lines of ships like a parking lot attendant and dropped us dead in the water right between the two buoys. All we had to do was drop the lines over. There were a lot of jaws hanging open on the bridge. Although all of Wren's OD's could dream of attaining that level of skill, it just wasn't in the cards. They wouldn't be around long enough. In February 1954, when Wren was completing a tour of very intensive operations in Korea, the average experience in destroyer type ships of the Wren's officers (excluding the captain and exec) was 9.9 months. The Wren officers assigned a prime responsibility such as Operations Officer, Gunnery Officer etc. had been in that position on an average of only 3.8 months. Most were fulfilling a reserve commitment and would shortly return to civilian life.

That was true for most of us. Very few of us planned a Navy career. It was a great tribute to the Navy training methods that we did our jobs quite well but would never get to the level of experience and skill as some of our "lifer" shipmates. But that was OK. We were, by and large, "citizen sailors". Our country was in trouble and we volunteered. Most of us had joined up during the winter of 1950/51 at a rather desperate point in the Korean War. The Chinese had just entered the War and the UN forces were being driven south in retreat down the Korean peninsula. The demands of the sea war in Korea required large numbers of sailors to man all of the ships, such as Wren, being refitted and recommissioned. From 1950 to 1953 the navy jumped from 137 destroyers to 247 destroyers. On June 25, 1950 when North Korea invaded South Korea, U.S.S Wren (DD-568) was lying in mothballs, encased in plastic and cosmoline in the Reserve Fleet up the Cooper River near Charleston, SC. After a distinguished WW-II combat record in the

Pacific, she was decommisioned in 1946 to wait her country's need again. Four short years later she was needed and the navy needed men to man her. We joined the Navy, went to boot camp and some of us went directly to places like Charleston to take these much needed ships out of mothballs. Others went to school from boot camp and then to a ship. Some like myself went to school after boot camp and then to shore duty before reporting to a ship. The Korean War and naval service was a major perturbation in our young lives. Most of us had volunteered for four years. And most of us got out of the navy after those four years and resumed our civilian lives. But our lives would never be quite the same.

Almost without exception, however, we would not have traded that experience for anything in the world. I feel that I was particularly fortunate in having had such a variety of experiences. I rode many different ship types while in Sonar School and I worked with divers and torpedo operations at Piney Point Naval Torpedo Test Range. In Wren, I not only worked in sonar but also had the opportunity to stand Radar watches in CIC and Quartermaster watches on the bridge. Most of the time I was in Wren I stood my Special Sea Detail (in and out of port) watches on the bridge where I got to see everything that was going on.

The discipline, responsibility, danger, travel and camaraderie of those four years forever changed our lives. Habits learned in that experience are carried with us to this day. There is a unique sense of community and belonging among the crew of a small hard riding ship such as Wren. It meant a hell of a lot more then just standing with your shipmates when the bar brawl starts. It was the sense that we all very much depended on one another. If any of us didn't do our job, it affected all of us. If one person made a mistake, some of us could die. As Shakespeare put it so well "We few, we happy few, we band of brothers". We also had a deep sense of pride in the shared experience and tradition with all of those who have gone to sea in men-of-war over the ages. In Wren we lived in many traditions built over hundreds of years by others who took ships to sea to go "in harms way". We awoke in the morning to the call of the same bosun's pipe and the cry "heave out and trice up" heard by John Paul Jones crew in Bon Homme Richard,

Nelson's crew in Victory on the morning off Cape Trafalagar and the crews of Admiral Oldendorfs line of battleships approaching Surigao Strait.

"Real sailors don't wear zipper pants." The author in his "flat-hat", tailored jumper and bell-bottom, 13-button pants on the French Riviera. (A.T. Miller Photo)

We took pride in looking like sailors too. When most of us were in boot camp, we were issued dress blue uniforms with the traditional tight, 13-button, one-pocket pants. Shortly thereafter, the navy switched to loose fitting, zipper-front pants with big pockets. Most of us treasured the old pants and if we needed new ones we searched all over to find a Small Stores that still had them. We were proud of what we did and wanted to look like salty sailors not "blue soldiers".

We shared not only the appearance but also the experience of sailors from nations around the world. I have often thought that the commonality of that experience was shown in a brief encounter of Wrens in Colombo, Ceylon.

Colombo in the spring of 1954 was a third world city. Despite many years of British colonial rule, many of the streets were nothing more then dirt roads replete with water buffalo and an occasional elephant. It didn't look like a great liberty port to us. A taxi driver suggested to us that we might enjoy the Mount Lavinia Hotel[1] on the outskirts of Colombo. This resort hotel had been built by the British during their colonial rule and was a very nice place indeed.

The Mount Lavinia Hotel Colombo, Ceylon. The meeting of Wrens occurred on the patio at the left side of the hotel behind palm trees. (Postcard)

A group of us Wrens sat out on a beautiful palm shaded patio overlooking the Indian Ocean drinking cool beverages. We had noticed some British sailors there but hadn't paid them much attention. Another sonarman, Kinlock, said "The Limey's hats say Wren on them". On closer inspection we found he was right. Inviting some of them to join us we found out that they were from H.M.S Wren. H.M.S Wren was a 300-foot Black Swan class destroyer carrying six 4.2-inch guns. H.M.S Wren was named after the bird while U.S.S. Wren was named after a marine sergeant who had distinguished himself in Tripoli battling the Barbary pirates. Having decided that we Wrens had much in common, we had a grand time. Toasts started with the queen and went from there. The combination of many toasts under the broiling tropical sun exacted its toll, however. Indeed we had such a good time that most of us were delivered back to U.S.S. Wren in the Royal Air Force paddy wagon.

---

[1] In the movie "Bridge On The River Kwai" William Holden is sent to the "Mount Lavinia Hospital". Those parts of the movie were made at the Mount Lavinia Hotel a couple of years after our visit.

HMS Wren. Besides the same names, we Wrens discovered that we also shared common missions. (Royal Navy Photo)

Although we didn't know it at the time, both of the Wrens were on almost identical missions for two different countries. H.M.S Wren had just come out of the Persian Gulf for a bit of R & R in Colombo. She was the British station ship in the gulf. Her primary mission was to insure that the government of Iran understood that Her Majesty's Navy was looking out for the interests of British Petroleum Ltd. A few days later when U.S.S Wren left Colombo, we went 2000 miles out of our way home to go into the Persian Gulf to Ras-Tanura in Saudi Arabia. The purpose of that expedition was to insure that the king and the princes of Saudi Arabia understood that the U.S Navy was looking out for the interests of the Arabian-American Oil Company. It's a small world after all.

We all treasure the experiences we had. They were funny, scary, awe inspiring, sobering and exciting. We still talk about them. There are some of these stories that we repeat again and again after almost fifty years. Sea stories. The stories have become as much a part of our life as were the original experiences. There is an old sailor's joke that goes "What's the difference between a fairy tale and a sea story"? The answer is " A fairy tale starts "Once upon a time....", a sea story starts "This is no shit...."".

Well . . . . ."This is no shit. . . ."

Down To The Sea . . . .

I enjoyed going to sea. It was always an adventure -- never the same twice. The sea in all its majesty and grandeur, its power and violence, its calm and serenity was always new. And very often going to sea meant going to some new and interesting place. Oh sure, there were the weeks on end of playing "Chesapeake Raider" out of Norfolk which got pretty old after a while. Underway early Monday morning to join in the long stream of ships headed for the Virginia Capes Operating Areas. Play with a submarine or shoot at sleeves or target sleds all week and then back to Norfolk on Friday afternoon.

But there were also days of getting underway to Canada, Cuba, Guatemala, Panama, Hawaii, Midway, Japan, Korea, Hong Kong, Singapore, Ceylon, Saudi Arabia, Egypt, Italy, France, Portugal and the Azores and all the seas between. Transits of the Panama and Suez Canals, welcoming Davy Jones aboard on the equator 70 miles south of Singapore and riding out three hurricanes at sea and one alongside a pier were never to be forgotten experiences.

I also cherish the opportunities that I had to go to sea in many different types of vessels -- most of them small and some of them wooden. Navies no longer use these small and lightly armed ships and they have all long since been converted to razor blades or tooth picks. It was a unique experience to share the Spartan life at sea in these small ships that will never be seen again. Most of them were built in a hurry during World War II in shipyards or boatyards in Tennessee, Wisconsin, Michigan, Pennsylvania and other places far removed from the sea. At that time, the US was losing the Battle of the Atlantic and every possible resource was being thrown into the effort to build anti-submarine ships.

When I encountered these ships in 1951 and 1952 they were assigned to the Sonar School Squadron in Key West, Florida. They were used to take fledging sonarmen (like myself) to sea to get experience operating with real submarines under actual sea conditions. Mostly equipped with obsolete WW-II vintage sonar equipment, they nevertheless gave the sonarmen an opportunity to work with a submarine in the noisy and difficult sonar conditions of the tropical ocean. Every morning during the Sonar School "Sea Phase" weeks we got up early to be at the harbor by 6:30 AM to pick up the ship we were assigned to that day. We sortied from Key West to meet our submarine in the deep water operating areas between Florida and Cuba.

PCS stood for Patrol Craft, Small and they certainly were. They were a broken deck, high bow, wood construction ship about 136 feet long with a 24-foot beam and displaced about 250 tons. With the shortage of steel during the World War II, even the superstructure was constructed of plywood and 2x4's. Their twin GM diesels could drive them through the water at a maximum of 14 knots. If a submarine of that time really felt threatened by a PCS, he could always surface and outrun it. They were designed to patrol off harbor entrances and escort slow coastal convoys. Armament consisted of a single breech loading 3-inch gun forward and a single 40mm gun aft with depth charges for anti-submarine weapons. On some of the PCS's, the 3-inch gun was replaced with a Hedgehog mount that could fire 24-rocket-like projectiles ahead of it at a submarine.

An inland sailor must have designed PCS's because they sure didn't like rough blue water. They had to be the worst sea-keeping ships I have ever been in. Round bottomed, sitting high out of the water with a lot of their weight way up in their structure, they wallowed and rolled in the slightest breeze. Looking at one bow on was like looking at Noah's Ark. The bridge was relatively high above the water so the sensations and effects of the ships motion were magnified even further for the bridge crew. I stood bridge phone talker watch one day in PCS-1384 when the Captain, the Officer of The Deck and the Quartermaster were all sharing a bucket. Fortunately, most of the time seas off Key West were calm - but not always.

Even in a flat sea the round bottom PCS-1385 rolls on its way to Dry Tortugas. The Hedgehog ahead-thrown antisubmarine weapon mount is at right side of picture. (A.T. Miller Photo)

Usually there were six to ten sonar students on board. On more then one occasion four or five of them were laid out in life jackets on the fantail feeling as if they were going to die and afraid they wouldn't. The least sick of the group was given the sound-powered phones, the concussion grenades and dye marker (used to simulate depth charge firing) and was designated the fantail phone talker. Most of them tried to keep their eyes shut so they wouldn't watch the mast sweeping across the sky. The effect of the awful rolling motion of these ships was made even worse by the persistent smell of diesel fumes wafting over the fantail from the water-level exhaust pipes.

I never got seasick and those of us who didn't got a lot more time on the sonar equipment on rough days while the others lounged on the fantail. One morning as the PCS-1384 pulled away from the pier in Key West, I stood at the rail next to a Naval Research Laboratory (NRL) engineer who was testing some experimental equipment on the ship. He had been in the Navy prior to working for NRL and considered himself an old salt compared to the sonar students, most of whom were right out of boot camp. We were watching the high seas outside the harbor and the waves breaking against the mole sheltering the harbor from the ocean. He observed that "This was a day that would separate the men from the boys." He got separated about the time we cleared the mole and hit the long rollers. By coincidence I ran into him again when both of us were working for RCA about seven years later. I never let on that I was witness to his "unsalty" embarrassment.

The PCS 1397 at full speed ahead (14 knots). The PCS high center of gravity and round bottom gave them very poor sea keeping ability. This PCS had the 3-inch, 50-caliber gun forward instead of a Hedgehog mount. (U.S.Navy Photo)

The only saving grace for the PCS's is that they were "good feeders." Small ship, small crew with only a couple of cooks. No serving line or steam table on these ships -- all meals were served right from the galley stove. We would go aboard early in the morning and get breakfast served to order - as much as we wanted. Of course, given the other dismal characteristics of these ships this great breakfast often ended up as fish or sea gull food.

I made a short, but interesting, cruise in the PCS-1385 to the Dry Tortugas in the fall of 1951. The Dry Tortugas are a small group of islands about 70 miles west of Key West in the Gulf of Mexico. The 1385 transported a group of Sonar School students to the Fort Jefferson National Monument for a Saturday of fishing and sightseeing. Fort Jefferson had an interesting history. Early 19th century military planners had thought that an armed presence on the Dry Tortugas could "control navigation of the Gulf". In 1846 work was started on a fort whose 8-foot thick walls would stand 50-feet high with three gun tiers containing 450 guns. Work continued for 30 years but it was never completed. Rifled artillery technology in the 1860's and poorly constructed foundations ultimately doomed the fort as a strategic outpost. It continued to be used as a prison, however, and Dr. Samuel A. Mudd and three other Lincoln assassination conspirators were imprisoned there. Dr. Mudd, who had set the broken leg of the fugitive assassin John Wilkes Booth, was sentenced to life imprisonment. He was later pardoned for his efforts in fighting an outbreak of Yellow Fever and saving many lives after the fort surgeon died in the early days of the epidemic.   In the late 19th century some efforts were made to develop Fort Jefferson as a naval base. The battleship Maine stopped there on its way to Havana where it was blown up thus starting the Spanish-American War.   A coaling station to refuel naval vessels was built outside the fort walls but was destroyed by a hurricane shortly after completion.   On the day I was there, we explored the old gun galleries around the mile-long perimeter of the fort and examined the ruins of the other structures. A number of sailors were fishing off the steel ruins of the old coaling pier. One of them hooked a rather large shark, which caused quite a bit of excitement. Not knowing what to do with it, a couple of the sailors worked their fishline and the shark off the pier, along the beach and out on to the pier where the PCS-1385 was tied up.   A Gunners Mate brought out an M1 rifle and shot the shark. No sooner had the echoes of the shot ceased reverberating through the fort walls, then the park ranger came running through the fort entrance waving his arms and screaming at the sailors.   "This park is a national bird sanctuary and all firearms are forbidden." He told the commanding officer of the PCS, in no uncertain terms, to get everybody back on board and get the hell out of his park as soon as possible.   Having incurred the wrath of the National Park Service we cleared the harbor and returned to Key West.

Fort Jefferson, Dry Tortugas. The Federal Specification for forts must have required a moat, which seems a little silly for a fort completely covering an island in the middle of the ocean. The pier at the left edge of the photo is where the PCS-1385 was tied up. The remnants of the old coaling pier is in the lower foreground. (National Park Service – 2006 Photo)

Submarine Chasers or PC's handled the open seas better then PCS's. They were flush deck, steel hull ships about 170 feet long with a 23-foot beam. The twin GM diesels gave them a 20-knot top speed. A submarine on the surface probably couldn't outrun them but it would certainly be a horse race. Like the PCS's, armament consisted of a single breech loading 3-inch gun up forward and a single 40mm Bofors gun aft with depth charges for anti-submarine weapons. On some PC's, the forward 3-inch gun was replaced with a Hedgehog antisubmarine rocket mount. Most of the PC's were built in 1942 during the dark days of the German submarine onslaught along the East Coast.

PC-472 at full speed (20-knots). As can be seen in this photo, PC's had a rather small superstructure making them very cramped as more antisubmarine equipment was added. (U.S. Navy Photo)

Although they had a larger hull then PCS's the PC's superstructure was smaller. Electronic equipment added during the war and after was jammed in wherever it could be fitted. The sonar equipment was sandwiched into the pilothouse, which wasn't very large to begin with. The Sonar Range Recorder and Attack Plotter were against the pilothouse aft bulkhead. As a result the recorder and plotter operators faced aft and were butt to butt with the helmsman and lee helmsman who faced forward steering the ship. Further complicating the arrangement was a plastic curtain pulled around the plotter and operator to shield the CRT from sunlight. There was no problem giving course and speed orders to the helmsmen during an attack - they were literally at your elbow.

On the starboard side of the pilothouse was a three-step ladder in a stair well leading down and aft to the radar room (laughingly called CIC because it also included a Dead Reckoning Tracer (DRT)). The sonar stack was mounted on the ledge between the stairwell and the pilothouse starboard bulkhead. A round swing-out seat similar to those on school lunch tables was mounted so that the sonar operator could sit out over the stairwell to operate the sonar equipment. The seat was varnished wood and it was a slippery precarious perch under the best of circumstances. In rough weather the sonarman braced his feet against the sonar stack lower panels, hung on to a handle on the stack with one hand and operated the azimuth control with the other. More then one sonarman who didn't hang on ended up unceremoniously dumped down the stairwell. The sonar system in these ships was crude and inelegant but it worked. We found and tracked submarines and successfully attacked them. I have great admiration for those who went to sea searching for enemy submarines for days on end in those small, cramped ships.

Destroyer Escorts (DE) came in many different configurations. The hulls were identical (306 feet with 36-foot beam) but they had different combinations of 3 inch, 5 inch and 40 mm guns. They were built on almost an assembly line basis from 1942 to 1944 at naval and private shipyards. Many were completed in less then six weeks. They were fitted with whatever type of propulsion plant was available at the time they were built. As a result, their twin screws may have been powered with diesel engines, diesel/electric drives, steam powered geared turbines and steam powered turbine/electric drives. Altogether 457 were built in US shipyards and used by the US, Canadian and British navies.

U.S.S. Chatelain (DE-149) an Edsall class, diesel powered destroyer escort used in the Sonar School Squadron. Note the open unsheltered bridge immediately forward of the T-shaped gun director. (U.S. Navy Photo)

I liked the DE's. They were the closest thing to a destroyer that I had been in at that point in my naval career. I had the opportunity to ride many of the different types of this class. Unlike other US destroyer types where the bridge was wrapped around the pilothouse, the DE's had open platform bridges very similar to those on British man-of-war. A wooden grate decked the conning station that was at the top of the superstructure, three decks above the main deck. As in British ships, there was only a compass binnacle and voice tubes to the pilothouse on the conning platform. They had a splendid view in all directions. On bridge watch under the Florida sun, it was very easy to imagine you were in H.M.S. Exeter standing off the River Plate waiting for the German pocket battleship Graf Spee to attempt to sortie from Montevideo. Other then high risk of sunburn, this breezy open bridge was quite pleasant while cruising in the Gulf of Mexico. I don't think I would like to stand watch in it in the North Atlantic in the winter, however. I have vivid memories of some interesting experiences in destroyer escorts

I seemed to have spent more time as the bridge phone talker on DE's then on the other ships we students sailed in. On one occasion on one of my early sea-phase days, we broke off exercises with the submarine to go alongside another DE to high line over a repair part. I thought that a ships company phone talker would be brought up to replace the inexperienced student for a critical evolution such as this. The OD appeared to have no intention of doing so. I was scared to death. I could just picture getting instructions mixed up to the engine room, helmsman or highline station and causing a collision or other catastrophe. At about 12 knots with many engine and helm orders, we slowly maneuvered within about 75 feet of the port side of the other DE. Everything went fine and the part was transferred without incident. My fear must have been apparent to all because the OD patted me on the back afterwards and told me I did fine.

Late one afternoon I was again bridge talker when a torpedo exercise was scheduled with the submarine just before we surfaced it for the day and returned to Key West. The submarine was going to fire a torpedo directly at the DE. The 1000-pound, high explosive warhead had been removed from the torpedo and replaced with a bright yellow exercise head filled with water. The torpedo was set to run at about 20 feet below the surface so it would pass well below the DE's keel, which was 11 feet below the water. At the end of its run, the water would be blown out of the exercise head and it would float to the surface to be recovered. The submarine got experience in firing a "live fish" and the student sonarmen on the DE got to hear what a torpedo sounds like coming right at you.

The sub fired and all of us on the DE's bridge were watching the torpedo wake coming right at us. So far, so good. When the torpedo was about 100 yards away, it suddenly broached on the surface. The bright yellow exercise head could clearly be seen headed right for our waterline. DE's hulls are only 3/8-inch steel and even an exercise head traveling at 40 knots could put a two-foot hole in our starboard side. It was headed for one of the large engineering compartments where a two-foot hole could have serious consequences. There was an almost simultaneous sharp intake of breath by everyone on the bridge followed by a number of expletives describing the technical competence of submarine torpedomen. The captain started to give an order to turn into the torpedo to try and avoid it but it was obviously too late for that. All I could think about was what the student phone talker would do in the midst of a severe damage control incident. Images of the World War II unexploded-torpedo-through-the-destroyer-hull movies flashed before me. When everyone was bracing themselves for the hit, the torpedo submerged and passed harmlessly under our keel. As all eyes turned to the port side to assure that the torpedo had made it, there was a quiet sigh of relief - - not least of all from the student phone talker.

The end of the day on the DE's was always an interesting experience. The sonar students got to watch the young ensigns and jg's try to put the ship alongside the piers in Key West in rather challenging currents. The DE's didn't berth at the harbor on the main naval station, as did the PC's, PCS's and submarines. They tied up at the Surface Anti-Submarine Development Detachment (SURASDEVDET) piers on the west-end of Key West. Henry Flagler originally built these piers as part of his scheme to extend his Florida East Coast Railway to Cuba. Flagler, who was one of John D. Rockefeller's partners in Standard Oil, had built a railroad bridge 120 miles across the keys from the mainland between 1903 and 1912. In Key West the rail cars were transferred to a ferry to carry them to Cuba - thus the big concrete piers. Unfortunately, a disastrous hurricane destroyed the tracks and killed many people, most of them WW-I veterans on Islamorada Key, in 1935. The rail service to Cuba was abandoned. The State of Florida took over the solid granite bridge foundations and extended US Route 1 on what was called the Overseas Highway to Key West. The Navy inherited Mr. Flaglers' piers.

Unfortunately, Henry didn't pick the best site for piers. Directly off the end of the piers were Wisteria Island and a little further east Sunset Island. These islands necessitated a turning approach to the piers and funneled the tidal flow between the Atlantic and the Gulf of Mexico through the Key West Bight. If you were fortunate enough to be making the pier at slack tide the approach was pretty straightforward. If you were making it when the tide was running it could get pretty exciting. Sometimes DE's ended up too far from the pier to get a line over and had to back out and start all over again. If they were fortunate enough to get lines over they often couldn't maneuver (or even use the winches to haul themselves in) against the current. Some, believing that speed meant control, made fast approaches filled with flying splinters of wood as they crashed into the pilings. These approaches were usually accompanied by the base First Lieutenant running down the pier shaking his fist and threatening to assess damage costs. The US Navy wasn't the only one to have trouble making these piers. I once observed the British Frigate H.M.S. Rocket broached ninety degrees from where it should have been with its bow against one pier and the stern against another. As amusing as all this was, however, the students stood on the ship looking at their bus waiting on the pier and realizing that the beer was getting warm.

Maybe because of their British looking bridges, American sailors often compared DE's to the famous Canadian Corvettes. Not even close! DE's were huge by comparison - almost twice as large. The corvettes were tiny ships. Although wider and a having a greater displacement, they were 15 feet shorter than American PC's! They had only a single boiler powering a triple expansion reciprocating steam engine. The ship was so small that the top of the boiler extended through the main deck and was enclosed in the superstructure. Armament consisted of a single 4-inch gun and depth charges. I had an opportunity to go aboard HMCS Sackville, the last remaining Canadian corvette, in Halifax, Nova Scotia. Sackville had a distinguished war record and had engaged in several fierce battles with German submarines in the North Atlantic. As far as I am concerned, the Canadian sailors who took these tiny men-of-war into the winter Atlantic to meet and defeat the German U-boats displayed a high level of seamanship and great deal of courage.

HMCS Sackville, the last surviving WW-II Canadian Corvette.(Wikimedia Commons Photo)

As part of our sonar school training as submarine hunters, we were sent out on a submarine to get the perspective of the hunted. The U.S.S. Medregal (SS-480) was an old fleet submarine built in 1944. It had a 5 inch, 20 caliber deck gun and two 40mm anti-aircraft guns on the cigarette deck. Diesel engines could drive it at 20 knots on the surface but submerged on batteries it could only do 4 to 6 knots. These were tiny cramped ships! With a full complement of crew, 10 students on board made it very crowded. When we got on board we were told to climb into a bunk and stay out of the way. Later, however, while we were running on the surface out to the operating area we were allowed one at a time to go up on the bridge. With the captain, the OD a quartermaster on the bridge and two lookouts in the shears, there wasn't much space for visitors.

After we were submerged at sea, an instructor went over all the ships systems with us. The diving officer hated us. We would all be in the aft torpedo room and he would sluice water from tank to tank to get the submerged trim right. At this point we would all troop forward, the ship would go down by the bow and he would have to trim again. Every time we went through the Control Room we got some not-quite-under-the-breath comments from the diving officer about tourists and pains in the ass.

It was kind of fun sitting at the submarine sonar equipment listening to the PC's and PCS's making runs at us and hear fellow students dropping concussion grenades on us. It certainly gave us an appreciation of how the "enemy below" saw us.

Late in the day cruising back toward Key West at 100-foot depth, we were laying in bunks in the forward torpedo room listening to the instructor.   One of the crew came in muttering about leaky grease fittings in the forward escape trunk.   He equalized the pressure and undogged and opened the overhead hatch.   About ten gallons of water suddenly dumped into the forward room.   I don't know whether this was a trick they played on students or inadvertent.   In any case it was very effective -- it scared the hell out of me.

Fourteen years after I rode her, in July of 1965, Medregal turned up as one of the footnotes to the Vietnam War.   She was in the Gulf of Tonkin assigned to intercept and monitor foreign vessels that might be trying to surreptitiously deliver supplies to the North Vietnamese.   Medregal was under the command of a temporary skipper because the assigned captain broke his neck diving into the shallow end of a swimming pool while on liberty in Subic Bay.   As she approached a suspect Greek freighter, she made a little closer surveillance than planned and collided with the freighter taking it out of the war. Medregal survived.

The smallest ship I ever served in was a Yard Diving Tender (YDT). The YDT-1 was a 97-foot wooden hull, steel superstructure, trawler type vessel used for diving operations. The YDT had started out as a coastal minesweeper and was converted to a diving tender after World War-II. It had a main heavy lift boom and two finger booms and anchors fore and aft for laying two point moors over a diving site.   There was a small diving decompression chamber on the starboard side of the mess deck. The YDT was powered by an air-start six-cylinder Union diesel that would drive it at about 10 knots.

YDT-1 in its original life as a minesweeper. When I served in it, all of the sweep gear was removed from the fantail, which left a large open area for diving operations. A large main boom and two finger booms were also added. (U.S. Navy Photo)

YDT-1 was built during the World War II in the Oxford Boatyard in Oxford, Maryland on the Eastern Shore. In earlier and simpler times, the Oxford Boatyard had built Skipjacks, Luggers and other working boats for the Chesapeake Bay watermen. The skilled hands of the Eastern Shore craftsmen showed in the construction of this practical working vessel. The hull was of oak thick and rugged to take the banging about of diving and lifting equipment. All the bulwarks and rails around the main deck were made of oak shaped for strength and low maintenance. The Pilot House, Masters Stateroom and Mates Quarters on the upper level were trimmed in carefully finished gleaming varnished mahogany. The ships wheel was a beautifully finished mahogany spoke design about four feet in diameter. No power steering here!

I was stationed at the Naval Torpedo Testing Range, Piney Point, Maryland when I sailed in the YDT-1. The sonar equipment I maintained was on the bottom of the river and the divers had to retrieve the hydrophones for me to work on them. Although I wanted to dive I couldn't be qualified because I was colorblind. Go figure that one. The Potomac was so dark and murky you could barely see shapes no less colors. I dressed and tended the hard hat divers even if I couldn't dive myself. I lived on the YDT-1 most of the time but still kept a locker and bunk in the barracks because of limited space on the ship.

The base had a small sheltered harbor (Cherryfield) where the 2 YDT's, 2 yard freighters (YF) and many torpedo retrieval and crash boats were moored. The Master of the YDT-1 was a First Class Bosun Mate named Smith who sounded like his vocal cords had been eaten out by cheap whiskey. All of the crew except me were divers. The divers were a rough and ready, hard drinking, gang of senior petty officers. They were all broad shouldered and very muscular from many years of working in the heavy, hard hat, deep-sea diving equipment. Most had served on Submarine Rescue Ships (ASR) and had many tales of the hard work and hazards of deep sea diving on air and helium/oxygen practicing raising submarines. A number of them had been trained at the diving schools conducted on the wrecks of the sunken battleship Utah in Pearl Harbor and the burned and capsized French liner Normandie in New York harbor. Two had tunneled completely under the bottom of the U.S.S. Missouri with washout hoses when it went aground in Hampton Roads. They were an all-American crew -- Smith, Sopchick, L'Hereaux, Messerschmitt, Anderson. Chief Boatswains Mate Tom Reid who was a tall, lean, tough bird with another deep whiskey voice was in charge of the diving crew. All the divers were in awe of him as the most knowledgeable diver they had ever known. And he was. He made many changes to procedures and equipment that improved operations and made them safer. He was a tough teacher too. When a seaman trainee diver "blew up" to the surface because he had his air valve open too wide, we were going to bring him back aboard. "Nothing doing," said Tom, "he goes back down". We turned off his air and he dumped the air in the suit with his chin valve until it deflated sufficiently for him to get his hand on the air valve. Then Tom had a discussion with him over the intercom about what went wrong and about watching the air in your dress as he slowly sank back to the bottom. Tom later became Chief Master Diver of the Navy and after his retirement a world-renowned salvager. There was a sizable obituary in the New York Times when Tom Reid died.

Smitty would sometimes let me handle the ship. The harbor at Piney Point was in a cove behind St. Georges Island and there was a long, winding and narrow channel out to the Potomac. There were a number of buoys and markers for the twisting channel. The channel was really for oyster boats and the boats that buy the oysters and so it was a tight squeeze for the YDT. So in addition to the buoys and markers we had our own set of unofficial landmarks (trees, rocks etc) that we used to navigate the twists and turns.

The small ship handled very nicely.   Although the big wooden wheel was connected directly by cables to the rudder (no power assist), they were kept lubricated and it turned easily and responded well . . . most of the time.   As long as you were in the center of the channel the YDT responded very nicely. If you got toward the edge of the channel in shallower water the ship would "take a suction" on the channel wall and not want to turn. The navy definitely considered it poor form to put the ship aground.   My first indication of trouble was when those beautifully finished mahogany pilothouse window frames started to rattle.   That meant I was in shallow water.   A quick look aft at our brown wake showed that the screw was throwing out mud balls. I would apply pressure to the wheel to turn away from the channel edge.   It wouldn't go.   I would quickly go around to the edge of the wheel and put my full weight behind pulling the spokes down.   Slowly, slowly, slowly it would start to respond.   And then all of a sudden it would break loose and go shooting toward the other side of the channel.   I'd leap to the front of the wheel and spin it back amidships and try to get the ship settled down in mid-channel.   On a cold winter day with both pilot house doors open to navigate on landmarks, my foul weather jacket would usually end up on the deck as I worked up a lather ricocheting down the back channel walls to the Potomac.   Smitty, sitting behind me up on the chart table, kept up a running commentary about the seamanship of the dumb-ass, ping jockey and what he would do to me if I ran us aground.

After you were in the navy for a while (an old salt) you never went on liberty on pay nights. "Amateur Night" you would say disdainfully. Not so the divers! These old salts hit the beach hard every pay night. Drink, gamble and fight.   They always organized a crap game in the head at the barracks as soon as the money was passed out and then on to the Red Barn or the White Fleet Inn down the road for some serious drinking. Much to the chagrin of these tavern owners, the night wasn't really complete until there was a fight.   It was not unusual to see divers sporting black eyes or facial abrasions the day after payday.   Fighting was just part of partying. When Smitty married Tom Reid's daughter the divers had a grand fight at the wedding reception.

Hot, Straight and Normal

Out of my Fleet Sonar School class of 60, I was one of only three guys assigned to shore duty -- everyone else went to sea, mostly in destroyers.   In those days, there were very few shore duty billets for sonarmen.   When I got orders to the Naval Torpedo Testing Range, Piney Point, Maryland I was not only surprised, I couldn't even find it on the map.   It turned out to be located in St Mary's County in southern Maryland on the Potomac River.   I had no idea what a sonarman did at a torpedo range nor could anyone at the sonar school enlighten me.   I got answers like "Beats me!" or "Never heard of the place."

When I arrived at Piney Point in late February, 1952 I found out that I was the only sonarman and that the Electronic Technicians (ET) had been doing the sonar repair work since the last sonarman left about a year before.   Boy, were they glad to see me!   It turned out that the sonar equipment was used to track the torpedoes and consisted primarily of hydrophones (underwater microphones) installed on the bottom of the Potomac River.   The ET's were used to working in warm and cozy electronic shops. When I arrived, they were pretty fed up with riding around the lower Potomac in cold, damp, small boats to repair "my" sonar equipment.   Divers in "deep sea" hardhat equipment had to go down and bring up the hydrophones so that they could be repaired and then return them to the bottom. The ET's were eager to tell me everything they knew about the system hoping that I would take over its maintenance as soon as possible. The system was not very complicated and it didn't take me long to learn the mechanics of splicing submarine cables, replacing hydrophones and using a magnetometer to align hydrophone mounts.   I was soon spending long hours in small boats getting damp and cold and the ET's were back in the shop drinking hot coffee.

Being assigned to the shop with the Electronic Technicians was actually a good deal for me.   Sonar maintenance was not a full-time job so I was also put to work helping the ET's.   I welcomed this because it gave me an opportunity to acquire new electronic skills particularly in maintenance of radio equipment.   Because we were in such a rural area far from TV shops, we also repaired television sets and radios for base personnel. The TV and radio repair skills I acquired at Piney Point helped to put bread on the table while I was going to electronics school after discharge from the Navy.

I learned to repair and align the Link MN-2 and MN-5 FM Mobile Radios used for communications between all the boats and shore facilities on the range. Every firing day we had to have at least half-dozen radios ready to go to replace failed units in the boats. The transmitters in these old WW-II vintage radios were only 2-Watts and were marginal over the communications distances on the range under the best of circumstances. With the vibration from the 225-horsepower diesels on the boats, the radios drifted out of alignment and quit working. We always ended up replacing a number of them before everyone could communicate. I also worked on High Frequency (HF) Radio equipment used for long-range voice communications. I also learned to repair, align and calibrate the magnetic detection equipment used to locate lost torpedoes.

My electronic mentors in the shop were the Schumacher brothers who were both 2nd Class ET's. They may have been a couple of Kansas farm boys but they were both smart as hell and good technicians. Lou had been an ET during World War-II and had re-enlisted when his younger brother Cort joined up during the Korean War. Besides being good ET's, they were also pretty good drinkers and card players. I was the only technician in the electronic shop with a Navy Drivers license. If things were pretty well caught up in the shop, Lou would tell me when I arrived in the morning to go to the motor pool and draw out a panel truck. "I think we need a trip to the Range House," he would say. We would all pile into the truck and would stop by the sick bay to pick up a couple of card playing medical corpsmen. We would then proceed out the base main gate, over the bridge and on to St. Georges' Island. St. George's Island was a low lying wooded island inhabited by some oystermen, a few summer cottages and a girl's camp. The Range House was on a swampy point about half way down the island. A little way down the island was a small general store that sold beer. The card players provided the funds and I bought the six-pack. Then we would proceed ever so slowly down the only road on the rural island.   The card players sat on the floor of the windowless truck and played poker. I kept watch in the rear view mirror and if a car that looked like it might be from the base appeared, I would increase speed to near normal but slow enough to let them pass.   We proceeded down to the eastern end of the island where there was another small general store.   At that point we had consumed the first six pack so again the card players provided the funds and I bought the beer.   We continued this idyllic back and forth journey (interrupted with occasional roadside stops) until about mid-morning when we would actually turn down a dirt road and go to the Range House.   The corpsmen stayed in the back of the truck while we three technicians went in the Range House and tried to maintain a sober demeanor. We went through the motions of checking out some equipment and then left.   The civil servants at the Range House were on to the game and if anyone called looking for us they would attest that we had been working there.   The cruising card game continued until noon when we returned to the base, put on our most decorous demeanor and had lunch.   The afternoon was usually spent with the shop door locked and all of us taking a nap.   We had to rest up because the gedunk opened at 4:30 and they were serving beers for 15 cents.

The Naval Torpedo Testing Range (NTTR), Piney Point had been built during World War II to test and proof torpedoes built in the Naval Torpedo Plant in Alexandria, Virginia. The torpedo plant was just south of Washington, DC on the Potomac. The torpedoes were shipped back and forth between Piney Point and Alexandria by small (130-foot) Yard Freighters (YF) cruising the Potomac.   By 1952 the main torpedo plant on King Street was closed but torpedoes were being assembled and overhauled in the Naval Gun Factory Annex at the foot of Franklin Street in Alexandria.   It had its own pier so the two yard freighters (YF-418 & YF-419) from Piney Point could tie up right alongside the plant.

The torpedo range ran from Piney Point to Point Lookout, where the Potomac River met Chesapeake Bay.   The Potomac was about 5 miles wide at Piney Point and about 7 miles wide at Point Lookout.   The torpedo range ran eastward down the Maryland side of the river. The ship channel was several miles away close to the Virginia side.   Torpedoes were fired from a large multi-deck barge anchored in the river off Piney Point. Although the range was officially 22,000 yards (11 nautical miles) long, it was only instrumented for 14,000 yards (7 nautical miles) because that was about the range limit of torpedoes at that time. There were pairs of hydrophones mounted very accurately on pilings on the river bottom so that they were precisely parallel to the range axis. There was a hydrophone station about every 1000 yards down the range to pick up the torpedo propeller noise.

The cables from the range can be seen coming off the pier to the right to go into the Range House. The billboard warned ships against anchoring near the cables. The tower with the triangle and circle on it is a survey marker used to locate the underwater hydrophones. The platform tower in the foreground was a never-completed project to install an old fire control radar to track boats on the range. (A.T. Miller Photo)

The noise signals were fed into submarine cables that carried them to the Range House about halfway down the range on St. George's Island. Equipment in the range house displayed and recorded the torpedo signals. The torpedo distance from the range axis was determined by some simple geometry calculations. Two Civil Service operators in the range house monitored the signals in real-time and broadcast the torpedo position to the boats that recovered the torpedo at the end of its run. The signals were analyzed in greater detail later to determine each torpedoes exact course and speed during its entire run on the range.   This range data combined with data from a Depth and Roll Recorder carried in the torpedo itself gave a pretty complete picture of its performance.

If there was a problem with one of the hydrophones on the bottom of the river, a diver went down, removed it from its mount, fastened a line to it and we would haul it to the surface.   I would remove the hydrophone from the end of the armored submarine cable and replace it with a new one.   It was a long and tedious process involving not only electrical connections but also all of the mechanical seals required to keep the hydrophone watertight under the water pressure at the bottom of the river.   When I finished the repair, we sent the magnetometer down to the diver and he installed it on the mount in place of the hydrophone.   I then instructed the diver how to adjust the mount based on the magnetometer readings on the equipment in the boat.   We used the earths' magnetic field to align the hydrophones parallel to the range axis.   Because of this, only nonmagnetic materials such as brass and phosphor bronze could be used for the mounts. Unfortunately, these are relatively soft metals and the divers would often bend or break parts of the mounts while working on or adjusting them.   Every time we made a magnetometer reading the diver would have to move away from the mount because metal in his diving dress disturbed the earth's' magnetic field.   It made for a very slow process. Finally after we were sure that the mount was aligned on the range axis, the magnetometer was removed and the hydrophone was sent back down and installed in the mount.   We all crossed our fingers and hoped that the diver didn't break one of the soft metal parts on the mount during installation.   If that happened, we would have to replace the mount and start all over again.   Sometimes a simple hydrophone repair ended up taking all day.   There was not much shelter and only very little heat on the small diving boat.   Trying to do critical repair work with cold bare hands further complicated a hydrophone replacement in the winter.   In addition, everything on the boat was cold and damp because of the water brought aboard from the wet hydrophones and their cable and the dripping diver.

On the hydrophone jobs we often used a 50-foot motor launch that had been converted to a diving boat instead of one of the larger YDT's.   The crew consisted of myself, one of the senior petty officer divers and a seaman diver.   Although it took two people to dress the diver, I had learned to dress and tend divers so the three of us could handle the job. There was a spherical buoy anchored near each of the hydrophone stations. We would moor the diving boat to the buoy. When we got the diver dressed in the full hard hat rig and he had gone down the ladder into the water, we would haul him forward by his lifeline and air hose until he could grab the buoys anchor chain and slide down the chain to the hydrophone station. One day, Seamen Grantham and I had gotten First Class Bosun Mate Smith to the bottom. I was getting my magnetometer equipment set up while Smitty was on the bottom removing the hydrophone. I could hear Smitty grunting over the intercom as he worked and he suddenly yelled "slack the diver". I went over to the large coil of lifeline and air hose hanging on the bulkhead, took off about ten feet and let it go over the side. A few minutes later he again yelled, "slack the diver" and I got up from my equipment and threw over another 10 feet or so of lifeline and air hose. A few minutes later an exasperated Smitty yelled "how about a little damned slack for the diver?" I threw him some more slack, looked out and saw that the buoy we were supposed to be moored to was about 50-feet away – we had broken loose. The snap-hook on the end of the mooring line had broken. I yelled to Grantham to get the engine started and I threw all of the remaining lifeline and air hose over the side. By this time we were drifting pretty fast. Smitty was trudging along on the bottom trying to keep from being pulled over and dragged. I could hear him huffing and puffing over the intercom between expletives describing Grantham and me. I told him to put some extra air in his suit to make himself light as I tried to haul him up by myself. Grantham was trying to maneuver the boat back toward the buoy. Smitty opened his air valve and lightened up and I got him pulled up to the surface and over to the ladder. He could hold on there while Grantham and I got the boat moored back to the buoy. Smitty accompanied our efforts with a running monologue over the intercom about what dumb asses we were that had dragged him all over the bottom of the Potomac River. Fortunately the water was only about 50-feet deep and Smitty had not been down long enough to be threatened by bends from his rapid surfacing. After a short rest, we lowered him to the bottom and he completed the repair. We took a lot of ribbing from the divers about making Smitty jog behind the dive boat. Despite the kidding, we all realized that if the bottom hadn't been sandy, hard and clear of obstructions we could have had a serious accident.   Needless to say all of our mooring equipment underwent a rather rigorous inspection.

The diving operations for hydrophones, while long and sometimes cold, were not anywhere near as dangerous as the diving operations to recover lost torpedoes.   If a torpedo sank at the end of its run it had used up all the fuel and most of the high-pressure air so it was not likely to start again.   Nevertheless, the first thing that the diver did on locating the torpedo was to put a locking bar on the screws so that they couldn't turn. The far end of the range had a hard sandy bottom so that the torpedo was usually laying on the bottom or at worst the nose was stuck a couple of feet into the sand.   Although potentially dangerous, it was fairly easy to get to and work on.

Torpedoes that were fired from the barge and never started running at all were an entirely different matter.   They had a full 3000-pound charge of air and the fuel and oxidizer tanks were full of alcohol and hydrogen peroxide.   The exercise head still contained 800 ponds of water so it plunged straight to the bottom.   Unfortunately the river bottom under the barge and for the first 1000-yards of the range was not hard sand but soupy black muck.   The failed torpedo would dive straight down and bury itself 15 to 20 feet in the mud.   Recovery was a very difficult and extremely dangerous procedure and only senior experienced divers were used for these operations.   After the locator boat found the torpedo either from the sound of its "pinger" or its magnetic signature, a buoy was dropped to mark the location.   Then one of the YDT's would moor over the position in "two-point-moor" using anchors fore and aft.   For this job, the divers wore diving shoes with the protective steel toe removed.   This allowed the diver to use the front of the wooden sole to dig into the mud and push himself along.   The diver used the anchor line from the marker buoy to guide himself to the bottom.   He would usually sink up to his knees in the mud when he arrived on the river bottom.   The divers handline was used to send him down a hand held hydrophone.   The hydrophone was wired into the diving intercom system so that the diver could hear the sound pulses from the torpedo's pinger. He would point the hydrophone around until he picked up the pinger signal. After he located the general direction to the pinger (and thus the torpedo), his handline was used to send him down the washout hose. This was 2-1/2-inch fire hose with a special washout nozzle. The front jet washed out a hole in the mud. Several rear facing jets carried the mud back up out of the hole and prevented the forward jet from knocking the diver over. The diver then started washing his way down to the torpedo. With the washout hose in one hand and the hydrophone in the other he would listen to the pings and push down the hole and toward the torpedo. When he thought he was close, he would wash slowly and feel around gingerly for the torpedo. This was a very dangerous point in the operation. He had to feel around and try to figure out where he was on the torpedo. If he inadvertently hit the firing latch, he could be killed or seriously injured as the two counterrotating screws started to turn at high speed. As soon as he found the aft end of the torpedo, he installed a screw lock to prevent the propellers from turning. He also installed a lock on the firing latch. All of this was slow and very difficult even in the summer when the diving dress had rubber wrist cuffs and the diver could work with his bare hands. In winter when the dress had bulky waterproof canvas gloves and the diver was wearing woolen gloves, it was orders of magnitude more difficult.

Divers working in deep water have to be brought to the surface gradually to keep them from getting the bends.[2] The amount of time they have to decompress is based on the water depth and the time that they had been at that depth. If they have been working hard, they have to decompress even longer because exercise forces more oxygen and nitrogen into the blood. The YDT's had a decompression chamber on board that allowed a diver to be "taken down" to depths of a couple of hundred feet by increasing air pressure in the chamber. It was installed on the ships primarily for the treatment of bends, however, we used it to recompress the diver rather than have them recompress sitting on a stage in the cold water for 20 or 30 minutes. This was particularly important in the winter when the divers would get very cold sitting on the stage decompressing. It became critical get them to the surface quickly to prevent hypothermia if the diver had torn the diving dress and was soaking wet. Often they would tear the palm of the glove while working. Not too much water came in as long as they kept their hand down. If

---

[2] The "bends" or what was originally called "caisson disease" is caused by the fact that dissolved nitrogen in the blood has larger molecules and thus takes longer to exit the bloodstream when pressure is reduced than does oxygen. If the pressure is reduced too quickly (as in ascending from deep water) the nitrogen expands and forms bubbles in the blood which tend to congregate at joints making them painful to bend – thus the name.

they had to reach up above their head, the air would rush out and the water in. I have seen divers come to the surface with the dress filled with water to hip level.

On a typical dive the diver might have to decompress for 4-minutes at 30 feet, 6-minutes at 20 feet and 10 minutes at 10-feet. The procedure we used was that he would decompress in the water for 4-minutes at 30 feet and then we would quickly haul him to the surface. Two of us would be standing by with T-wrenches in hand to get the helmet and chestplate off and the diver undressed as quickly as possible. The medical corpsman would have put a hot cup of coffee, a miniature of GI Brandy and towels and dry divers wool underwear in the chamber. As soon as we got him out of the dress he would tear off the wet underclothes and dive into the chamber. The door was shut and dogged down and the compressed air was turned on. The air pressure was increased until it was at the equivalent pressure of 30-feet of water and the complete decompression cycle was restarted. Fortunately compressing the air makes it warmer which helped the diver recover from his exposure. These guys were tough experienced divers who took pride in their work and would often resist being brought to the surface before finishing the task at hand even though there was water in the dress. Longer time on the bottom also meant longer decompression. I have helped undress divers with blue lips and chattering teeth who were exultant in the fact that they were able to complete the job and that someone else would not have to make a dive to finish a job that they had started.

Torpedoes are fired on a range for two reasons. One is to test new or modified torpedo designs to insure that they worked correctly and achieved the desired performance. Most of these tests were conducted under direction of engineers and ordnance experts from the Naval Ordnance Laboratory (NOL) in White Oak, Maryland. These tests represented only a small percentage of the total range firings. When I was at Piney Point most of the NOL work was concentrated on the development of the Mk-27 and Mk-30 antisubmarine acoustic torpedoes.

The bulk of the torpedo firings on the range were for proof tests. I had never realized it, but every new or rebuilt torpedo must be fired successfully three times to prove that it can operate acceptably before it is issued to the fleet.   Not only that, but the proof-test data from Piney Point went with each torpedo to the fleet.   When the torpedo was actually fired, this data was entered into the fire control computer to compensate for the torpedo's biases.   When I was at Piney Point, most of the torpedo firings were proof tests for the Mark 16 torpedo.   The Mark 16 was a long range, high-speed torpedo that used Navol, which is 70% pure hydrogen peroxide, as an oxidizer.   This allowed storage of much more propulsion energy in the standard 21-inch diameter, 21-foot long torpedo than in earlier marks.   The torpedoes that we were proofing were being issued to fleet submarines to replace the old Mark 14 torpedo.   The Mark 14 Torpedo could only go 4500 yards at 47 knots whereas the Mark 16 could go 11,000 yards at 47 knots. This high performance of the Mark 16's made for some interesting and exciting events when something went awry during proof firings.

Normally the range did proof firings on Monday.   The torpedoes were fired from the barge with a bright yellow exercise head replacing the 1000-pound explosive warhead. The exercise head was filled with water, which was blown out of it at the end of its run causing the torpedo to come to the surface.   The exercise head also contained a Depth and Roll Recorder that made a permanent running record of the torpedo depth and how much it rolled during its test run.   In case the torpedo didn't surface at the end of its run, there was also a small sonar transmitter or "pinger" mounted in the exercise head that could be used to locate the errant torpedo on the river bottom.

The Range Barge had a large superstructure containing a high-ceilinged main deck where torpedoes were handled, enlisted berthing and mess hall on the deck above and chiefs and officers quarters above that.   An enclosed bridge structure on the forward end above the officers quarters was used by operations personnel during firing.   During World War-II range operations were conducted around the clock so the barge was manned with a full complement of officers and men.   In 1952 we were only firing a couple of days a week so there was only about 30 enlisted men and a couple of chiefs on board.   The mess hall was fully operational, however, because they had to feed all the small boat and yardcraft personnel in addition to the barge crew on firing days.

The Range Barge. The above water torpedo tubes can be seen protruding from the forward end. Range operations were directed from the tower directly above the tubes. (A.T. Miller Photo)

Single tube torpedo launchers were mounted on the port and starboard sides of the forward end of the barge.   They could be trained to point them at an aiming marker about 1000 yards down range.   The torpedoes were launched from the tubes with compressed air.   A submarine type submerged tube was mounted in the front of the barge below the waterline in the hold.   The hold also had an engine room containing generators, air compressors and pumps.   The barge was anchored in a four-point moor from each of its corners.   Chains ran out from four windlasses to large mushroom anchors buried in the bottom.   Before firing started the barge position over the range zero point was verified from the bridge.   Bearings were taken on survey towers on the shore on Piney Point and St. George's Island.   Anchor chain was taken in or let out on each of the four windlasses until the barge was directly over the zero point and aimed straight down range.

It took quite a flotilla to support range operations.   On firing days, there were ten to twelve 42-foot torpedo retrieving boats deployed in the area where the torpedoes were expected to surface.   These boats had thick oak hulls, were powered by a 225-

horsepower Gray Marine diesels and contained several flotation tanks so they would float if hit by a test torpedo. They would go alongside the floating torpedo, connect a line into an eye in the nose of the exercise head and tow the torpedo over to a yard freighter. The 130-foot yard freighter (YF) stood by downriver from the expected torpedo surface point. As the torpedo retrieval boats brought the torpedoes alongside they were hoisted aboard and stowed in the hold or on the deck. A 36-foot, plywood hulled, crash boat carried the Range Safety Officer. He directed the deployment of the retrievers and moved them around in response to tracking information from the range house as the torpedo proceeded down range. The crash boat had twin 225-HP diesels and could go about 35 knots. Sometimes torpedoes ran wild and the crash boat would be used to chase it down and warn civilian boats and oystermen out of the way by blowing its siren. A 50-foot motor launch had been converted to a Torpedo Locator Boat. It had sonar equipment to pick up the sound pulses from the pinger in a sunken torpedo. It also had magnetic detection (magnetometer) equipment to locate lost torpedoes by their magnetic signature after the pinger battery died. The locator boat usually stood by about halfway down and off-range in case it was needed. One of the 97-foot Yard Diving Tenders (YDT) was always standing by and ready to dive on a sunken torpedo and retrieve it.

Normally all of the torpedoes would be fired and retrieved on Monday and bright and early Tuesday morning the yard freighter with its load of expended torpedoes would get underway for Alexandria and Washington. It was about 100 miles to Alexandria via the winding Potomac and it took the YF most of the day to get there. It was a pretty routine trip except for passing the Naval Proving Ground at Dahlgren, Virginia. The Potomac River was quite wide below Dahlgren. The Main Range Gun Line at Dahlgren was located on a point facing down the Potomac River. From this location, guns could be fired for over 90,000 yards downriver without crossing land. The proving ground tested and proofed gun barrels manufactured by the Naval Gun Factory in Washington, DC before they were issued to the fleet. In 1952 and 1953 they were proofing a lot of 5-inch, 38-caliber barrels as replacements for destroyers that were wearing them out firing at shore targets in Korea. On the Dahlgren Range they fired inert, sand-filled 5-inch projectiles for the tests. The projectiles didn't explode but they did weigh about 58-

pounds and could do quite a bit of damage if they hit something. Dahlgren Range Boats monitored local pleasure and fishing boats and kept them out of the range. The Piney Point Yard Freighter had to stay in the ship channel and was in radio contact with Dahlgren Range Control. Dahlgren Range Control would clear the YF to cross the range but they never stopped firing. As the YF proceeded across the range, they would fire a few hundred yards in front of it and as it got further into the range they would drop behind it. The chiefs who were masters of the YF's said it all worked fine but it did make them a little nervous. Late in the afternoon they would arrive at Franklin Street Alexandria and offload the torpedoes. After this was completed, they would get underway, proceed up the Potomac to the Anacostia River and tie up at one of the piers at the Naval Gun Factory in Southeast Washington, DC. There the YF would be refueled and any freight for Piney Point would be loaded. The return to Alexandria to pick up torpedoes and return to Piney Point was generally on Thursday. So the crew of the YF got a couple of nights in Washington often spent in the bars lining Eighth Street SE right outside the Gun Factory main gate.

Yard Freighter (YF) used to transport torpedoes back and forth between Piney Point and Alexandria. (US Coast Guard Photo)

The person in charge of yardcraft was designated the Master. These Masters were generally First Class or Chief Quartermasters or Boatswains Mates. The Master of the YF-418, one of those that plied the Potomac from Piney Point, was a rather rotund Chief

Boatswain Mate.   We always figured that he became rotund because of his fondness for malt flavored beverages.   He was particularly fond of a beer brewed in Baltimore called Gunthers.   Now real connoisseurs of beer had a pretty low opinion of Gunthers.   The local joke was that some Gunthers was sent to the state lab for testing and the results said that the horse had diabetes.   The main thing Gunthers had going for it was that it was cheap.   The Master of the YF-418 would sit in the gin mills on Eighth Street and as it got late in the evening, and many Gunthers had been consumed, he would start telling people how he was the captain of a ship.   Before long, along Eighth Street SE he became known as "Captain Gunthers".   His fame and title eventually spread back down to Piney Point.   If we ever knew his real name it was quickly forgotten because to one and all the Master of YF-418 was always Captain Gunthers.

Proofing any torpedo often results in erratic or unexpected behavior with unintended consequences.   Proofing Mk 16's with their high speed and long range resulted in some interesting and potentially dangerous accidents.   Because they were going so fast for so long, it was hard to keep the torpedo retrievers and other range craft out of their way.   As long as they were running "hot straight and normal" at their assigned depth there wasn't much danger.   The compressed air flasks in the torpedoes were charged to 2800 pounds per square inch pressure.   At the end of their run when the pressure dropped to about 1500 ponds, a valve opened and the water was blown out of the exercise head causing the torpedo to come to the surface.

The torpedo was still running pretty fast even after it surfaced and we occasionally "torpedoed" one of our own small craft.   A torpedo hit one of the 42-foot torpedo retrieval boats up forward.   The exercise head penetrated the thick oak hull and knocked the big diesel engine off its mounts.   Fortunately, anticipating this problem, the torpedo retrievers were equipped with flotation tanks that prevented it from sinking.   One of our 36-foot crash boats wasn't quite so lucky.   A Mk-16 went in one side and out the other side of its thin plywood hull.   It promptly sank and the crew was rescued by one of the torpedo retriever boats.   At the end of its run, when it surfaced, the torpedo was usually going fast enough so that it actually porpoised out of the water.   One jumped right over the after deck of one of the torpedo retriever boats as it surfaced. No one believed the coxswain's "jumping torpedo" story screamed over the radio until he pointed out his boats bent awning stanchion with yellow exercise-head paint on it. Fortunately no one was injured in any of these incidents.

Firing days got even more interesting when we started proofing pattern-running torpedoes. These were special versions of the Mk-16 equipped with a gyroscope that allowed them to run straight out to a predetermined range and then execute a pattern (usually a circle or a cloverleaf). The idea was that if the torpedo didn't hit the target ship it might hit another one in the convoy. If all else failed, convoy ships might collide while trying to avoid the circling torpedo in its midst. The design was based on German torpedoes captured during World War-II. Normally, there was enough trouble positioning the recovery flotilla with torpedoes that ran straight. Trying to figure out where a torpedo on a 1000-yard circular or cloverleaf pattern was going to end up was a real challenge. The torpedo was still in pattern-running mode when it surfaced which resulted in mad scrambles with throttles to the firewall to get out of its way. On some of the retrievers, the engineman was stationed on the roof of the cockpit to try to spot the errant torpedo's steam wake. Fortunately we didn't have any serious accidents but it all provided great material for beer-altered tales at the bar in the gedunk afterward.

Most of the torpedoes we proofed ran "hot, straight and normal" and after three runs were issued to the fleet. There were a few, however, that were "dogs" and kept coming back and failing. Alexandria would overhaul and test all the components and swear that they were perfect. We would fire them and they would do all sorts of wondrous things. They would run off the range and up on the beach at St. George's Island. They would run in erratic courses all over the river. Some dropped out of the tube and the pitch pendulum stuck in the "up" position. The torpedo would then drop toward the bottom, turn around and come straight for the surface at 47 knots where they would go about 20-feet in the air. Some of them were fired out the tube, the engine never started and they sunk. Some were "cold shots" where the alcohol never ignited and the torpedo only ran a few thousand yards. When we neared the end of the proof program there were still 12 Mk-

16's that couldn't be proofed.   I understood that they completely disassembled all 12, mixed up all their parts and reassembled 12 "new" Mk-16's.   I left Piney Point before these were visited upon the range.

The most benign weapons we proofed on the range were the Mk-1, Mod-1 Mine Vehicles.   These mines looked exactly like a torpedo and were launched from a submarine torpedo tube.   They were built by General Electric and were powered by a battery and a small motor.   They were designed to mine an enemy harbor from a submarine located outside the harbor. They ran slowly and quietly for a predetermined distance and then sank to the bottom of the harbor and armed themselves.   When a ship came near to them, a magnetic influence fuse exploded the large warhead.   We had a problem in proofing them because they were so quiet we couldn't track them with the range sonar system.   To solve that problem, an electric noisemaker was mounted in one of the handholes in the exercise head.   All of us hated proofing mine vehicles because they were so slow that it took all day to complete a small group of them.

The most interesting part of the mine vehicle program was when we tested a new more sensitive magnetic influence fuse designed to explode on the smaller magnetic field of a submarine.   The U.S.S. Tench (SS-417), a guppy submarine, came to Piney Point with a loadout of Mk-1 Mod-1 mines.   I rode Tench during the exercise to assist them with range communications.   Tench fired a mine, which ran for several thousand yards and then settled to the bottom. Tench then sailed over where the mine had planted on the bottom.   If the new magnetic fuse detected the Tench, its firing mechanism released a small plastic buoy on a light nylon line and recorded some magnetic signature data in the exercise head.   Then the Piney Point divers would carefully follow the line down to the mine, connect a cable to it and haul it to the surface and on to the YF.

U.S.S. Tench fired mine vehicles at Piney Point in early 1953 to proof a new magnetic exploder.   The author rode on the bridge operating one of Piney Point's Link MN-2 radios to provide range communications. (US Navy Photo)

In July 1953 I received orders to the U.S.S. Wren (DD-568).   I had only been at Piney Point for about a year and a half, however, my boot camp and sonar school time all counted as shore duty and my time was up.   I enjoyed duty at Piney Point.   I learned quite a bit, met some very interesting characters and was only 2 hours from home.   So, I packed my seabag and was on my way to Norfolk to pick up Wren.

U.S.S. Wren

By May of 1953 I was overdue to go to sea and I finally got notice that my time was up. In those days, when the Navy Bureau of Personnel (BUPERS) notified you that you would be transferred to sea duty, they asked you for your ship type preference. I knew that 95% of sonarmen ship assignments were to destroyer types. I requested transfer to a Fletcher class destroyer specially modified for anti-submarine warfare and designated as a DDE. These ships included the latest sonar equipment, sonar fire control systems and weapons including the new anti-submarine Mk 30 torpedoes …..state of the art. When my orders arrived at Piney Point, I got my wish … kind of. It was a Fletcher all right, but just a garden variety DD. U.S.S. Wren (DD-568) was a WW-II destroyer that had been hurriedly brought out of mothballs and recommissioned for service in Korea in September 1951. It had been modernized somewhat during a shipyard availability in late 1952. Although it did not have the fire control system and weapons of a DDE, it did have a modern AN/SQS-10 sonar system that was newer than anything I had studied in sonar school. I was pleased with my assignment as I packed my gear in late July and headed for Norfolk to pick up Wren.

Wren was named not for the small bird but for Marine Master Sergeant Solomon Wren, a hero in Tripoli during the war with the Barbary Pirates in 1804. U.S.S Wren (DD-568) was a Fletcher class, 2100-ton displacement destroyer built by the Seattle Tacoma Shipbuilding Corporation. She was laid down April 24, 1943, launched on January 29, 1944 and commissioned May 20, 1944. Wren was initially assigned to patrol and escort duties off the Aleutian Islands.

Wren in the Aleutians in dazzle camouflage paint, 1944. Notice how the censor whited out the then-secret radar antennas (US Navy Photo).

She participated in several bombardments of the Japanese held Kurile Islands. Wren earned three battle stars in the Pacific during World War II and was one of the "Sacrificial Lambs" in the destroyer screen around Okinawa that were heavily attacked by Kamikaze suicide planes. Although Wren sustained no major damage she is credited with downing four Japanese aircraft. Wren was present in Tokyo Bay for the formal Japanese Surrender ceremony. After returning to the US, she was mothballed in the Cooper River at Charleston, SC on July 13, 1946. Wren was recommissioned on September 7, 1951 during the Korean War. Wren went around the world in 1953 and 1954 as part of her deployment to Korea. Wren blockaded Puerto Barrios Guatemala in May and June 1954 during the CIA overthrow of the Arbenz regime. She participated in a couple of Med cruises, midshipman cruises and major Atlantic Fleet exercises. Her final assignment was as a reserve training ship operating out of Galveston, Texas. Wren was decommissioned again in December 1963 and put into "mothballs" in the Philadelphia Reserve Fleet. She was stricken from the Navy list in December 1974 and sold to American Smelting of Wilmington, DE for scrap on October 22, 1975. Some former crew who were members of the USS Wren Association got wind of her demise and were able to get a few mementos for the association. Included was her mahogany name board (U.S.S. Wren – DD-568) that hung alongside the gangway in port. It hung on the wall at all of our reunions.

The design that would ultimately become the Fletcher class was started in 1939. The design goals were 38-knot speed, 1600-ton (max) displacement and 6500 nautical mile endurance. The Navy wanted a smaller, stronger and faster ship than the existing Benson and Sims class destroyers. As World War II started, operational requirements were added based on British combat experience and the need for antisubmarine and antiaircraft weapons. The design kept getting bigger and heavier. When the first Fletcher (U.S.S. Nicholas) was commissioned in June of 1942, her top speed was 37 knots and displacement was a huge 2589 tons because of extra equipment added to meet new wartime requirements. Ultimately 175 Fletcher class destroyers were built. They were undoubtedly the most famous and well known of all of the WW-II era destroyers.

Wren launching a Mk-15 Torpedo from one of its five torpedo tubes while steaming at 35 knots in an operating area south of Key West, FL, May 1954. Spectators are crowded into the starboard 40mm Gun tub. (A.T. Miller Photo)

Originally, the main battery of the Fletcher class was 10 torpedo tubes in two 5-tube mounts. During World War II there were many instances, such as the action off Samar during the Battle of the Philippine Sea, where destroyers made almost suicide torpedo attacks against Japanese battleships and cruisers that turned the tide of battle.

When I encountered Wren in 1953, during the primacy of the aircraft carrier, the likelihood of major surface actions by badly outgunned destroyers had diminished substantially. The forward torpedo tube mount located between the stacks had been removed and replaced with radar controlled Quadruple 40mm Gun Mounts on the port and starboard side. The huge carbon arc searchlights were removed from the sides of the stacks. The five remaining torpedo tubes were really "just in case" because it was highly unlikely that we would ever use them. The main battery then became the 5 inch 38 caliber dual-purpose guns with the 40mm's as secondary battery mostly used for antiaircraft fire. The five 5 incher's were mounted in single-gun, enclosed (but not armored) mounts along the ships centerline. All of the 20mm Oerlikon anti-aircraft guns had been removed.

Antisubmarine ahead-thrown Hedgehog weapon mounts had been added port and starboard on the 01 level aft of Mount 52. Each of these mounts could fire a pattern of 24 rocket-like projectiles each with a shaped charge warhead that could punch a hole in a submarine pressure hull. There were two depth charge racks on the stern and six (three per side) depth charge K-Guns to allow Wren to deliver 11-charge antisubmarine depth charge patterns. Originally the depth charges were the classic Mark 6 "ash cans" containing about 600 pounds of TNT. Although the Mk-6 had a big bang, it tumbled end-over-end and sank rather slowly limiting its accuracy, particularly against newer, faster submarines. Later these were replaced with the Mk-12 Depth Charge which only carried 250 pounds of TNT but was tear drop shaped and had stabilizing fins that made it sink very rapidly. Although the Mk-12's were our standard weapon, we continued to use the Mk-6's for training and demonstrations.

Wren in 1952 before upgrading. Note the stick mast, torpedo tubes between the stacks, searchlights on aft stack and Mk-12 Radar on Mk 37 Gun Director. (US Navy Photo)

The old cable-guyed stick mast had been replaced with an aluminum tripod mast so that larger radar and electronic warfare antennas could be installed. Although Wren had the new mast, it still had its old WW-II vintage Raytheon SG-1b Surface Search Radar and SC-3 UHF Air Search Radar. Even though these radars were old and required frequent tuning and maintenance, they performed very well. In fact, the navy was just beginning to realize that the old UHF air search radars could pick up planes at longer ranges than the new L-Band AN/SPS-6 and AN/SPS-12 radars. Although they continued to install SPS-6's and 12's, the Bureau of Ships directed that one destroyer in each division should retain its old UHF radar.

Unlike later destroyers where it was buried deep in the hull, the "Sonar Shack" on the Fletchers was on the 02 bridge level. Sonar was across the after part of the bridge superstructure with the Captains sea cabin on its port side and the ladder to the 01 level on the starboard. The gun director room (about 8 feet in diameter) was immediately forward of sonar with the pilothouse forward of it. The pilothouse and the bridge were just a few short steps from sonar. We could always stick our nose out of sonar and find out what was going on. The sonar shack was small (about 6 by 10 feet) and filled with equipment. There was the control "stack" for the AN/SQS-10 sonar with the Sonar Range recorder next to it. The Antisubmarine Attack Plotter (ASAP) completed the line of equipment along the after bulkhead which was covered with dial indicators and control switches.

In the 18-inch space between the range recorder and the ASAP a sturdy aluminum shelf had been rigged to hold the coffee mess.   An aluminum cover over the top of the ASAP allowed its use as a table for maintenance work (or card games) when it wasn't in use. At General Quarters with the ASW Officer and 4 or 5 sonarmen in the space, there was barely breathing room.

U.S.S. Cone (DD-866) a Gearing class destroyer.   Cone was the flagship of Destroyer Division 61, which also included Wren, Noa and Stribling. (G. Hipp Photo)

The Fletcher's also provided the basic hull and machinery design for the later Sumner (2200 ton) and Gearing (2250 ton) destroyers.   The Sumner class used the same 376-1/2 foot long and 40-1/2 foot wide hull as the Fletchers and the same 60,000 horsepower engineering plant.   The Gearing class used a"stretched" Fletcher hull with a 14-foot hull-section inserted, however, the engineering plant was the same.   Our compatriots in Destroyer Division 61 Noa, Cone and Stribling were all Gearing class 2250-ton destroyers. In addition to being longer, their superstructure (above the main deck) was wider allowing a fore and aft passageway throughout the ship. We envied them for that because in bad weather we got wet going fore and aft on the main deck.   Although the 2250's longer hull allowed them to carry more fuel than Wren their increased weight and displacement made them about 6 knots slower.   That is why we had to duck into Santa Maria in the Azores to refuel while they continued to steam across the Atlantic. It is also why we left them in our wake when we responded to the Empire Windrush SOS in the Mediterranean!

Wren refueling in the fishing port of Vila do Porto, Santa Maria, Azores. To save time refueling, all the black oil had been sluiced aft before arrival so that we only had to fuel from the forward station. This is why Wren was sitting down at the stern (A.T. Miller Photo)

Although the original Fletchers didn't make the 38-knot design goal, Wren exceeded it! In 1952 Wren was the guinea pig for a new four-blade screw design. The new screw, based on testing at the David Taylor Model Basin, was primarily designed for improved fuel economy but it also increased maximum speed. Wren first did speed tests over the measured mile at Guantanamo Bay, Cuba with her original three blade screws. She was then put in the floating drydock in Gitmo and the new four bladed screws were installed. Afterwards on the measured mile with all four boilers at max output and throttles completely open she did 38.6 knots. At that speed with the stern dug down, a rooster tail behind and the vibration knocking out light bulbs aft, she seemed to be flying. The requirement for that kind of speed was primarily driven by the need to be a fast moving evasive target during close-in torpedo attacks. By the time I was in Wren there was little chance that we would be involved in that type of high-speed gun and torpedo surface action. Thank God!

In the 1950's most sailors knew Norfolk, Virginia as "Shit City".   That reputation probably goes back to the local attitude that resulted in the infamous "Sailors and Dogs Keep Off The Grass" signs there during World War II.   It was still a pretty raunchy navy town.   Although most of the bordellos had been closed down, East Main Street was still famous throughout the fleet for its shoulder to shoulder bars, strip joints and B-Girls. With my luck, I always seemed to catch "Easy Main" when I had Shore Patrol in Norfolk.   We would usually spend the night breaking up fights and carting drunks away.

I arrived in Norfolk late on a Monday night. I called Ship Operations to find out where Wren was berthed and was told that she was "at sea with return date unknown". I turned in to the receiving station at Naval Operating Base (NOB) Norfolk to await Wren's return, which hopefully would be on Friday.   The Receiving Station had lots of casual petty officers waiting for ships so I didn't catch many work details. I spent most of each day in the gedunk drinking cokes and reading magazines.   Sure enough, Friday morning after quarters I got orders to Wren at Pier 22 at the Convoy Escort (CE) Piers.   She had just returned home from a week at sea playing "Chesapeake Raider".

I got off the navy bus at Pier 22 clutching my seabag, "blue bag" and orders.   A Chief Bosun Mate with orders in hand also got off the bus.   "What ship" the chief asked. "Wren" I answered. "Me too" he said "she's leaving for Korea in a few weeks".   That was great news for me. I firmly believed in the old recruiting poster that said "Join the Navy and see the world". The chief didn't share my enthusiasm. He was due to retire in about six months and was trying to get his orders changed. I guess he did because after we reported aboard, I never saw him again.

As the bus pulled away, I looked around for a Fletcher with the hull number 568, hopefully right alongside the pier. Not a chance! There she was, the fourth ship outboard of the destroyer tender Shenandoah (AD-26).   Couldn't have been further away.   It was a scorching hot and humid August day. By the time I climbed the steep gangway to Shenandoah, crossed through the tender, climbed down from the 01 level on the first can and dragged my gear across two more my whites were soaked through with perspiration and streaked with dirt and my hat was askew.   In my disheveled state, I came across the brow to Wren, saluted the ensign and the quarterdeck and asked permission to come aboard.   The OD took one look at me with my orders in hand and exclaimed "not another one!" He turned to the watch petty officer and said "and where the hell do you think we can put this guy?" The problem was that people were being ordered aboard Wren to bring the ship up to full war complement to go to Korea. At the same time, the short-timers who couldn't make the eight-month cruise had not yet been ordered off the ship. The ship was temporarily way above complement and had run out of bunks.   The PO took me down below and back aft in the First Division compartment and found a bunk with the mattress folded over.   "Take this one" he said, "the guy is on leave".   "We don't have any spare lockers so you'll have to live out of your seabag".   Welcome aboard! "Oh yeah" he added "we have admirals inspection tomorrow morning so we'll have to get all the seabags out of here and over to the next ship before 0900". Terrific!

Bright and early Saturday morning, dressed in work uniform, I went up to sonar and helped to get the sonar spaces squared away for inspection (including polishing the water faucet). When we were finished with the spit and polish, I went below to take a shower and get dressed for inspection.   Coming back after my shower I found that my seabag had already been moved over to the next ship.   Fortunately I had taken my inspection whites and shoes out before I showered.   My big problem was what to do with the dirty dungarees.   It was getting close to time to muster for inspection so I smoothly folded the dungarees and carefully flattened them out as best I could and put them under my mattress.

With suitable pomp and circumstance, white gloves and swords the admiral and his staff inspected us and found us suitable to depart for Korea.

The Wren Engineering Department standing for the Admiral's Departure Inspection. (US Navy Photo)

Afterward, returning to the First Division compartment, I found that the assistant division officer, Mr. Davis was very displeased with me. It seems that the admiral had found my dungarees under the mattress during his inspection of the compartment. My protests about not having a locker and my seabag being removed fell on deaf ears and I was informed that the XO wanted to see me. The Executive Officer turned out to be much more reasonable and understanding than Davis and just encouraged me to do better in the future. Departing the XO's office, I went down to the Ship's Office to pick up my liberty card. I figured as long as I was all dressed up I might as well hit the beach. The Duty Yeoman couldn't seem to find my liberty card and kept muttering "I was sure we made up one for you". "Well, no problem" he said "I'll type one up and get the XO to sign it". In a few minutes, with my newly signed liberty card, I headed for the quarterdeck and liberty. As I approached the quarterdeck, I noticed Mr. Davis, who had been talking to the OD, looking at me with a funny expression on his face. Remembering the absent liberty card, I immediately suspected what was up. As I saluted the quarterdeck, he said "Miller, I thought we pulled your liberty card". Now, pulling a liberty card is an illegal punishment (only the captain can restrict persons to the ship) frequently imposed by junior officers for minor infractions. They know that they can get away with it by threatening to write you up for Captains Mast if you protest. "No sir", I replied with a big smile. "I've got it right here" and saluted the ensign and went over the side. Davis looked like he was going to have apoplexy. He didn't forget it, however, and got his revenge a year later in Quebec. But, that's another story.

Although Wren was my first assigned shipboard duty, I was not a complete landlubber. I had several weeks of sea duty on various kinds of antisubmarine vessels when I was in Sonar School. For thirteen months at Piney Point, I had worked on and been assigned to various types of yardcraft operating in the lower Potomac River and the Chesapeake Bay. The Masters of these craft were First Class or Chief Petty Officers and were all deep sea divers. They were tough "old salts" who were quick to point out any mistakes in seamanship by a "dumbass ping jockey" (sonarman). I learned fast! Arriving on Wren as a Sonarman Third Class, I felt quite comfortable and adapted quickly to life on a destroyer.

Unlike the chief I had met getting off the bus, I thought that doing a world cruise in a "tin can" was just great. The prospect of visiting interesting ports all over the world was pretty exciting. Shortly after reporting aboard, I had bought a copy of Rachael Carson's new book "The Sea Around Us". I found it fascinating and was looking forward to experiencing and understanding many of the wonders described in her book. During the cruise, I referred to the book often to explain what I was seeing in "The Sea Around Us".

We had a full complement of 10 Sonarmen as we got ready to leave the states. Archer Kinlock was a third class and the leading sonarman and had been aboard since the ship was recommissioned in Charleston (a plankholder). Sonarmen Seamen were Gene Staunton, Jim Roberson, Gene Updegraff, Jim O'Connell, York and Ed McDonald most of whom were plankholders. O'Connell and York were on "kiddie cruises" which were special enlistments for 17-year olds who would be discharged the day before they turned 21. Al Berndt and Al Dodge, both third class had recently transferred aboard from the U.S.S. Ingersoll. I was also third class. In another one of those small world things, I ran into Al Berndt again 12 years later when I was working for RCA Service Co. at Goddard

Space Flight Center.   I used to wonder why he visited so often until I realized that the attraction was my secretary not me.   Jodie and Al were married in 1974.

Al Berndt, on left and Gene Staunton in September 1953 when Wren stopped in Hawaii. Gene and I became close friends as shipmates in Wren. Gene died in 1989.   (A.T. Miller Photo)

In the weeks leading up to our departure, we did some ASW and gunnery training exercises out in the Atlantic in the Virginia Capes Operating Area with Noa, Cone and Stribling. We spent several days loading ammunition from trucks on the pier.   Loading ammo is a backbreaking all-hands evolution.   I certainly didn't have much trouble sleeping after a day of lugging 58-pound 5-inch projectiles from the truck, up the gangway, across the deck and down several decks to the ammunition magazines. I couldn't believe that we had space for all the ammo we took aboard. We loaded 765 5-inch, 38-caliber projectiles, 835 5-inch powder cases and 4930 rounds of 40mm fixed ammunition.   We also spent a couple of days loading provisions - another back-breaker. It became painfully obvious that the ammunition and provisioning requirements for peacetime destroyer operations were only a fraction of those required for warfighting.

Hurricane Barbara interrupted our preparations for deployment to Korea.   On that morning, cup of coffee in hand, I stepped out on the wing of the bridge to view the activity at CE piers and shoot the breeze with the quartermasters. I noticed that they were watching a flag hoist being broken from the mast of the tender Grand Canyon. Grand Canyon was the flagship of the commander Destroyer Flotilla Fours (DesFlot4). I read the flags and asked, " What does PREP EASY VICTOR 14 mean". One of them said, "It means prepare to get underway at 1400 hours". "A hurricane is coming up the coast and we have to move out to the hurricane anchorage in Chesapeake Bay." Almost immediately preparations were started to get underway and to prepare for heavy weather. Later that afternoon we backed away from the pier and headed for the hurricane anchorage just south of Tangier Island. It turned out to be a pretty rough hurricane. We had a hard time maintaining our position and ended up losing our port anchor. More about that ignominious evolution later. For the moment, suffice it to say that we survived and returned to CE Piers late the next day.

Finally on August 28, our preparations complete, we got underway for Korea. Everybody was a little sad and a little excited. Sad for those left behind and excited about the unknown adventures ahead. It would be more than seven months until we returned. I thought of the old sailors prayer "God save us and keep us – the sea is so big and our ship is so small".

Path Between The Seas

Destroyer Division 61 (including Wren) departed CE piers, Norfolk Naval Operating Base, and was underway for duty in Korea and circumnavigation of the globe. Before we returned again to Norfolk, Wren would steam some 55,000 miles. Wren, in company with Cone, Noa and Stribling steamed south from Norfolk headed for the Isthmus of Panama. We were following approximately the same route used by the battleship U.S.S. Louisiana when it carried President Theodore Roosevelt from Norfolk on his famous inspection trip to the canal construction in 1906. We proceeded south past Cape Hatteras and down the East Coast trying to stay westward out of the Gulf Streams' northbound 1-1/2 knot current. We steamed across the Straits of Florida to within sight of the lush, green, northeast coast of Cuba. I was taking depth soundings as we passed Cuba and was amazed at how deep the water was here within easy sight of land. There certainly was no coastal shelf on Cuba. DesDiv-61 continued southwest across the Caribbean and arrived at Colon, Panama Canal Zone early in the morning on September 2, 1953.

Because of the large amount of ship traffic awaiting transit, we could not immediately enter the canal so we anchored in Limon Bay off Colon. Later, as we prepared to get underway to transit the canal, the Panama Canal Pilot came on board. Panama Canal Pilots have a unique responsibility shared by no other pilots in the world. When the Panama Canal Pilot takes control of the ship and it is entered into the log, the captain effectively relinquishes command and the pilot is totally responsible for the ship. Anywhere else, the captain remains responsible for the ship and can take back control from the pilot at any time. In fact, Captain Johnson took the conn of Wren from the Suez Canal Pilot in Port Said when he thought that the pilot was endangering the ship. The Panama Canal Pilot brought aboard his own line handlers to assist in attaching the ship to the small, electric "donkey engines" that towed the ship through the locks. He also brought aboard a couple of World War II vintage "walkie-talkie" radios to communicate with canal line handlers and lock controllers.

Wren with Cone astern in Gatun Locks, Panama Canal.   East lock gate is still open.
Donkey engines are atop the lock wall. (A.T.Miller Photo)

As we got underway at about 9:30AM, we passed the Cristobal breakwater and entered the canal. The 50-mile long canal is located in the narrowest and lowest saddles of the long and mountainous isthmus. Contrary to popular belief, the canal actually goes north and south (not east and west) because of the east-west curve of the isthmus at that point. The first 6 miles, or so, is at sea level and through a rather uninteresting mangrove swamp. The three Gatun Locks raise the ship from sea level up 85 feet to the level of the huge (over 160 square miles) Gatun Lake. The locks are each1000-feet long so they can comfortably handle two destroyers at a time. As we came toward the approach walls for the Gatun locks, lines were heaved over and used to pull in the steel tow cables contained on the large horizontal reel atop the electric "donkey engines". The electrically driven reel allowed the towing operator to slack or tighten the cables from the cab of the engine. As ships were moved from one lock to the other, the operator slacked the cable so the 2 mile-per-hour engine could climb the 45-degree grade between locks. As soon as it got to the top, the reel hauled in the slack and the cable again took a strain on the ship.   We proceeded into the first lock followed by Cone.   Everyone not assigned sea-detail duties were topside with cameras in hand.

Slowly and very smoothly, the great lock gate closed behind us.   These hollow, buoyant gates are a marvel of engineering design and despite their huge size are so perfectly balanced that they can be driven by relatively small electric motors.   As the gates became completely shut, water started boiling up all around the ship from 100 inlets and we started to rise.   All of us were amazed at the amount of water flowing in and how fast the ships were moving upward.   It was an impressive sight to see two destroyers rising so quickly.   I had always thought that the water was pumped in and out of the locks. Wrong! The system is powered completely by gravity.   All the water flows from Gatun Lake through 16-foot diameter culverts.   Going up, they just open the valves and the lock fills up with water from the lake.   Going down the water is drained from the locks into the ocean.   After going up the three steps of Gatun Locks, we cast off the lines to the "donkey engines" and exited the locks into Gatun Lake under our own power.

Wren with Cone astern leaving Gatun Locks after being lifted up to Gatun Lake level. Lock control tower is alongside rear lock gate. (A.T. Miller Photo)

Gatun Lake was formed by damming up the Charges River, which flows out of the rain forest in the interior of Panama.   At the time it was built. The 1-1/2 mile wide dam was the largest earthen dam in the world.   It is a half-mile thick at its base.   As we entered the lake, word was passed that we would anchor in the lake for a few hours to wait for other traffic to clear the canal.   Fresh water, which is made by boiling sea water using heat from the boilers, is a very precious commodity on a destroyer.   Normally all swabbing down of decks is done using seawater from the fire fighting and flushing system and a small amount of fresh water for the final damp mopping.   After a while at sea, the ship accumulates a coat of sticky grimy salt.   Now we had the unusual situation of sitting in a lake with fresh water flowing through the fire system.   Hoses were broken out all over the ship and we used this opportunity to wash all of the salt rime and grime off the sides and superstructure and even the mast.

When the cleanup was completed, word was passed that we would have "swim call" in a 20-minutes. Everyone not on duty went below to don bathing suits.   Who among us was going to miss the opportunity to be able to tell our grandkids that we had swum in the Panama Canal?   The whaleboat and the gig were put in the water to act as lifeguards. Although we all had to pass a swimming test to get out of boot camp, anyone who wanted one could have a lifejacket before going over the side (Gatun Lake was pretty deep and, as we shall see, also strong currents).   I was an experienced swimmer, had swum competitively and worked as a lifeguard.   In fact, during Service Week in Boot Camp my job was to teach Non-Qualified Swimmers to swim.[3] When we were cleared to go in the water, I dove in from the 40mm gun tub on the 01 level.   The water was cool and I was having great time swimming around.   All of a sudden I noticed that I was drifting past the stern of the ship.   I started swimming forward against the current and got back alongside in a few minutes.   The whaleboat and gig had to rescue some of the less accomplished swimmers.   Where did the current come from?   It didn't take us too long to figure out that they were flooding down the Gatun Locks and the current was caused by the rush of water out of the lake and into the 16-foot culverts for the locks.   We were

---

[3] In the summer of 1954 I tried out for and made the Destroyer Force Atlantic Fleet swim team. We were the Atlantic fleet champions that year.

about a mile from the locks and yet the amount of water moved was so huge that it caused a substantial current even where we were. The XO decided that we had enough swimming for one day.

After another hour, we got underway again and proceeded slowly south in Gatun Lake with Cone in trail. As we got to the south end of the lake we passed the wreckage of the French construction equipment sticking out of the water to starboard. The rusted steel stood as a monument to the 20,000 who died in the ill fated $40 million, 20-year French attempt to build a sea-level canal. Although the $387 million, 10-year American project was successful in conquering disease and building a canal with locks, it also cost 25,000 lives.

Proceeding slowly, barely making a wake, we passed the mouth of the Charges River at Gamboa and entered Gaillard Cut. Although named Culebra Cut during construction, it was renamed for GeneralDavid DuBose Gaillard the engineer in charge of this section of the construction. The cut was the most challenging and trouble-plagued section of the whole project. It required an enormous amount of explosive demolition and the largest amount of soil and rock removal of the entire construction. There were landslides, explosive accidents, railway accidents and mudslides. There were probably more people killed in Culebra Cut than in the rest of the project. Slides continued in the cut even after the canal was opened. During the 1930's Gaillard Cut was widened from 300 feet to 498 feet in some of the more slide prone areas. As we glided along, we were all surprised at how close we were to the jungle on the starboard side. The excavated side must have been very steep because the navigation buoys were right alongside the bank. The jungle was lush and dense and we saw a number of monkeys and brightly colored birds in the trees. The nearby undergrowth resonated with a steady cacophony of bird and other animal noises.

As we approached the Pedro Miguel locks, we again had to stop because of traffic ahead. As we approached Pedro Miguel, we were moving very slowly and just sidled up to the concrete approach wall leading to the locks.   We put over a couple of lines to keep us from drifting away.   Less then an hour later we got underway again, transited the single lock and entered Miraflores Lake.   Miraflores Lake is another man-made lake about mile wide leading from the Pedro Miguel to the two-step Miraflores Locks.   The Miraflores Locks have the tallest lock gates because of the large tidal variations on the Pacific Ocean side.   We transited the two locks without incident and headed for the Baker Piers at the naval base at Balboa.   Balboa is the port for and is across the canal from Panama City.

With all of our stops during our transit, it had taken all day and it was now beginning to get dark.   Those of us who had liberty that night were beginning to get antsy about when we were going to tie up and when liberty would be called away.   We knew that Panama City had "Cinderella" liberty and we would have to be back to the ship by midnight.   As we approached Balboa, word was passed that liberty would be called away as soon as the Special Sea Detail was secured.   My sea detail station was on the NMC Depth Sounder and I only had to man it until the first line was passed to the pier and we were officially "moored".   As soon as the quartermasters whistle sounded that the first line was on the pier, I secured the NMC and bolted below for the showers.   I quickly showered, put on my "dress canvas", picked up my liberty card and headed for the gangway.   As I came on deck, I was amazed and chagrined to see that we still weren't alongside the pier.   I couldn't believe it.   It had been more then a half-hour since the first line went over and they were still struggling to get the ship against the dock.   The difference between low and high tide at Balboa is about 16 feet resulting in very strong currents when the tide is changing.   Evidently the tide was running out and the current was holding Wren away from the pier.   No combination of engine speeds and rudder angles seemed to work. Finally, when the stern got fairly close to the dock, another line was passed over back aft. The forward and aft lines were put on capstans and the ship was slowly hauled against the current and in to the pier.   At one point both lines were stretched tight, getting thinner and looked as if they might part at any time but we finally got moored alongside.   Not very graceful – but as they say in the airplane business " A good landing is any one that you can walk away from". The brow went over and a stream of white hats surged toward the waiting buses for Panama City.

We only had a few hours, so most of us just wanted to look around this famous Central American city and have a few beers. There was of course the contingent that wanted to get laid in Panama City's infamous four-floor bordello the Villa de Amour. We had been told before leaving the ship that the villa, and in fact that whole section of town, was off-limits. The Army Military Police (MP's) would arrest anyone caught in the off-limits section. Of course, sailors will be sailors and where there's a will there's a way! It turned out that Panama City cabbies were experienced at penetrating the Army MP gauntlet. For a bonus fare, they would run the checkpoint with the sailors on the floor under a blanket. Nevertheless, a couple guys from Noa got caught and were returned to the ship charged with a number of offenses starting with " disobeying a lawful order".

Al Dodge and I had been wandering around looking at the sights in this very old town. It had started out as a fishing village (Panama means "many fish") and had grown to be a large city and the capital. We had passed by the MP checkpoint and could see the famous four-floored bordello from a distance. We had checked out a couple of bars and were looking for another. We were walking down a street crowded with sailors when we noticed quite a commotion in one of the bars. When we got there, we looked in and saw a pretty good fight in progress. The sides seemed to be drawn between Wrens and Noas. Still staying outside, we checked to see if the Wrens needed help. Just at that point a Noa took a rum bottle off the bar and hit a Wren Gunners Mate over the head. Didn't phase him a bit. He turned around and decked the Noa with one punch. Seeing that, Al and I figured the Wrens would probably do OK and continued on down the street.

Our trip northward from Panama was uneventful. The weather and seas were calm as we approached Point Loma, the high peninsula overlooking the entrance to the San Diego harbor. We proceeded slowly northward around North Island and then east toward downtown San Diego. We had expected that we would tie up at the Naval Station down at National City.   Imagine our surprise and joy when we realized that we were headed for the Navy Pier at the foot of Broadway right in the center of town.   You could look right up Broadway from the ship.

When liberty was called away, I headed for the bus station and a bus to LA.   I wanted to take this opportunity to catch some West Coast Jazz.   And I did.   Shelley Manne's band was playing down near the beach.   The ex Stan Kenton drummer had a group that included trumpeter Shorty Rogers, alto player Art Pepper and tenor man Bob Cooper.   The following night in the heart of Hollywood I caught the Dave Brubeck Quartet with Paul Desmond.   I got a late bus back from LA somewhat worse for wear from overconsumption of malt flavored beverages while I was listening to all that great music.   As I walked down Broadway on my way back to Wren, I made an amazing discovery - - San Diego bars opened at 7 AM!   I caught a few cool ones and just made it back on board by 8AM.   In fact I had to go direct to quarters and muster with the 1st Division still in my dress uniform.   Mr. Davis gave me a funny look and made some remarks about mustering in the uniform of the day but fortunately didn't pursue it further.

The one-week passage to Hawaii was calm and uneventful.   We moved along Ford Island past the old "Battleship Row" heading for Baker Piers at the Pearl Harbor Naval Station.   As we passed the shattered remnants of her hull, we rendered honors to the U.S.S. Arizona sunk during the attack on December 7, 1941.   The U.S. Ensign flew above her as she was still considered a ship in commission.   We were all very quiet and sobered by the realization that the bodies of over 1100 of her crewmen were entombed in the hull.[4]

While in Hawaii many of us took a tour of Oahu.   It was very interesting including Diamond Head, the Pali and the Punchbowl Crater Military Cemetery where many WW-II dead are buried including Ernie Pyle the famous war correspondent.   We also toured the Dole pineapple factory where the drinking fountains served pineapple juice.   At that

---

[4] Forty-nine years later in May of 2002, Catherine and I visited the U.S.S. Arizona Memorial. After seeing the exhibits and movie, we took the Navy boat out to the Arizona.   Standing in the bridge-like memorial structure looking down at the hull with the barbette of Turret-3 poking through the water is a powerful emotional experience that brought us both to tears.

time, the windward side of the island was completely undeveloped.   The beaches at Waimea and others that are now the hot surfing spots were deserted and marked with big signs warning about the dangerous surf and currents. We had lunch at a tiny restaurant across the road from a beautiful and deserted tropical beach. Now those areas are jammed with people and apartments, condos and time-shares.

Highlining the division chaplain to Wren from Cone.   In calm seas it is a pretty routine operation. In bad weather you can get dunked. (A.T. Miller Photo)

It was a long 10-day haul across the Pacific to Japan.   The division did a lot of high speed maneuvering exercises and communication drills in preparation for what we would need in Korea.   All of the ships also practiced highline drills to transfer people and material between ships.   This is another evolution we would use often during Korean operations.

We stopped at Midway Island to refuel.   Midway is a beautiful atoll with a crystal clear lagoon. It is actually a group of small islands.   Sand Island across the inlet from Midway itself is where the World War II airstrip was located.   It is still there but another field was built on Midway.[5] When Wren was there in 1953, a Squadron of PBM seaplane bombers

[5] After the navy abandoned Midway in the mid-1990's, it reverted to the jurisdiction of the Department of Interior as a wildlife refuge. The Phoenix Corporation was contracted to operate the airport and tourist facilities. Conflicts between Interior and Phoenix over

flew patrols from the lagoon. We had swim call in the lagoon during the few hours we were there. We were disappointed because we didn't get to see any of Midway's famous Gooney Birds. It seems that in the fall they migrate somewhere else.

Sand Island in the foreground with Eastern Island behind and coral reef surrounding. The remains of the Eastern Island airfield used during the Battle of Midway can still be seen. Wren came through the inlet and around to the fuel pier. Note the large concrete seaplane ramp at the enclosed harbor near the atoll entrance. The large runways on Sand Island are of more recent vintage. (US Navy Photo).

Mr. Arnason held a special pay call after we left Midway. We could draw pay in U.S. Occupation Money (script) or Japanese Yen. We were also told to exchange all US Dollars (greenbacks) that we had for script or yen. It was illegal to use greenbacks in Japan. Even so, everyone I knew kept back some greenbacks because we knew that you could exchange them for Yen on the black market for way more than the current rate of

tourist access to wildlife areas resulted in Phoenix abandoning their contract in 2002. Aloha Airlines cancelled their weekly service to Midway. The Midway Atoll National Wildlife Refuge reopened for visitors in January 2008 with access possible through organized tour companies or as a Fish and Wildlife Service Volunteer.

365 Yen to the dollar. The script, which Japanese were not supposed to use, was supposed to cut down on black market activity. Every so often, the US Armed Forces would restrict all military personnel to their ship or station for one day and reissue script. The new script would be a different color and military personnel could exchange their script on a one-for-one basis. The black marketeers were then stuck with a lot of worthless script.

We crossed the 180-degree Longitude meridian, also known as the International Date Line over a weekend. When you cross the line westbound you lose a day and the chaplain was bemoaning the fact that we lost Sunday. We were all presented with cards proclaiming that we had entered the Domain of the Golden Dragon. As we approached Japan, we hit very severe weather and had some injuries. One man was cut seriously on the face. We had to highline Dr. Plummer, the division doctor, over from Cone and almost dunked him in the water.

After the 10-day transit from Hawaii we were glad to see the rugged mountainous coast of Honshu, Japan. We proceeded into Sagami Wan and turned northward toward Tokyo Bay. As we passed the Miura Peninsula we turned westward and toward Yokosuka. Yokosuka is a large port and was one of Imperial Japan's major naval bases in World War II. It has several enormous dry-docks, one of which (Dock 6) was used to build the super Yamamoto class battleship Shinano. As the war progressed, the Japanese decided that they needed aircraft carriers more than they needed battleships so Shinano was converted to a carrier. The conversion was not completed when the Japanese got Shinano underway to move it from Yokosuka to Kure in the Inland Sea. They were trying to escape US B-29 bombers that were pounding Honshu almost every day. Unfortunately for the Japanese, Shinano was sunk on this maiden voyage by the U.S. Navy sub Archerfish in the lower reaches of Sagami Wan. Commander Joseph Enright was awarded the Navy Cross for sinking the huge 59,000-ton carrier that US Intelligence didn't even know existed.

The four destroyers of DesDiv-61 tied up alongside the Destroyer Tender Bryce Canyon (AD-36) for 10 days of much needed maintenance after our long cruise from Norfolk. Destroyers are small ships and have only limited on-board repair facilities. Destroyer tenders contain machine shops, large electronic shops with special test equipment and an optical shop in addition to heavy lift cranes and divers to do underwater repairs. They also have a large selection of spare parts. Our AN/SQS-10 Sonar had been down since we left the Panama Canal. The Scanning Switch, which is a large heavy electro-mechanical assembly that isn't supposed to fail, had burned out a bearing in the assembly that rotated at 6000 RPM. We had tried to get a replacement in supply depots and tenders in San Diego and Pearl Harbor with no luck. The Bryce Canyon didn't have one either. I was elected to see if I could find one in Yokosuka. I tried another tender and the base supply depot and finally found one on the USS Proton, an old Landing Ship, Tank (LST) that had been converted to a floating electronic supply depot. The only problem was getting it back to the ship. It was in a two-foot square wood box and weighed about 60-pounds. It took a cab ride to the fleet landing and a ride in a landing craft to get it to Wren with help from some willing hands along the way. Installing it was a big job involving removing and reconnecting hundreds of screw terminal connections. Fortunately after we turned it on everything worked and we were ready to go hunt submarines.

Task Force 77

Fast Carrier Task Force 77 was always at sea. No triumphant returns to port with welcoming gushing fireboats for the primary strike force of the US Seventh Fleet. Like the Ancient Mariner it was sentenced to a life of roaming the high seas. Ships left it and joined it. Its composition changed almost continuously, but it never came home. It prowled the Asian seas where there was trouble or where trouble was expected. During the Korean War it was usually in the Yellow Sea, the East China Sea or the Sea of Japan within jet fighter striking distance of the Korean combat areas. Later during the Vietnam War it was in the South China Sea or the Tonkin Gulf near Vietnam.

Task Force 77 was big. During the Korean War it usually consisted of from one to four aircraft carriers, one or two heavy cruisers or an Iowa class battleship and always about twenty destroyers. The carriers and their air groups were, of course, the task forces' main weapon. The primary mission of the other ships was to protect the carriers. The aircraft carriers carried hallowed names of historic battles such as Yorktown, Princeton, Oriskany, Lake Champlain and Valley Forge or names of famous old ships-of-the-line such as Essex, Wasp, Boxer, Kearsage or Hornet. They were all Essex class carriers built during World War II.

Unlike modern angle-deck carriers that allow aircraft to "go around" if they don't catch an arresting wire, the Korean War vintage carriers had straight flight decks with a steel cable barrier about two-thirds of the way down the deck. If a landing aircraft didn't catch a wire with its tailhook, it made a controlled crash into the barrier. The barrier could be lowered to allow aircraft to taxi forward and park. There were no mirror landing systems or radar approach systems as on today's carriers. There was only the Landing Signal Officer (LSO). The LSO stood on a platform on the port aft side of the flight deck and directed landing aircraft with a set of brightly colored paddles during the day and lighted "wands" at night. It was a very difficult and demanding job under the best of circumstances. It was orders of magnitude worse in rough weather when the

LSO not only had to monitor and correct the approaching aircraft but also judge and compensate for the rolling and pitching deck. If endangered by an off-course approaching aircraft, the LSO jumped over the side and into a net rigged outboard of his platform.

A Landing Signal Officer (LSO) directing aircraft landing operations on a straight deck aircraft carrier. Note the escape net in the lower left corner of the photo. (US Navy Photo)

These were the early days of carrier flight operations with jet aircraft. The primary Navy jet fighter at that time was the Grumman-built F9F. The first version of the F9F had a straight wing and was called the Panther. Later versions with a swept wing were called Cougars. The carrier's aircraft catapults were driven by hydraulic rams and were much less powerful than todays steam powered catapults. Because of this, the carriers had to turn into the wind and increase speed to 25 knots to launch the jet aircraft. Reorienting the carriers and all the accompanying ships in the task force for one of these course and speed changes was a complex and dangerous evolution.

The battleships with Wren in TF-77 in the winter of 1953/54 were either Wisconsin or New Jersey. Cruisers included Albany, Rochester, Des Moines, Bremerton, Quincy and

Helena. The destroyers were Gearing class 2250 or Sumner class 2200-ton ships or recently reactivated Fletcher class 2100-ton ships such as Wren. Although the destroyers were primarily used for antisubmarine and antiaircraft protection they were also used as radar pickets (birddogs) patrolling between the task force and the coast to detect incoming attack aircraft. Operating close to the enemy coastline put the task force in constant danger of air attack with only a short advance warning.

Wren steaming away from USS Wisconsin at high speed. Wren had just arrived in TF-77 from Sasebo and had delivered mail and new crewmen to BB-64 by highline. (A.T. Miller Photo)

The radio voice call for Commander Task Force 77 was "Jehovah" and the collective voice call for the task force was "Magistrate." I think they particularly picked guys with deep booming voices to operate the task force commander's radio. When you heard "Magistrate.. this.. is..*Jehovah*......." it always seemed to sound like a command from on high.

Destroyer Division 61, which in addition to Wren included Noa, Cone and Stribling, operated with Task Force 77 a number of times in the fall and winter of 1953/54.

Destroyer assignments to 77 were usually for 30 or 35 days. The crew did not look forward to them. It was a long stretch at sea in a small, hard riding ship with very cramped living spaces. The pace of activity was very high and everyone was always tired. Once in the combat zone all night operations were at darken ship without any running lights. The danger of collision under those conditions was always a concern. By the end of one of these tour's tension was high, tempers were short and everyone was counting the days back to Japan.

Wren leads DesDiv-61 to sea from Sasebo, Japan at high-speed enroute to Task Force 77. Noa, Cone and Stribling follow Wren. Depth charge racks are at the left and the fan shaped device in the center of the stern is a smoke generator. (A.T. Miller Photo)

Before our first deployment to Korean waters a Republic of Korea (ROK) Navy Ensign was assigned to Wren to act as interpreter. Mr. Kim reported aboard in Sasebo and stayed with us until we until we left Japan to return to the U.S. He was a shy quiet man and seemed a bit awed by the rather boisterous American junior officers. We only had a couple of occasions to use his translating skills - both dealing with fishermen in distress.

Wren arrived in Task Force 77 for the first time on October 12, 1953. A truce, stopping the fighting on and around the Korean Peninsula, had been signed a few months before on July 27, 1953. No one was sure, however, about North Korean and Chinese intentions. Although the shooting had stopped, peace discussions at Panmunjon continued on a number of volatile issues including prisoner repatriation. Since the truce, Chinese and North Korean aircraft and ships probed the edges of the United Nations defenses on a fairly regular basis. The U.S Forces in the Korean Theater remained on a high level of readiness. All naval operations were conducted as if we were still at war and a Combat Zone still existed in the seas around Korea.

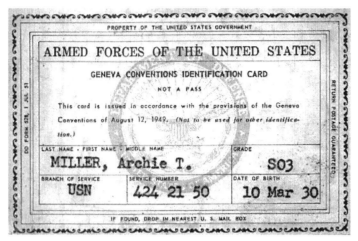

Because Wren was operating in the Korean Combat Zone, we were all issued Geneva Convention Cards to be used in the unlikely event that we were captured by the North Koreans or Chinese.

There was also serious worry about the more then twelve thousand explosive mines planted by the North Koreans in the seas around Korea. The weather in the winter was terrible with storms blowing out of Siberia and Manchuria resulting in high seas and limited visibility. These storms dislodged the anchored mines and swept them out to sea where the task force operated. We saw and destroyed enough mines to know that the threat was real and always worried about the ones we didn't see and destroy. To some extent the crew anticipated the adventure and excitement of a deployment with Task Force 77. They also knew, however, that it was going to be three to four weeks of decidedly ungracious living in terrible weather in a ship that would again prove why they were nicknamed "tin cans."

The level of operations was intense. Gun firing exercises were scheduled even during the transit from Japan to the TF-77 operating area. A plane towing a target sleeve or a full-size, drone target aircraft was flown out from Japan or South Korea to provide targets. The four ships formed a column one behind the other and the target aircraft flew various patterns to exercise different defense plans. Large cloth sleeves were towed about 1000 feet behind the tow plane. The destroyers fired their 5-inch and 40-millimeter guns at the target sleeves. Remote controlled obsolete airplanes (drones) were sometimes used as targets for more realistic exercises. Fixed offsets were put in the fire control computer so that while the ships' proficiency could be judged, the drone would not be shot down. One time, however, the drone, an old WW-II vintage Grumman piston engine fighter was inadvertently damaged so that it was unable to land. It had to be destroyed before it ran out of fuel. The offsets were taken out so we could shoot straight and we had at it. Splash one Hellcat.

Once we joined the task force, destroyers were assigned as part of the curved "bent line screen" that swept the seas ahead of the capital ships for submarines while keeping a lookout for mines. The ships were spaced one and one half times the expected sonar range for the day so that their sonar search patterns would overlap. The idea was that the screen would detect any approaching submarines and they could be attacked before they could get near the aircraft carriers and other capital ships. In those days, the diesel/electric submarines were too slow to catch a task force from behind while submerged. They had to lie in wait in the path of the task force and hope to get through the screen and sink a carrier. Two destroyers were assigned as "pouncers" in the rear of the task force ready to attack any submarine that managed to get through the screen at the front of the task force.

Wren was an anomaly in Destroyer Division 61. The other three destroyers, Cone, Noa and Stribling were newer Gearing class ships. They were a little larger, could carry more fuel and had one more five-inch gun barrel in two less gun mounts. The older Fletcher class Wren was prettier and faster but not nearly as comfortable. Unlike the other three, Wren did not have a fore and aft inside passageway. That meant you had to transit the open weather decks to get between the forward and the after parts of the ship. Those of us who slept back aft and stood watch up forward got this lovely exposure to sea breezes on our way to work. There was almost always some spray in the air so at best you got damp going back and forth even if you kept to the lee side of the ship. You almost always carried a light coating of salt, which felt greasy and dirty. Even going up the lee side wasn't completely safe. There was a break in the superstructure between 5-inch gun mount 53 and the torpedo mount that allowed waves on the weather side to come across the ship. As you approached the break you would stop and peer around the edge and then make a dash forward -- hopefully without getting wet. If your timing was bad you could be in cold water to your knees (or worse).

U.S.S. Wren at sea with Task Force 77, off the Korean coast, October 23, 1953. Photographed from a helicopter from U.S.S. Yorktown (CV-10) while delivering guard mail (US Navy Photo).

At worst, in really bad weather, we had to don foul weather gear and life jackets, climb up a deck through gun mount 53 and work our way carefully along the lifelines on the deck above the main deck (01 level). The deck was pitching and tossing and wet and slippery. There was a narrow catwalk with lifelines over the break connecting the after and forward superstructure. Unfortunately there was also a crane for loading torpedoes in the break. As you went forward on the catwalk, you had to climb over the torpedo crane and your body was above the catwalk and lifeline. I always alerted the starboard lifeguard watch to keep an eye on me when I was going over the crane at night so I wouldn't be thrown overboard undetected. Many a night with Task Force 77 I arrived in sonar wet and cold to go on watch and thought enviously of our compatriots in Noa, Cone and Stribling going fore and aft inside in their shirtsleeves.

Eating was difficult in heavy winter weather. The Fletchers also used the mess deck for berthing the mess cooks. During the day the bunks were folded up against the outer bulkheads. Most of the bench seats for the mess tables were free standing and not fastened down so they could be stowed out of the way at night. We tried lashing them to the tables but in very rough weather only the fixed benches along the bulkhead were really usable. Chow was served in one compartment and eaten in the next one forward. A critical operation in rough weather was stepping over the foot high hatch coaming between compartments while carrying a fully loaded food tray. This became increasingly slippery and hazardous as sailors spilled food while navigating the hatch. Another complication was that the mess deck was not level but sloped up toward the bow. It was literally an uphill fight on a slippery deck to get to a table. As soon as you got to a table a slice of bread was slipped under the tray to keep it from sliding all over the table. A tablemate was asked to hold onto your tray while you went back to get a cup of the drink du jour. Glass salt and pepper shakers had long ago been replaced with ones improvised from plastic bottles that wouldn't break when dashed to the steel deck. Those sitting on the benches lashed to the table had to use their feet to maintain their seat. As the ship rolled one way you extended your foot under the table to brace yourself. As it rolled back you bent your knee and braced your foot under the bench. These were folding benches that had a brace that hooked into the legs to keep them from folding up. All this foot motion often resulted in the foldup benches' leg brace being kicked loose. After a while everyone's ear was attuned to the sound of a brace popping out. If you saw four people on a bench suddenly jump to their feet you knew the brace had been kicked loose and the bench was in imminent danger of collapsing. The rule was that whoever kicked it loose had to grovel on the deck to refasten it while the others held on to his tray. Of course in rough weather some sailors lost their appetites so there wasn't as much demand for seating in the mess deck. I never got seasick and I didn't mind the rough weather because the chow lines were always a lot shorter.

Another annoyance was the requirement to darken ship any time we were in the Korean Combat Zone (which was almost all the time we were with 77). All external lights and running lights were extinguished after sunset and door switches were set so that adjacent interior lights would go off if any external doors were opened to the night. In most of the ship where doors were off passageways or ladders it wasn't too much of an inconvenience. In the First Division berthing compartment, it was a real pain in the neck. It was the largest berthing compartment on the ship stretching the complete width of the ship. A pair of side-by-side ladders (stairs) from the main deck accessed it. At the top of the ladders was a short passageway ending in external doors on the port and starboard side. During darken ship, whenever one of these doors was opened, all the lights in the compartment below went out - - and about 50 sailors were in the dark. When the door was closed, the lights came back on - - maybe! The door was held closed by steel dogs operated by a large wheel on each side of the door. Most of us were in the habit of going through the door and giving the wheel a desultory spin just sufficient to engage the dogs and prevent the door from swinging open as the ship rolled. That was OK during the day but at darken ship it wasn't enough to make the lights come back on. To compound the problem the traffic not only from the 1st Division compartment but also from the 2nd Division and the Engineering Division further aft also used these doors. I slept back in one corner of the compartment against the starboard hull. If you were trying to read or mend clothes or write a letter, you did it in short spurts. As soon as the lights went off everybody yelled "Shut the door – TIGHT". Most of the time they did and the lights were back on in a few seconds. If they had gone out the door and didn't spin the wheel enough, we all were in suspended animation waiting for light. It then became a contest to see if someone else would come through the door and close it right or one of us would have to get up and trudge up the ladder to get the lights back on. The whole thing with the lights wasn't really that big of a deal except that after a couple of weeks of it on top of everything else it got everybody pretty touchy.

The inconveniences to living in the rough sea environment paled in comparison, however, to the real hazards to life and limb in operating and fighting these ships in serious winter weather.   Inboard lifelines were rigged and every precaution taken but people got banged up or scraped from slips or falls.   Some were serious.   A fireman slipped on a boiler room ladder while trying to close the hatch against the sea.   He was seriously cut across his face when the hatch pinned him against the coaming knife-edge with his feet kicking out in empty air.   The doctor was highlined over from Cone (and almost dunked) to suture his face.   Actually, the doctors' hands were shaking so badly after his highline experience that our senior corpsmen did the sutures.   The sea was so rough that the ship was slowed and turned into the wind until the sutures were complete. Another man fell going down a ladder, caught his ring on a hatch dog and seriously tore up his finger.   One of the sonarmen was not standing in the correct position while loading hedgehog projectiles.   When the ship rolled he lost his balance, fell forward and the hedgehog rocket smashed the small bones in his hand as it fell against the mount.   We highlined him over to a carrier, where there were better medical facilities, and he never returned to the ship.

One January night about eight o'clock while we were with TF-77 in the Korean Straits, three men in Cone were trying to secure the motor whaleboat that had come loose in the heavy seas.   They all had lifejackets, helmets and lifelines on when they were deluged in green water. Two of them went over the side their lifelines popping like string.   Cone immediately executed the man overboard maneuver as other ships in the task force got out of her way.   As they came about on the return track, the men and the floats thrown overboard to them were spotted in the water.   Wren and Ozbourn (DD-846) maneuvered up wind of Cone.   We were putting oil in the water to try to calm the seas.   All our spotlights and signal lamps were used to try to illuminate the rescue scene.   We were trying to position the ship to provide Cone some shelter from the wind and seas while illuminating the rescue area. Cone had an accommodation ladder over the side and was trying to maneuver the ship near the men without sucking them into the screws. One of the men was able to help himself and take a lifeline and after some time he was hauled on board. The other man appeared to be unconscious although the life jacket was keeping his face out of the water.   A volunteer swimmer in life jacket and lifeline went overboard from Cone and tried to swim to the injured man.   With the 30-degree water and heavy seas the swimmer couldn't get to him and finally had to be hauled in exhausted.   A float type life raft was released from Cone and four men tried to paddle to the unconscious man.   They were unsuccessful and had to be recovered from the cold sea.   Finally, despite the danger of the man being sucked into the screws, more aggressive ship handling put the ladder alongside the man.   A couple of men donned lifelines and descended the ladder.   As the ship rolled they were plunged up to their waist in the frigid water.   They tried to hoist him from the water but they could only grab him by the life jacket and he was a dead weight.   In trying to lift him, the collar of his life jacket tore off.   Finally the ship took a great roll and he was gone.   There was no sign of him on either side of the ship.   We were all stunned.   He may have been dead already but it had seemed that his rescue was so close.   The next day as the task force steamed back through the area of the accident we manned every high place on the ship to look against all hope for a trace of the lost man.   I stood atop the after 40mm Gun Director, the highest place aft of the stacks.   The front that had caused the horrendous storm the night before had passed and it was crystal clear, windy and very cold.   Although visibility was perfect, the seas were still mountainous.   We all knew that the chance of his body even being there no less our being able to see him were nil but we all strained to look anyway.   In the vastness of the sea under the great blue arc of the sky there was nothing. I think we all said a prayer ". . . for those in peril on the sea".

Wren photographed from a helicopter from the U.S.S Yorktown (CV-10) delivering mail to the fantail just aft of Mount 55, which has been turned to starboard. Note FOX flag for Flight Operations flying from starboard yardarm. Although I can't be seen in this photo, the author was standing in the door on the bridge immediately below the Mk37 Gun Director. (US Navy Photo).

Destroyers took turns as the Plane Guard or Rescue ships astern of the carriers during flight operations. The Plane Guard was closest behind the carrier and was there to rescue pilots of planes that went off the carrier deck. The Rescue destroyer was further back to back-up the Plane Guard and assist in rescue operations. Both ships had their whaleboat rigged out over the side ready to be lowered into the water. Some of the crew sat in the boat, exposed to the elements and ready to be lowered away at a moment's notice. The ship was going at 25 knots into a wind that may have been 15 or 20 knots so the boat crew was exposed to high, cold winds mixed with spray or rain. No fun. Flight operations went on constantly. Aircraft were launched and recovered at all times of the day or night in every kind of weather. In those days before angled flight decks and mirror landing systems, the Landing Signal Officer still used fluorescent paddles (or lighted wands at night) in each hand to direct the planes onto the pitching deck. Miraculously, considering the number of flight operations and the beastly winter weather, there weren't many accidents. We only had to put our boat in the water once to assist in the rescue of a plane. The F-9F went over the side of the carrier Essex after its landing gear collapsed.

Wren approaches the USS Yorktown (CV-10) to assume plane guard station prior to the beginning of Task Force 77 air operations. (A.T. Miller Photo)

The helicopter, that hovered astern of the carrier during flight operations got the pilot almost immediately. The plane was still afloat and the pilot just stood on top of his seat and grabbed the rescue loop from the chopper. All we had to do was pick up rafts, floats and other rescue equipment that had been thrown in the water.

The task force usually steamed at 18 knots. Launching or recovering aircraft during carrier flight operations required the task force to steam into the wind at 25 knots. The task force turned back to its original course at the end of flight operations. Changing the task force direction into the wind was a complex and dangerous operation. It was done at high speed and there was always a danger of collision. The task force commander would order the turn. "Magistrate this is Jehovah...Turn zero niner zero.. Standby... Execute". On "Execute", the capital ships in the center of the formation turned to the new course. The screen of destroyers was then on the wrong side of the formation and going in the wrong direction. With the task force now going at 25 knots each of the destroyers had to steam close to 30 knots to get back into the bent line screen in front of the task force. The task force commander signaled the intention to turn the task force by voice radio or signal flag hoist. On receipt of this initial message both the bridge and Combat Information Center (CIC) crews plotted the problem on a Maneuvering Board to determine the required course and speed and compared their results. The OD reviewed and approved the course and speed. The captain was always on the bridge for these evolutions. On the order to execute, all of the ships came to their new course and speed. It looked like a free for all. Ships were speeding in every direction. CIC crew, lookouts and quartermasters tracked the other ships to insure no one was on a steady bearing that meant a collision course. Particular attention was paid to the aircraft carriers and other large ships, that considerably outweighed, and could do great damage to a destroyer. Everyone had in the back of their mind the terrible accident involving Wasp and Hobson. A little more than a year before on April 26, 1952 in a similar operation off the coast of South Carolina the 27,000 ton aircraft carrier Wasp (CV-18) had literally rolled over the 1,630 ton Ellyson class Destroyer Mine Sweeper Hobson (DMS-26). Hobson was cut in half and sank in four minutes. A mistake on the bridge of Hobson caused the collision and the loss of 176 of the Hobson's crew. A sonar school classmate of mine was lost in Hobson. We were in company with Wasp in Task Force 77 for several weeks. I think it was almost meant seriously when lookouts were cautioned to keep an eye on the "can opener." There were times when it was touch and go to stay out of the carriers path as ships maneuvered at high speed. On October 14, 1953, while with TF-77, Wren's log contained the entry "1932 – Changing course and speed as required to avoid Boxer". USS Boxer (CV-21) was a 27,000-ton Essex class carrier that could easily have sunk Wren.

Although a truce was in effect, the North Koreans or Chinese tested us from time to time. One or two Russian built Mig fighter aircraft would fly out toward Task Force 77 from North Korea. They were detected by the ship's radar and identified as potentially hostile aircraft. Immediately General Quarters were called away on all ships. The task force prepared to launch interceptor aircraft. The North Koreans usually launched these feints at two or three o'clock in the morning for maximum disruptive effect. They sure scared the hell out of me. I can remember clearly jumping out of my bunk, pulling on my clothes and running forward to General Quarters. The ship was heeled over at high speed and spray was cascading over the deck as the task force turned into the wind to launch planes. Going to General Quarters you don't have a choice of using the wet or dry side of the ship. To avoid confusion and prevent collisions between running sailors, the rule for going to General Quarters was "up and forward on the starboard side and aft and down on the port". As I'm running in the dark through the spray in the blacked out ship I'm wondering what the hell is going on and if this is a real attack. Usually about the time we got planes up, the Migs would turn and hightail it back into North Korea.

One Wednesday after several days of very rough weather and strenuous replenishment and refueling operations with much loss of sleep, the executive officer declared the afternoon as "Rope Yarn Sunday". Rope Yarn Sunday is an old naval tradition going back to the days of sailing ships. It was an afternoon (usually Wednesday) of in-port relaxation and an opportunity to repair clothing. The exec declared it at sea to let everyone (except the watch standers) rest and catch up on their sleep. We had not been resting for more then half an hour when General Quarters sounded for one of our Mig antagonists. We swore there was a commie spy in Wren that had reported Rope Yarn Sunday to the North Koreans.

Task Force 77 was kept in a constant state of readiness in case something happened requiring a fast response. The entire task force was refueled every three or four days. They didn't want us to get below 80% fuel. On a refueling day one or two tankers from Pusan, Korea rendezvoused with us before dawn and at first light refueling began. Tankers were named for Indian-named rivers. With TF-77 we fueled from Taluga, Passumpsic, Cimmaron and Tolavana. A carrier rigged to the tanker's port side to receive black Navy Special oil for its boilers and jet fuel for its aircraft. Fueling a carrier could take several of hours. A succession of destroyers came along the tankers starboard side to receive black oil while the carrier refueled. They rigged two 6-inch fuel lines to the destroyers, one forward and one aft. With two fuel lines Wren took about thirty-five minutes to take on 45,000 gallons of fuel if the weather wasn't bad. For the destroyer, fueling was an all-hands evolution. The fuel hoses were hauled in by hand and it took many men to do it. The crew for the forward fueling station was on the foc'sle and if the weather was bad, they were continually hit with spray and green water coming over the bow. The crew for the aft fueling station was better protected but still sometimes took green water if we got too close to the tanker. At the same time the tanker also highlined over light cargo, 55-gallon drums of lubricating oil, mail and movies. The designated duty of the signalman on our bridge during refueling was to wigwag to the tanker signalman to try to negotiate for the best movies available.

U.S.S/. Taluga, which fueled Wren while with TF-77, is shown fueling the U.S.S. Oriskany (CV-34) to port and the U.S.S. Cecil (DD_835) to starboard. Unfortunately during the winter of 1953/54 the sea was rarely this calm. (U.S. Navy Photo)

We did this so often that after a while most of the crew believed they could fuel at sea in their sleep. It was true; we worked well as a team and got pretty efficient. It was still brute force work, however, involving a lot of what the old salts called "heaving around". Fueling from a tanker was pretty straightforward. They had special booms and used what was called an Elwood or "close-in" rig to almost drop the hoses over to you. We could maneuver quite close and the crew had the timing and techniques down very well. Occasionally we fueled from an aircraft carrier. Though not as good as a tanker, it wasn't too bad. The carrier was high and they rigged the fueling hoses from the hangar deck so they dropped down to us and came aboard reasonably well. The absolute worst was to fuel from a battleship. They rigged the fuel hoses from a tripod on the top of a five-inch gun mount, which was about 20 feet in from the side of the battleship. The combination of low height and long distance insured that the hose would hit the water before it got to us. As soon as we started pulling the hose over, it was down and dragging in the water. With about 15 guys on the inhaul it was almost impossible to move. One winter day with TF-77 off the coast of Korea it took us 45 minutes just to get the first fuel hose over from Wisconsin. Everybody was soaking wet, cold, exhausted and pissed off. To add insult to injury, Wisconsin whose crew was high and dry on their large ship had their band out to play tunes for us. There was some discussion among the crew about whether seawater from our fire hoses could reach across to the band.

While Wrens, soaking wet and cold, struggled to fuel from Wisconsin, their band (03 level aft of 5" mount) serenaded us. Just what we needed! Note Wisconsins ' fueling line handlers high and dry just below the bridge. (A.T. Miller Photo)

When I was first in Wren my fueling station was on the forward inhaul on the foc'sle, a particularly wet location. Later, I was moved to the aft inhaul which is amidships and better sheltered. Finally I was made the phone talker for the 'midships highline station which was high and dry on the 01 level. One time with 77, when I was on the aft inhaul we were fueling from a fleet tanker. We quickly got the fuel hose hauled over and then we had a break of 20 to 30 minutes while they pumped fuel. Although it was cold weather, the course we were on put us on the lee side out of the wind and the winter sun felt warm in the calm air. We were right over the after fireroom so the deck was nice and warm. We all laid down on the deck warm and cozy in our multiple layers of foul weather gear, bulky kapok lifejackets and helmets. We got so comfortable that almost everyone immediately dozed off. Evidently Wren's course drifted a little left and we got close to the tanker forcing a large wave up and over Wren's deck. I woke up underwater and sputtering wondering where the hell I was and what was happening. As the water receded and I struggled to my feet, my first view was of the fueling crew up on the 01 level in hysterics at our surprised and shocked faces. We gave them an index finger greeting as the freezing cold water poured down inside all of our foul weather gear. Fortunately they finished fueling about that time and with chattering teeth we expeditiously got disengaged from the tanker. I was almost blue by the time I got all the gear off and went below to get into dry clothes. What a wakeup call that was!

About every 10-days or so we would replenish dry and refrigerated stores. This was a very difficult procedure made much worse by the generally bad winter weather. Wren would go alongside an Attack Cargo Ship (AKA) and rig highlines. The stores were highlined over to us in big cargo nets. We had so little deck space that sometimes the net would come down in the Hedgehog Mount and food cases would dump out all over the deck. Crewmen worked frantically to get the area cleared before the next load came over. Carrying heavy cases across wet rolling decks was very treacherous. During replenishment in very heavy weather in January, the operation was finally called off after the highline parted because we were rolling so badly. The Replenishment Force Commander gave Wren a "Well Done" for being able to replenish as much as we did under terrible conditions.

Fresh water was a precious commodity on an old Fletcher class can. We only had one salt-water evaporator (newer destroyers had two) to make fresh water. The four steam boilers that propelled the ship used most of the water. Whatever was left over, after boiler feed water requirements were met, was available for drinking and washing. In normal operations water for the crew was not a big problem. Most of the time we could steam on two boilers and had more then enough water. With TF-77 we operated on four boilers most of the time. In addition, the constant speed changes and steaming at 25 knots for long periods during flight operations used up lots of water.

As a result, most of the time we were with TF-77 we were on water-hours. That meant that the showers were padlocked by the Master-At-Arms except for a couple of hours in the evening. We were encouraged to use the salt-water shower at any time. Most of the crew passed on that one. It was of course impossible for all of the crew to shower in those couple of hours. Besides the physical logistical problem of everyone using the few shower stalls in this short time, many people were on watch or otherwise occupied during the time the padlocks were off. Sailors being resourceful creatures devised the "water hours bird bath". There were several rows of small stainless steel sinks in the head. It was quite a sight to come into the after head and see rows of stark naked sailors standing in front of the filled sinks throwing water into the air and over themselves like so many robins in those pretty ceramic fixtures on front lawns. Throw on the water, lather up and throw on the rinse water. I think we probably used almost as much water as if they had left the showers on. The biggest problem in this operation was finding a dry place to stash your towel in a compartment filled with flying water. We managed!

Toward the end of a tour with TF-77 tempers became short. Confrontations and minor fisticuffs occurred. We were all physically tired, tired of doing the same things every day, tired of being damp and salty and tired of seeing the same people at close quarters all the time. We just wanted to get back on solid land and lift a few cool ones. Everyone was very careful about what they said and how they said it. Even in bad weather you would see guys standing out on deck letting the wind blow in their face just to get away from the confines of the ship. I used to stand out on the 01 level just forward of the mast under the shelter of the bridge overhang. I was out of the worst of the gale and could watch the sky and sea and take deep breaths of fresh air. We all counted the days.

Usually our approach to Sasebo Japan was timed so we were just off the harbor entrance anti-submarine nets at dawn. The nets were closed at night and no ships could enter. We tried to time it so that we would be the first ship through when the nets were opened at daybreak. As soon as we entered we went to the fueling piers in the outer harbor to refuel. A boat usually came over to the fueling piers with our mail. Spirits and anticipation were high. We could see and smell Japan. In an hour or so after we were refueled we moved to our anchorage in the inner harbor. As soon as we were anchored, the water taxis and "bum boats" started circling us. They weren't to be disappointed. As soon as the anchor detail was secured, liberty was called away for the two sections not having the duty. The navy LCVP liberty boats and the water taxis swarmed alongside and Wrens with a couple of paydays stuffing their pockets hit the beach to do Sasebo. Those in the duty section wistfully watched them go. Tomorrow would be their turn. For most, the first stop was the closest place to the fleet landing that served Nippon, Asahai or Kirin beer in those big one liter bottles for 200 yen (55 cents in those days). Many had their favorite places among the bars lining Paradise Alley. Some went shopping for the many bargains available in cameras, china and silk. Some went to the Sasebo Enlisted Mens Club famed for its steak dinners. Whatever they did, however, it was all over at midnight. Except for a few with overnight passes "Cinderella Liberty" was the rule in Sasebo or Yokusuka. If you weren't inside the gate at the fleet landing at midnight, you were "over the hill".

Sonarmen on liberty in Sasebo Japan. Note the 200-Yen (55 cent US), one-liter bottles of Asahai on the table. From left to right the author, Al Dodge, Gene Staunton and Archer Kinlock. (A.T. Miller Photo)

As it got later in the evening sailors started drifting back to the fleet landing to return to the ship. Having either had enough to drink or run out of money they were ready to return. Because it got so crowded in the street in front of the fleet landing, taxis and pedicabs had to drop off their passengers at a taxi area about half a block from the landing. I had the great good fortune to get shore patrol at the taxi stand about a week before Christmas 1953. A large portion of the 7th Fleet was in port in Sasebo for the holidays. On top of that the Marine Air Squadron from the U.S.S. Saipan was having their Christmas party in town that night. Marines in various stages of inebriation had been stumbling out of cabs as midnight approached. My partner was a third class from Cone who I didn't know. About 11:45 PM a cab approached weaving and rocking from side to side. The cab driver was waving at us out the window. It was obvious that there was a serious fight going on in the back seat. As the cab slid to a stop, the door opened and this huge marine came bouncing out. He had lost his hat and his blouse and as he stood up he flexed his shoulders and arms and the sleeves ripped out of his tailored shirt. My partner took one look at him and with a trembling voice said, "I'll go for help!" and bolted off toward the Shore Patrol Headquarters leaving me to deal with the monster marine.   The other guy got out of the cab and the fight resumed with the cab driver dancing around and demanding his money.   I tried to stay under the blows and started hitting the big marine in the shins with my billy club.   He didn't go down easily. Some other sailors jumped in to help me out but the marine dragged all of us out into the road where we were in danger of being run over by assorted taxis, trucks and pedicabs. Finally the shin blows got to him and as he collapsed, we all sat on him in the middle of the road.   About this time my partner returned with the Chief and a detachment of Shore Patrol.   I jumped all over my partner about how we were supposed to work together.   After commenting on his mental capacity and ancestry, I told him at some length and no uncertain terms that the procedure was to SEND for help and stick together. Fortunately the rest of the evening was relatively calm.

Motor launches and LCVP and LCM landing craft were used for liberty boats. They made one round trip after another to the many ships at anchor in the harbor. From about 10:30 on the fleet landing became increasingly unruly. There were literally thousands of mostly tipsy sailors waiting for boats to take them back out to their ship.   The numbers of sailors for each boat were carefully counted off at the gate to make sure boats weren't overloaded.   Only a safe number was allowed through the gate for each boat. Nevertheless, when their boat was announced, the previously counted, drunken sailors pushed, shoved and ran down the sloped ramp to be sure they wouldn't miss the boat. It was like a cattle stampede down the ramp to the boats.   Shore patrol on the boat float tried to slow them down and insure that none went over the side. On the 15 to 20 minute trip back to the ship, fights often broke out in the boats.   The LCM landing craft were the worst. Their big open well deck designed to carry a tank was like an arena with the fights surging from one end to the other. But eventually it all got sorted out and everybody got back to the ship to dream of another week in Japan and then back to 77.

Whale Bangers

When I joined the Navy I thought I would serve as a musician. I had been music major in college and had passed a preliminary audition for the U.S. Navy School of Music in Anacostia, D.C. Unfortunately the final audition was a lot tougher then the preliminary and I ended up in boot camp with no defined career path. Navy boots with musical background and good technical test scores were encouraged to become Sonarmen. Good ears and pitch discrimination were valued for listening to and analyzing sonar echoes from submarines. All you had to do was pass the Seashore (pitch discrimination) Test and you were off to Fleet Sonar School, Key West. There were lots of musicians in sonar school. There were a number of musical groups made up of students. Most of them just played for fun. I worked in a small band that had some paying jobs at the enlisted men's and chiefs clubs on the base and an occasional off-base job. We got extorted into playing for free, however, for the cocktail parties at the Sonar School's Echoasis Officers Club. At that time, it was against navy regulations for sailors to have outside paying jobs. The officer in charge of the club threatened to blow our cover on the paid gigs if we didn't do their cocktail parties gratis. The only redeeming feature of that gig was that the Stewards Mates who were running the bar would sneak us gin bottles filled with premixed martinis. A sonarman by the name of Robert Morse sang and danced with our group. Subsequent to his Navy experience, he went on to star in "How To Succeed In Business Without Really Trying" and more recently won awards for his performance in "Tru". You never know!

U.S. Fleet Sonar School, Key West graduation ceremony February 1952. The World War-II vintage wooden school and barracks buildings are in the background. Only the Sonar Simulators were air-conditioned. (A.T. Miller Photo)

Sonar school included six months of training in electronics, equipment maintenance, sonar operations and ear training. It was pretty interesting and I learned a lot. I had dabbled with electronics for years and this training filled in the gaps and built on what I already knew. Navy training methods were interesting too. Once the Navy decided that you could be trained, they employed methods to insure success not available to civilian institutions. For instance, if you fell asleep in class, the guys on either side of you got extra duty. If you ever started to doze, you would get an elbow in the ribs. Anyone failing the weekly test had their liberty privileges revoked and went to night school for the following week. It was made plain to all of us that if we flunked out our next assignment would be scraping rust and chipping paint on mothballed LST's in Green Cove Springs, Florida. I graduated from Sonar School in February 1952. After a short stint of shore duty at the Naval Torpedo Testing Range, Piney Point, MD, I was transferred to the U.S.S Wren in July 1953.

Antisubmarine warfare during the Korean War had not changed much since World War II. True, the sonar displays were better and the equipment was easier to use but you still had to be within 5000 to 6000 yards (best case) of a submarine in order to find it. The system was still highly dependent on the skills and particularly the sharp ear of the operator. Sonar school trained us to recognize the sound characteristics of submarine echoes and other non-submarine returns (ship wakes, decoys, the bottom, etc.) Particular training was given in recognizing the change in echo pitch caused by the movement of the submarine. This change caused by doppler effect made the pitch lower for a submarine moving away and higher for one coming toward you. The echo from an object dead-in-the-water (not moving) did not have any doppler. In sonar school we spent hours and hours in the Student Recognition Group Trainer (SRGT) listening to recorded and simulated echoes. This training was reinforced constantly with exercises at sea with friendly submarines and in shore-based Sonar Attack Teachers that very realistically simulated shipboard antisubmarine exercises.

It was known that the Soviet Union had given North Korea two submarines. There were also persistent intelligence reports of Soviet and Chinese submarine activity in Korean waters. Although there was never a confirmed enemy submarine contact in Korean waters there had been 80 reports of possible submarine contacts and a number of attacks by destroyers on promising looking contacts. On June 12, 1951, several hours after a mine had seriously damaged her, USS Walke (DD-723) reported a sonar contact classified as possible submarine. USS Hubbard (DD-748) launched repeated depth charge and hedgehog attacks on the contact. Hubbard reported two underwater explosions and a slight oil slick. On July 20, 1951 an escort operating with the British aircraft carrier HMS Glory depth charged an ASDIC (sonar) contact in the Yellow Sea that had been classified "suspected submarine". A few oil patches surfaced in the depth charge area but no debris was recovered. An American destroyer depth charged a contact in the Formosa Straits that turned out to be the wreck of the submarine U.S.S. Tang sunk by its own torpedo in WW-II. When we arrived in the Far East we were concerned about the possible submarine menace and our ability to combat it. Given the fragile truce situation, we felt that an easily deniable sub attack ("They struck a mine") was a very real possibility.

Enroute from Yokosuka, Japan to our first tour with Task Force 77 in Korea we had a submarine scare. We had come through the Inland Sea and were transiting the Shimonoseki Straits between the Japanese islands of Honshu and Kyushu. Earlier it had been raining and visibility was poor but now a cold front had come through and it was brisk and cold. The sky was bright blue, visibility was unlimited and there were whitecaps. The sonar conditions were good as the sun set. At 10:43PM as we came out of the straits and into the Sea of Japan, Noa reported a sonar contact as possible submarine. It was a logical place for a submarine to wait for naval targets traveling from Yokosuka to Korea. At 11:04PM Wren went to ASW General Quarters. All four destroyers held intermittent contact at various times. At 36 minutes past midnight, it was decided that the contact was not a submarine and we continued on our way. Every time we headed for the Korean combat zone, however, there was always apprehension about submarines.

Wren left Yokosuka, Japan for ASW exercises on November 14, 1953 and proceeded south into Sagami Wan, the large body of water south of Tokyo Bay. We rendezvoused with the U.S.S. Ronquil (SS-319) to conduct antisubmarine training exercises before returning to Korea. The seas were moderate, the sky clear. Fujiyama with its snow frosted topping floated on a cushion of haze in the distance. The ship rolled with that easy motion that sailors naturally absorb without even thinking. The sonar conditions were good and we had no trouble maintaining sonar contact on the submarine. At night we anchored in the small, protected Aijro Ko harbor at Atami, an old Japanese hot springs resort that unfortunately was off limits to US sailors. It was a pleasant operation -- easy steaming, good operating conditions and no steaming at night.

For three days we hunted the submarine and used concussion grenades and dye marker to simulate depth charge attacks. At the sound of our grenade the sub would release a slug of compressed air and we could judge our accuracy by how close the air bubble was to our dye mark. We did very well (sunk Ronquil many times) and were confident that when we returned to Korea we could take on any submarine that we met, Russian or Chinese.

On November 19, 1953 we got underway for more antisubmarine exercises. This time we were part of Hunter Killer (HUK) Force Pacific. The HUK Group consisted of DesDiv 61 and DesDiv 82 and the Aircraft Carrier U.S.S. Sicily (CVE-118). The Sicily was a small escort carrier built on a T-3 Tanker hull during World War-II. The destroyers of DesDiv-82 were Ingersoll, Ammen, Knapp and Cogswell. Our adversary submarines were USS Sea Fox (SS-402) and Pickerel (SS-524). The HUK strategy was that the carrier aircraft would hunt the submarines down and make an initial attack. The destroyers would then go in and finish the kill.

Captain Green and phone talker observing U.S.S. Sicily (CVE-118) in heavy weather (note spray from Sicily's bow) during HukPac operations in Sagami Wan, Japan. (AT Miller Photo)

The carrier aircraft were Douglas AD Skyraiders. These huge, single-engine, attack aircraft could carry a bigger bomb load than a WW-II four-engine B-17 Flying Fortress. There were two versions of the antisubmarine AD's and they operated in pairs. One plane had radar and other detection equipment to locate the sub. The second plane had a searchlight and weapons to attack the sub. The AD's looked very large when parked on the deck of the small escort carrier. Fortunately the design of the AD's allowed them to make a relatively slow approach to the small flight deck that was only steaming at about 19 knots.

These ASW exercises were conducted on fairly realistic conditions with full evasive submarines. We had good hunting with the Huk group and returned to Yokosuka on November 24.

One of the antisubmarine versions of the AD Skyraider (US Navy Photo)

On November 29, 1953, in company with the U.S.S. Stribling (DD-867), we steamed south and then west around the south coast of Kyushu to meet the Australian aircraft carrier H.M.A.S. Sydney in the Yellow Sea. Sydney was a medium size carrier with an air group of piston engine Seafury fighters and Firefly antisubmarine aircraft. Sydney's captain was commander of the task group. The weather was typical early winter conditions off the southwest Korean coast. Winds were brisk and cold, sky filled with fair weather cumulus and seas in the Cheju Straits were moderate with occasional whitecaps.

Wren and Stribling provided escort and plane guard for Sydney flight operations for about five days. We provided an antisubmarine screen during normal steaming. During flight operations one destroyer would steam astern of the carrier ready to assist personnel or aircraft in the water from an aircraft accident. One day we towed a target spar well astern of the ship. The crew got a big kick out of watching the Australians make attack runs and fire rockets at the geyser in our wake. It was pretty easy for us. Not at all like the fast paced, round the clock, high-pressure operations with Fast Carrier Task Force 77 up north.

HMAS Sydney in the Cheju Straits December 2, 1953. A Seafury piston-engine fighter is on a downwind leg to land. (A.T. Miller Photo)

The water in this area off the tip of the Korean Peninsula was not too deep, usually less than 500 feet. We were in sight of land at times and in fact had been using the Konun Do light as a navigation reference. We were occasionally getting sonar contacts. They were good solid echoes similar to a submarine but when plotted they did not move and they had no doppler. They were probably rock pinnacles and the sonarmen called them "a piece of the bottom." They were taken seriously, however, because we were in the combat zone and there were current intelligence reports of possible Korean, Chinese or Russian submarine activity. Our duty as escort was to protect the carrier that undoubtedly would be the target if there were an attack.

It was shortly after 7:30 PM on December 2 near the end of our tour with Sydney. I had just gone on sonar watch with Seaman York, a young man (and alto sax player) with a great deal of confidence in his sonar skills. It was true that he had a pretty good ear for doppler and he was bright, but his brash and impulsive approach to his duties made the rest of the sonar gang just a little uneasy. We had both settled down with fresh cups of coffee. York was on the "stack," the sonar console, and I was sitting in the corner reading. The sonar shack, as it was called, was about six by ten feet and on the same deck level as the bridge. Most of the sonar equipment was arranged along the aft bulkhead with some small units mounted on the forward bulkhead. With just the two of us, the space was adequate though cozy. During General Quarters with six of us in the shack there was no place to sit (except for the stack operator) and hardly room to breathe.

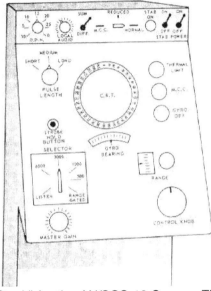

The control console or "Stack" for the AN/SQS-10 Sonar. The Sonarman sat with his left hand on the Master Gain and his right hand on the Control Knob conducting "Beam-to Beam" searches. - RCN illustration

York said, "I've got a contact." I could see the bright green blip on the screen as he slewed the audio cursor to pick up the sound. The echo was sharp and the blip was about submarine size. It sounded like "no doppler" to me. At 7:40PM York reported on the speaker to the bridge "Sonar contact bearing 160, range 1200 yards, echo quality sharp and clear." I said, "I can't hear any doppler, I think its a piece of the bottom." "No, no" York said, "I can hear slight low doppler." "He's going away from us." I said, "I don't hear doppler -- check it out a little longer." "No, no," he said, "its a submarine." He immediately keyed the bridge speaker and reported, "Sonar contact bearing 165, range 1100 yards, echo quality sharp and clear, doppler slight low, classified possible submarine." With that all hell broke loose. At 7:55PM the Bosun Mate on the bridge passed the word on the 1MC PA, "General quarters, general quarters, all hands man your battle stations." The metallic bong of the General Alarm sounded throughout the ship. I could hear the pounding of feet on the ladders up to the bridge level. Sonarmen came crashing into the sonar shack. I was struggling to get the metal cover off the top of the Attack Plotter and stowed behind it. York was continuing to classify the target. Other members of the attack team were getting phones on and checking equipment. Our ever-helpful Division Officer stuck his head in the door, handed me multiple copies of Action Report forms and told me to be sure that they got filled out. I dumped them on the deck behind the Attack Plotter. As the General Quarters team assembled, I assumed my station as Weapons Petty Officer and put on the phones connecting me with the depth charge station aft and the Hedgehog ahead-thrown weapons station forward. I had my left hand on the Weapons Selector switch and the gun-grip-firing key in my right hand.

As we headed in toward the contact, the Captain Green was trying to get permission from Sydney to drop a single depth charge. I called to the depth charge station on the fantail, "Stand by to roll one depth charge, depth set 200 feet." There was a long silence on the line finally broken by "Do you mean a real one? We don't have the covers off the depth charges." I said, "You're damn right a real one -- This is no drill." They were ready to drop hand grenades and dye markers! Fortunately for us, Sydney wouldn't approve firing and we passed over the contact with the depth charge crew still struggling to remove the canvas covers. On another phone circuit to the Chief Torpedoman the captain was candidly expressing his opinion of the skills, intelligence and ancestry of the depth charge crew.

As we passed over the contact and it came out of the baffles, Stribling said she also had contact. The captain, quoting intelligence reports of possible acoustic torpedo danger, ordered our anti-torpedo noisemaker (FOXER) towed behind the ship. After some delay, (this was also a depth charge crew responsibility) FOXER was deployed. We heard a tremendous noise in our sonar and there was a huge green noise spoke on the display because FOXER's sound bounced off the bottom in the relatively shallow water. On hearing all this noise, the Stribling sonarmen didn't know what it was and reported that the submarine had fired a torpedo at them.   At this point the captain of the Sydney had enough and advised over the radio "Operate independently, I'm leaving."   Sydney was last seen going over the horizon toward Sasebo, Japan.

Stribling was assured that the noise was the Wren's noisemaker and not a torpedo and everyone started to reassess the debacle that resulted in Sydney hauling ass for safer waters.   To reduce confusion, the captain ordered the noisemaker retrieved which the depth charge crew managed to do in reasonably short order and everything quieted down. CIC reported that the contact had tracked Dead In The Water (DIW).   If it was DIW it could not have had any doppler.   York held to his doppler story but the rest of us were convinced we had "a piece of the bottom."   The captain ordered a "spiral search" toward Sasebo where we arrived a day later then scheduled.   The delay caused by our little caper cost the crew a day's liberty in Japan so the sonarmen were not exactly the most popular guys on the ship.

Faces had to be saved so the official story was that we had mistaken a whale (which could have doppler) for a submarine.   Warming to the spirit of the occasion, the crew of Stribling made an elaborate plaque welcoming Wren to the Royal Order of Whale Bangers.   It was hung on the door of the Wren sonar shack with appropriate ceremony. From that time on the rest of Destroyer Division 61 referred to the Wrens as Whale Bangers.   Some months later, when we crossed the equator, my subpoena from Neptunis Rex stated " Big bearded Whalebanger caused all hands to lose half-nights sleep chasing a whale."   As far as the sonarmen were concerned, our experience with whales showed that they were gentle creatures generally innocent of imitating submarines.   Whales-sounding-like-submarines was a sonarman's sea story left over from World War II.   We all knew what the real problem was and we threatened York with serious harm if he ever did it again.

The Whalebanger Plaque presented to Wren Sonarmen by the crew of the USS Stribling. (Alfred W. Dodge, Jr. Photo)

The BT

Navy sonarmen in the fifties hated the BT. The things real name was the bathythermograph but that was such a mouthful that it was always just "the BT." Colorful adjectives were often included to further focus animosity toward this simple scientific instrument. The BT was a brass, torpedo-like device about three feet long and two inches in diameter with fins on one end that was used to determine expected sonar performance. How could such a small and seemingly insignificant device raise such passions in otherwise intelligent, highly trained sailors? Actually it wasn't the device itself so much as the effort it took to make it work that incurred all this wrath.

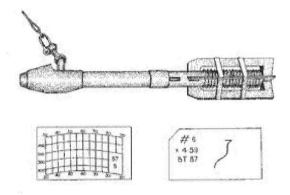

At the top is the BT as it was towed through the water. Bottom right is a glass slide with the BT trace on it. Bottom left is the calibrated viewer used to derive depth and temperature data from the slide. (gld.chariot.net.au illustration)

The BT measured sea temperature versus water depth and scratched a plot of this data on a smoked glass slide. To get it to do this, the BT was lowered on about a thousand feet of plastic covered stainless steel airplane cable from the stern of the destroyer -- every four hours night and day in all kinds of weather. Well, if the sea state exceeded State 7 (Huge waves) you didn't have to do it because they figured the water was so mixed up it was all the same temperature anyway. There was a widely held theory among sonarmen that the Officer Of The Deck (OD) would err on the side of declaring it was State 6 just to watch the sonarmen get wet. There was no question that some OD's had a lower Sea State scale then others. Conventional wisdom was that these OD's were all products of the NROTC program (some narrowed it further to Ivy League NROTC graduates).

It took two men to drop the BT. There were two sonarmen on watch and one had to operate the sonar equipment at all times. That meant that the other watch stander had to recruit an assistant to help him drop the BT. During the day this wasn't much of a problem, however, at night someone would have to be awakened to help. In warm calm weather it wasn't too bad. The helper would appear on deck in skivvies and flip-flops and as soon as the BT was retrieved he could jump back in the sack. However, having to get out of a warm bunk, put on foul weather gear and life jacket and get wet in bad weather added another level of surliness to an already unpleasant task. Also, someone had to wear a sound powered telephone set to talk to the bridge. If the Aft Steering helmsman (already wearing phones) could be cajoled into sticking his head out of the After Steering hatch, he could do the talking. His availability varied inversely with the amount of green water coming over the after deck and splashing into his hatch.

The boom and winch used to drop the BT were on the starboard side about twenty feet from the stern near the aft five-inch gun mount (55). First a smoked slide was loaded into the hated BT and the BT was shackled into the eye on the end of the plastic coated stainless steel airplane cable. Then, after the OD slowed the ship to 12 knots, the boom was swung out and secured. This was preferably done on the up roll so that the boom tip wouldn't hit a wave. Poor timing or misjudging the wave resulted in the boom and BT being slammed back against the ship followed by a loud chorus of epithets from the sonarmen describing the BT, the ship, the boom, the OD and anything else that came to mind. It was also conventional wisdom that the same OD's that had low Sea State guesses also waited the maximum time to slow to 12 knots to make sure that the sonarmen were suitably wet and chilled. While awaiting the order to drop the BT, the sonarmen would often while away the time by jumping up to the mount 55 five-inch gun barrel and lifting their feet clear of the water coming over the deck.

Dropping the BT was relatively easy. Just release the brake on the winch and when the counter indicated 1000 feet of cable put the brake back on. With the ship at 12 knots and 1000 feet of cable the BT would dive to about 350 to 400 feet. An electric motor drove the winch to retrieve the BT. One time, the BT had been dropped and the button punched to turn on the electric motor to pull in the cable. Nothing happened – not a sound. Several people punched the button to no avail. Someone got a swab and used the wood handle to punch the button. No joy! The motor was dead. The captain was fuming, eager to resume speed to rejoin the task force and here was the valuable BT dangling helplessly at the end of 1000 feet of cable with the ship proceeding at a leisurely 12 knots. There was a hand crank on the winch but hauling the BT up that way would be at least an hour-long job. The deck force was awakened and the cable hauled in by hand. Because the cable kinked very easily and could be damaged, it had to be carefully walked up the starboard side across the foc'sle, down the port side and up the starboard side again with someone holding it every few feet. Then they all had to hold the cable for the hour it took us to crank it in by hand. Needless to say the sonarmen rose to the top of one of the deck force's lists. Afterwards, the electricians who were responsible for the motor said they could understand why it didn't work. It was full of seawater. The electricians immediately jumped to the top of one of the sonarmen's lists. No one asked where we all were on the captain's list. In an attempt to lower the sonarmen's profile, a new procedure was instituted where the motor was checked before the BT was dropped.

One time the BT was dropped and then effortlessly winched in. The reason it was effortless was that the BT was no longer there. Only the eye remained on the end of the cable. The BT was a carefully calibrated expensive instrument and its loss was no trivial matter. Our division officer determined that the two sonarmen neglected to tighten the shackle and were thus responsible for the loss. The sonarmen pointed out that the Officer Of The Deck and the division officer (both Annapolis grads) should really have known better than to drop the BT. The sonarmen carefully explained that when the officers order the BT dropped and it tries to dive to 400 feet when there is only 300 feet of water under the keel there might be a problem. Probably with their fitness reports in mind, both ensigns rejected that scenario and concurred that the shackle and the sonarmen and not shallow water was the problem.

Then there were those damned smoked glass slides.   You had to take them out of the box carefully by the edges so that the smoked glass didn't get smudged.   They had to be inserted in the BT with notched edge up and then the brass sleeve carefully closed.   If the slide was in backwards or the sleeve didn't close all the way there was no trace.   The sonarmen had an unwritten rule; the BT only gets one chance to do the right thing.   A BT drop is never repeated because a slide is blank.   That's why we kept a straight pin in the slide box.   If the slide was blank, the sonarman's creative talent and the straight pin approximated the trace of the previous slide.   If a smudge or fingerprint obscured the trace the slide went over the side and a new slide and the straight pin provided the current conditions.   Dropping the damned thing once was bad enough -- we sure as hell weren't going to do it twice.

Even when you got a good slide that wasn't the end.   The slide had to be carefully washed in fresh water and allowed to dry.   Once it was dry it was dipped in lacquer and allowed to dry again and then filed in a box.   There was additional data to be collected, numbers to be calculated and reports to be made.   It is understandable that we who thought of ourselves as antisubmarine warriors were frustrated by and resentful of this little instrument that caused us so much grief.   Today expendable, sonobuoy, bathythermographs such as the AN/SSQ-36 are thrown over the side, automatically make temperature measurements down to 2500 feet and radio them back to the ship. Unfortunately that's not the way it was when I was a sonarman.

Collisions

On January 24, 1954, Wren was struggling through mountainous waves in the Sea of Japan off the coast of North Korea.   We were operating independently as part of Task Group 95.2.2 on patrol above the 38th parallel about six miles off Kosong, Democratic Peoples Republic of Korea (North Korea).   The Wren was not supposed to be here. We were supposed to be enjoying liberty in the fleshpots of Sasebo, Japan. Hazlewood (DD-531), another Fletcher class destroyer that was supposed to do this patrol, had to go into the shipyard in Japan for repairs.   To the chagrin of the crew, Wren was ordered underway and back to Korea to cover for Hazlewood shortly after returning from almost a month at sea with Task Force 77.   This time we were going to the East Coast of Korea and we weren't very happy about it.   There were a lot of glum faces as we passed through the anti-submarine nets at the entrance to Sasebo harbor and headed to sea.

We sortied northward from Sasebo in company with Heerman (DD-562) through the Tsushima Straits toward the Sea of Japan.   It was in these straits on May 27, 1905 that the great Japanese Admiral Heihachiro Togo humiliated the Russians and ended the Russo-Japanese War by crossing the "T" twice on the Russian fleet.   Leading the Japanese task force in his battleship Mikasa, Togo maneuvered brilliantly against the Russians and cut them to pieces. Togo sunk or captured thirty-one of the thirty-eight Russian ships.   Wren probably passed over the watery graves of 5000 men and the Russian ships Borodino, Alexandr III, Suvarov, Veliky, Navarin and Oslyabia that were all sunk by Togo's fleet in the 5-hour running Battle of Tsushima. Togo's losses were only 117 dead and 600 wounded.

As we turned northwestward out of the straits and into the teeth of the gale, we separated from Heerman to each go to our separate patrol stations.

The Korean Theater of War. Wren proceeded from Sasebo through the Tsushima Straits and northward into the Sea of Japan above the 38th parallel. (Naval History Branch)

Wren relieved the U.S.S. Rogers (DD-876), a Gearing Class 2250 ton destroyer, on January 21st in raging seas. The weather had not improved since then and on the 24th Wren was rolling heavily and its bow plunging under the water and then coming up and out of the sea until its bottom was exposed. I stood with one foot on either side of the superstructure slide joints on the 01 level and watched the distance between my feet change as the hull bent under the stress. A violent storm was blowing down out of Siberia. It had been snowing heavily all day and the seas were enormous. Visibility was about zero. The cover story was that we were on a "weather patrol". We certainly were seeing plenty of weather. The day before a small seagull had landed on the ship totally exhausted by the weather. Dan Bowers, one of the electronic technicians, put it in the radar transmitter room until it was warm and rested. We knew that the old joke about the weather being so bad that "the birds were grounded" could really be true. Actually, we were patrolling from 38 degrees 5 minutes North Latitude to 38 degrees 40 minutes to insure that Chinese or North Korean naval forces did not violate the recently signed Korean War truce agreement by crossing the Armistice Line and proceeding into South Korean waters.[6]   The area we were operating in was about 50 miles south of Wonsan, which the U.S. Navy held under siege from 16 February 1951 for 861 days – the longest naval siege in modern history.

Wren with bow underwater plowing through heavy seas. (A.T. Miller Photo)

The wind was very strong and the seas steep sided and very high. The old destroyers' bow would bury itself into the sea and then slowly come back up shaking itself sideways

[6] This naval standoff at the Armistice Line continues to this day. As recently as June 29, 2002, North Korean naval units crossed the line southbound and were engaged by South Korean gunboats. In the ensuing naval battle, four South Korean sailors were killed and 19 wounded. North Korean casualties were not known but were estimated "at about 30".

as tons of water roared across the foc'sle smashed against the bulkheads and poured over the side back into the sea.   On the up rolls the bow was coming completely out of the water as far back as the sonar dome.   As it came back down it would hit the water with a bang and then shudder as the bow worked its way back underwater.   Those bunking in the forward living compartments had only to put their hand out to feel the hull flexing under the water pressure.   The sonar was useless because of the quenching from all of the air bubbles being driven under the ship.   Passage fore and aft was impossible on the main deck so everyone was using the more difficult route on the 01 level (no inside passageway on these old cans).   No one was getting much sleep.   We loosened the bunk lacings to make the mattress sag and lashed or braced ourselves in our bunks.   I propped my pillow against the chain on one side and draped my leg over the edge on the other to stay in the bunk.   In addition to the ships wild motion, it was unbelievably noisy.   The sea pounded on the thin lightly insulated hull and the bubbles gurgled as they churned and slid upward. There were fuel tanks immediately under my bunk and the black oil fuel roared as it surged back and forth through the perforated baffles.

Wren taking a heavy roll while on patrol off the snow covered mountains of North Korea January 23, 1954.   The pelorus is gimballed and remains level as the ship rolls under it. (A.T. Miller Photo)

At 6:25PM we were detached for independent patrol about from the 38th parallel "demarc line" north to Sonchi-Ri about 7 miles offshore.   Heerman was on a similar track about 8 miles north of us.   At about 8:30PM our old Raytheon SG-1b surface search radar picked up a ship contact (designated a "skunk") and Wren turned to investigate it at 20 knots. Most of the off duty crew, myself included, were in the mess deck watching the movie. We were in the Korean Combat Zone and had been running at darken ship with all navigation and external lights off. In the Combat Information Center (CIC) the radarmen marked the track of the skunk on the face of the VK Radar Repeater with a grease pencil to determine the closest point of approach (CPA). As we approached the plotted position of the skunk we turned on our running lights so that they could see us and slowed to 15 knots. Bridge personnel kept sticking their heads into the pilothouse port side door to check the skunk's position on the VD Radar Repeater. When we got in to 1000 yards radar range we started sending blinker light challenges in the direction of the other ship. Captain Green[7] took the conn. The air was filled with swirling snow that reflected back the red blinker light. There was nothing but blackness where the other ship was supposed to be. CIC was having difficulty tracking the other ship because of the clutter on the radar screen caused by echoes from the high waves. CIC's track on both the VK and the Dead Reckoning Tracer (DRT) showed that the skunk was coming right toward Wren. When we were about 500 yards from the other ship, we lost contact completely because we were within the minimum radar range. The last radar track showed the unknown ship coming right at us. The lookouts and every eye on the bridge strained for sight of the ship as the blinker light challenges continued. Suddenly lights came on and appeared out of the dark right off our port beam. The red and green running lights of another ship were both visible. It was coming straight at our port side! Marv Dorson, the quartermaster operating the blinker, jumped back off the signal platform because the lights were so close. He thought we were going to be hit immediately. Someone on the bridge yelled "Oh my God, we've had it!" The Bosun Mate passed "Standby for collision port side" over the 1MC address system. The captain ordered "left full rudder" in an effort to turn into the other ship and swing our stern out of his way.

---

[7]Maurice "Fred" Green was the CIC Officer in USS Hoel when it was sunk during the "Action Off Samar" on October 25, 1944 while making a torpedo attack on Japanese cruisers and battleship. This battle has been characterized as "The last stand of the Tin Can sailors" LT. Maurice Fred Green, survivor of USS HOEL was not at all pleased with the rescue attempts or lack of attempts, submitted a narrative report which is a part of the National Archives.

I was down below in the mess deck engrossed in the movie. When they passed the word for collision quarters there was a mad scramble for the main deck. I was on the port side of the mess deck watching the movie. I didn't have a seat so I was standing behind the ice cream machine right near the open watertight door. I bolted through the door, through the serving compartment and up the ladder. When I came out on the main deck I looked out and saw this ship going down our port side about 30 yards away. Although it wasn't, it seemed close enough to touch. I could see 40mm guns with the pipe frames around them to protect the superstructure from "friendly fire". I thought that it was one of the Korean Asheville class PF's[8] that had been tied up next to us in Sasebo. The ship turned out to be a South Korean Navy gunboat that had been running at darken ship. The ship was far from where it was expected to be and the Koreans evidently didn't understand the United Nations recognition code for that day. The former U.S. Navy Landing Ship Support Large (LSSL-91)[9] was 158 feet long and displaced about 387 tons. It could have done severe damage to Wren in a bow-on collision. If he had hit us in the engineering spaces and flooded two of them, we could well have capsized and sunk. We were on our own and in terrible weather. There are no lifeboats on a destroyer; only two whaleboats that can hold about 30 men out of a crew of almost 300. Everyone else goes over the side into life rafts where you stand in the water or into the water to hang onto floating nets. The thought of going over the side at night in the northern part of the Sea of Japan in January far from other ships was very frightening. We were all sobered and shaken by the experience. I think that many of us repeated that ancient mariner's prayer "A prayer for the ship and all who sail in her".

---

[8] Four Asheville class frigates were transferred to Russia's navy under Lend Lease during WW-II. They were returned to the U.S. Navy after the war in rather poor shape and laid up in Yokusuka, Japan. They were reactivated at the beginning of the Korean War and transferred to South Korea. One of them, Apnok (PF-62) was badly damaged in a major collision on May 21, 1952, decommissioned and returned to the U.S. It was replaced with Imjin (PF-66).

[9] The LSSL's were developed from the Landing Craft, Infantry (LCI) to provide close-in firepower support for amphibious operations. The "Mighty Midgets" had 2 dual-40mm Bofors gun mounts aft and either dual 40's, a 3-inch, 50 caliber gun or rocket launchers forward plus two 50-caliber machine guns. . They were the most heavily armed ships per ton of displacement of any ship built during World War-II.

The USS LSSL-91 in Yokosuka, Japan shortly before she was transferred to the ROK Navy and renamed Kanf Hwa Man (LSSL-108). The ROKN designated the ship a gunboat. LSSL-108 narrowly missed colliding with Wren. (US Navy Photo)

The captain felt that his split second decision to turn into the other ship was wrong and that he should have turned away. He is quoted as telling the OD "don't ever do what I just did!" As far as the crew was concerned, it was the right decision. We were still high and dry and except for a few required underwear changes, we were all OK.

Destroyer sailors in the 1950's worried a lot about collisions - - and with good reason. There were quite a few of them and nearly all of us had observed close calls or near misses with another ship. One of the reasons for this was that naval formations at that time contained large numbers of ships operating close to one another and maneuvering at high speed. Another reason is that destroyers were often operated at high speed and in close proximity to other destroyers while executing closely timed attack maneuvers during antisubmarine exercises. Add to this the intensity of operations and the wartime-like conditions (darken ship) of the Korean Combat Zone and the odds of collisions increase. On February 19, 1953, while operating off the coast of Korea, the USS

Prichett (DD-561) and USS Cushing (DD-797) collided. Both ships required dry-docking in Sasebo, Japan.

In all cases, collisions happen because somebody makes a mistake. The navy has procedures and training for how to maneuver with other ships, rights-of-way, signaling intentions and notifying superiors of dangerous situations. The navy had expanded rapidly in the Korean War and almost all ships were manned with young and relatively inexperienced crews. This was particularly true of the officers who stood Officer Of The Deck (OD) watches. Most of them were reserves, with not a lot of training, who were having their first experience of sea duty.

Destroyers were usually severely damaged in collisions even with other destroyers. The ships were of light construction and carried no armor. The hull consisted of light steel frames on about two foot centers. The frame was covered with 3/8-inch thick steel plate. If you look closely at the bow area of one of those old destroyers you can clearly see the outline of the frames under the steel plate. This is because the pressure of heavy seas, such as those we encountered in Korea, has pushed the light skin in around the frames. No wonder they called them tin cans!

One of the objectives in antisubmarine warfare in the nineteen fifties was to keep attacking and not give the sub an opportunity to shoot or get away. The primary method of doing this was by the two-ship coordinated attack. Two destroyers would take turns attacking the submarine. The ships would remain fairly close together because of the relatively short (under 5000-yard) detection range of sonar systems. One destroyer would steam toward the submarine and fire weapons as it passed over it. At the same time the other destroyer was circling around the submarine on a 1000-yard radius. As soon as the attacking destroyer fired, it would turn out to the circle and the other destroyer would turn in toward the submarine. This required that both destroyers agree which way each would turn and when. The attacking ship would call on the radio; "I see starboard right." The other ship would answer, "Concur starboard right." As the attacking ship fired, it would transmit, "Starboard right - Standby - Execute" and both ships would turn. They were both steaming at about 20 knots and it only took about a minute and a half to come from the circle to the submarine. If one ship turned the wrong way things could go bad very quickly. To try to eliminate errors in this process, the sonarmen would mark the quadrants with grease pencil on the glass face of the bridge pelorus (compass) to assist the OD in making the turn decision.

In the spring of 1954 we were conducting antisubmarine exercises with a naval reserve destroyer escort, U.S.S. Robert E. Keller (DE-419), which was home-ported in Washington, DC. In those days naval reserve units were not maintained at anywhere near the level of readiness that they are today. A skeleton crew sufficient to perform required maintenance and painting and not much more manned Keller. The crew was brought to operating strength with reserve personnel (weekend warriors) when it was going to sea. It did not go to sea very often so the crew did not get much training and the reserves even less. We were working with Keller and a submarine in the Virginia Capes Operating Area.

I had a previous knowledge of Keller. I was stationed at the U.S. Navy Torpedo Testing Range at Piney Point, Maryland that was located on the Potomac River near its confluence with the Chesapeake Bay. The Keller was outward bound from Washington proceeding down the Potomac when it collided with and sunk an oyster boat off Piney Point. The crash boat from Piney Point retrieved the oystermen and the Officer in Charge (OIC) of the torpedo range was assigned to chair the board of inquiry. Despite objections from the Commandant, Potomac River Naval Command (PRNC), who had convened the board, the OIC in his final report was extremely critical of the captain of Keller. The Commandant PRNC thought that the findings might damage the career of the Keller's captain. The Piney Point OIC contended that he "had to call them as he sees them". Some time later when a chief warrant officer embezzled funds from the Piney Point Officers Mess, the Commandant, PRNC appointed the Keller's captain as chair of the board of inquiry. I understand that the Keller's CO took advantage of the opportunity to even the score with the OIC Piney Point.

Wren and Keller were to conduct coordinated two ship attacks on the submarine. It was a beautiful day with unlimited visibility. Both ships established sonar contact with the submarine and Keller started in to attack the sub while we held on the 1000-yard circle. Keller proposed a turn pattern, Wren concurred and we executed as Keller simulated depth charge firing. As we started in off the circle toward the submarine, it was obvious Keller had turned the wrong way. We broke off the attack and turned sharply away while blowing our whistle to indicate our turn direction. Keller blithely proceeded out to the circle. It wasn't a real close call thanks to an alert OD. If it had happened at night or when there was less visibility we could well have had a collision. Captain Johnson had a rather animated radio discussion with the captain of the Keller about two-ship attack procedures and turn coordination.

Having gotten everything straightened out (so we thought) we started an attack on the submarine with Keller out on the circle. We made a simulated depth charge attack with a concussion grenade and dye marker. I stepped out on the bridge wing to see how we did. As I looked aft to see how close the air slug from the sub was to our dye marker what did I behold but Keller following in our wake. Keller was supposed to be just turning in from the circle and here she is right behind us. Her timing was perfect -- she was going right through our dye marker! If we had fired a real pattern of eleven 600-pound depth charges, the Keller would have been right in the middle of it. At that point, our captain called off the exercise while he still had his ship intact and we headed for Norfolk. I guess he figured we had really sunk the Keller anyway so we won!

Keller had a history of collisions. Here she is colliding with starboard quarter of the aircraft carrier USS Sargent Bay (CVE-83) in the Pacific during World War-II. (US Navy Photo)

In November of 1954 we were engaged in a large Atlantic Fleet exercise called Lantflex. We were off Onslow Beach in North Carolina providing shore bombardment support for a marine landing. The night after the landing, a marine pilot had to ditch his plane at sea. The exact location of the ditching was uncertain. All of the destroyers were ordered out to sea to form a column steaming eastward. The plan was that after the column was formed all of the ships would make a 90-degree left turn and the line of ships would sweep northward through the area to search for the pilot.

It took a while for all the destroyers to gather. The column was steaming slowly eastward at five knots. The Officer of the Deck was a Harvard NROTC product who was definitely common sense challenged. The crew called him "Sneaky Pete". We were approaching the column at fifteen knots. All of the ships in the column were showing speed lights indicating that they were steaming at five knots. Everyone was waiting for the OD to give the engine orders to slow down. The quartermaster called out "ship ahead showing lights for 5 knots". We proceeded toward the column at fifteen knots. Instead of an engine order the OD gave a course change to steer us into our place in the column. At that point the captain called "I have the conn" and took us out of the column and in circle to make the approach at the right speed. After it was all over the captain said to the OD "If I hadn't taken the conn, it would have been bang, bang, bang." Fortunately the captain was there to take the conn and save Sneaky Pete . . . and us.

Two incidents on the morning of October 31, 1954 illustrate the dangers inherent in war-like naval operations even when conducted in peacetime. We were engaged in another part of the Lantflex exercise in the Atlantic off the east coast of the U.S. It was a huge exercise involving two battle groups with a battleship, two carriers, two cruisers and about twenty destroyers in addition to auxiliary and amphibious vessels. Submarines were attempting to intercept and "sink" the surface ships. Operations with submarines were always conducted with extra caution because of the special vulnerability of submarines to collision. Ships operating with a submarine had to keep moving so that the submarine could hear the surface ships on their sonar and know where they were. Submarines kept their running lights on even when submerged so that they could be seen as they approached the surface. Before surfacing, underwater telephone contact was established with the submarine. The sub released a green smoke flare and received confirmation that the surface ships could see where the sub would surface and were clear of the area.

Sometimes, however, when exercises are conducted in simulated wartime conditions safety precautions are relaxed in the interests of realism and an accident can happen. This apparently is what happened to the U.S.S Bergall (SS-320) a Balao class GUPPY submarine on October 31, 1954. Bergall was part of the submarine opposition force trying to attack the large Lantflex surface fleet. The day before the collision, Bergall had very aggressively penetrated the destroyer screen and had "sunk" (Bang-Bang your dead) the aircraft carrier Valley Forge which was also the task force flagship. As the Bergall slipped between the destroyers in the screen, the captain had raised her periscope and copied the date-time group of a blinker message being transmitted by Wren to another destroyer. This bit of evidence absolutely proved that they had slipped undetected between two destroyers in the screen. Actually, although no one involved would later admit it, Bergall had been detected by Wren's sonar. Gene Staunton and I relieved the morning watch at about 7:45 that morning. As we went through the shift change briefing Roberson said "Oh a pretty solid contact went down the starboard side about 5 minutes ago". "Well why the hell didn't you report it?" I shouted. "Well", Roberson said "if I did we would have gone to GQ and I wouldn't have gotten to breakfast." I could have killed him. Having gotten past Wren, Bergall then hid under an LST where her sonar echo would merge with the LST's. From that hideout they carried out the simulated attack on the "Happy Valley". About the time I took my seat at the sonar, I could hear Bergall on the underwater telephone declaring Valley Forge sunk.

At 3:32 AM on the morning of the 31st, Bergall was again submerged stealthily approaching the surface group. Her batteries were a bit low and the captain was concerned if they would be sufficient to use max speed after a simulated attack. Bergall came to periscope depth, raised its air-breathing snorkel and was using diesel engines to recharge batteries. As the captain was making a sweep with the periscope he saw the U.S.S. Norris (DDE-859) a Carpenter (converted Gearing) class escort destroyer bearing down on them. He yelled, "Oh My God she's going to hit us!" and sounded the collision alarm as the Norris hit. Although the Bergall's snorkel and conning tower was damaged, she had no flooding and was escorted by a submarine rescue ship (ASR) to Philadelphia Navy Yard for repairs. The Norris was severely holed and had five flooded compartments. Another destroyer escorted her into Norfolk.

Less then an hour and a half later and forty miles away Wren went to the aid of two destroyers involved in another serious collision. The task force was steaming northward in the hours before dawn. Two destroyers, Lind and English, had been deployed about 20 miles ahead of the task force as radar pickets and were now steaming south returning to the task force. They were steaming side by side and were at darken ship and radar silence, as was the rest of the task force. The exercise was being conducted under simulated wartime conditions. About every five minutes they would take one radar sweep to confirm their position. As they were approaching the task force one of the escort carriers, a CVL, broke away from the task force and proceeded westward to conduct flight operations for a dawn patrol. Just before 5:00 AM, the carrier radioed Lind and English to join up with her to provide plane guard and rescue support.

The Lind, which was the more westerly of the two, thought that the carrier was still in the task force and continued southward. The English knew that the carrier had gone westward and made a right turn to join up with her. At 5:01AM English collided with the Lind just below her bridge and slid forward along her port side opening an eight foot gash below the waterline. The force of the collision snapped the English's bow off just ahead of the forward five-inch gun mount. The 31-foot long bow section swung around and folded against the port side of the ship. Miraculously no one was hurt. A chief sitting in a bench against the port bulkhead of the Lind chiefs quarters was catapulted across the compartment but not injured.

USS English shortly after colliding with Lind. By this time, the damaged bow section had broken off and sunk. Although severely damaged, English did not have much internal flooding. (Sten Taube Photo)

At 5:22AM Wren was ordered to standby Lind and English and provide assistance as required. I was on the four to eight morning sonar watch at the time. One of the quartermasters came into sonar, which was right off the bridge, and said that we were going to assist Lind and English. When I went out on the bridge, the sky was just starting to get light in the east. I could barely see English lying dead in the water but even in the limited visibility she didn't look right. I used one of the signalmen's long glasses to get a better look. Her bow was gone as cleanly if it had been taken off with a meat cleaver. As it got lighter I could see that the bow was folded back against the port side. English started backing down to put her stern into the sea and take pressure off the forward bulkheads. As she did, the bow swung forward, broke off and sank. Evidently the bulkheads aft of the collision damage were holding pretty well and there was not a great deal of flooding.

Lind was another story. Even in the half-light of dawn it was immediately apparent that she was way down by the bow and had serious flooding. She too backed into the sea. As it got lighter a large hole could be seen in her port side forward near the anchor windlass and bosun locker. It was well above the waterline. It was obvious, however, that she had other much more serious damage below the water line. A motor launch from the battleship Iowa made the side of the Lind to bring them more submersible pumps and more timbers to shore up bulkheads. Although destroyers are divided into many watertight compartments, the bulkheads are not strong enough to contain internal flooding by themselves. Heavy timbers are used to shore up and reinforce the bulkheads of flooded compartments to prevent them from collapsing under the water pressure.

At 7:57AM Wren was ordered to escort Lind back into Norfolk. She was steaming very slowly. We steamed alongside about 100 feet away. Water poured over the side from a multitude of pumps trying to keep ahead of the flooding. Every time the Lind's bow hit a wave it bent to starboard and the deck folded up just in front of the forward five-inch gun mount. Apparently the keel and other structural members had snapped and the bow was close to breaking off. Our captain and the captain of the Lind used electric megaphones to discuss the possibility of getting rid of Linds anchors and chains to reduce weight in the bow. After much discussion they decided it was much too hazardous. The chain had certainly been thrown around in the collision and if it snagged while it was running out it would tear the bow off.

Lind underway for Norfolk after collision with English. Besides the visible damage, she was holed below the waterline and had severe flooding problems. (Sten Taube Photo)

About 11:30AM we rigged a highline over to Lind and sent them some more submersible pumps and more timber for shoring. We also sent them over several cases of toilet paper. All of theirs had been flooded in the bosun locker. They started to make some headway against the flooding and the bow came up some. As we got closer to Norfolk the seas quieted and we were able to increase speed. Both Lind and English would have to go into shipyard for repairs. Lind was repaired in Norfolk and English spent four months in the Philadelphia Naval Shipyard getting a new bow. Before even temporary repairs, however, they would have to offload all ammunition and most fuel. When we arrived in Hampton Roads about 4:30PM, Wren anchored in the ammunition handling anchorage, which is in an isolated section of the harbor. English's bow and anchors were at the bottom of the Atlantic so she obviously couldn't anchor and Lind's anchor windlass was smashed. They tied up on either side of Wren and waited for the ammunition lighters to come alongside.   The Wrens had an opportunity to observe and ponder the massive destruction caused in a split second by a wrong decision.

Lind moored alongside Wren in Hampton Roads.   The severe damage to the bow and the anchor handling equipment is clearly evident. (Sten Taube Photo)

Because of some fundamental laws of physics the heavier ship in a collision situation always wins.   In August of 1954, we had been in Quebec, Canada as part of a midshipmen cruise.   We were in company with our usual buddies Noa, Cone and Stribling, three destroyer escorts, the fleet tanker Canisteo (AO-99), the light anti-aircraft cruiser Juneau (CLAA-119) and the heavy (17,000 ton) cruiser Pittsburgh (CA-72).   We departed Quebec for the long trip down the St. Lawrence River in a heavy fog.   The ships were in a single long column.   Because it was slower then the rest of the ships, the Canisteo had left Quebec the day before.   By afternoon we were in the lower St. Lawrence River approaching the Bay Of St. Lawrence.   The river is very wide at this point and we were doing 25 knots even though it was quite foggy.   We were keeping track of other ship traffic on the river on radar.   As we approached Father Point, which is on the south side of the river near the town of Rimouski, a freighter was coming up the river on a track that would take her north and well clear of us.   Inbound ships picked up river pilots from a station at Father Point as we had in our passage up the river.   The freighter, which evidently did not have radar, turned southward toward Father Point to meet the pilot boat. Unfortunately, she turned directly into the path of Pittsburgh. Although Pittsburgh tried to avoid the freighter, a ship of that weight and speed is not easily stopped or turned and she plowed into the forward part of the ship. The freighter was severely damaged and one of the freighter crew was killed. It was so foggy; we never did see either ship. The next day out in the Atlantic we went alongside Pittsburgh to highline over Mr. Arnason our supply officer who was also a lawyer. He was to serve on the board of inquiry investigating the incident. The unevenness of the match was clearly evident. There were only a few small dents in Pittsburghs bow and some paint scraped off. A week later, one day out of Havana, the task force stopped dead in the water so that Pittsburgh could put painters over the side and boats in the water to remove the signs of the collision before entering Havana. The next day we steamed into Havana harbor with Pittsburgh's freshly painted bow looking no worse for the wear.

Mines

Whenever we were steaming in Korean waters we worried about naval mines. The North Koreans had made very effective use of mine warfare. Five US destroyers had been seriously damaged with 53 crew members killed and 154 injured. Five US minesweepers and a fleet tug had been sunk with a total of 43 dead and many wounded. Although a truce had been declared shortly before Wren entered the Korean combat zone, the mines were still there. Of the estimated 12,000 or more mines planted by North Korea, only 1535 had been officially swept or destroyed by the time Wren arrived in Korea. The other 10,000 plus mines were either still anchored where they were planted or were drifting loose in the seas around Korea. In any case they had the potential of either seriously damaging or possibly sinking a destroyer like Wren.

The mine is one of the oldest weapons of naval warfare and remains highly effective today even in its simplest and most fundamental form. In the period from 1950 to 2001, the U.S. Navy had suffered 18 ship casualties caused by hostile action. Of these, one was caused by a missile (USS Stark), one by a small boat (USS Cole) one by torpedo (USS Liberty), one by aerial attack (USS Higbee) and <u>fourteen by mines</u>! When Admiral Farragut commanded "damn the torpedoes, full speed ahead" in Mobile Bay during the Civil War, he really was talking about what we now call mines not torpedoes. The mines that severely damaged the U.S.S. Princeton and the U.S.S. Nassau off the coast of Kuwait in the Persian Gulf War in 1991 were not much different from those damned by Farragut. The mines that caused so much trouble for United Nations navies during the Korean War were mostly the same simple contact mines used in World Wars I and II. In October 1950, after encountering a field of 3000 of these mines in the waters off Wonsan, Admiral Allan Smith told the Chief Of Naval Operations in Washington that, "We have lost control of the seas to a nation without a Navy, using pre-World War I weapons, laid by vessels that were utilized at the time of the birth of Christ." In congressional testimony in May 1951, Admiral Sherman, the Chief Of Naval Operations, characterized mines in Korea as the "Navy's great problem".

The reason for this great problem is that these relatively simple devices are easy to plant in large numbers (which the North Koreans did) and require specialized equipment to sweep and neutralize. Unfortunately at the outbreak of the war in Korea the US Navy was not prepared to sweep mines on a large scale. Minesweeping is neither high tech nor glamorous. Whenever navies are short of money, mine warfare funding is usually the first to go. After World War II mine forces were cut drastically and in fact the Pacific Mine Warfare Command was eliminated completely! When the war started in Korea there were only a few minesweepers available in the East Asia. These being used to sweep Japanese waters for mines still remaining from World War II and were insufficient for the task facing the Navy in Korea. The South Korean Navy had only a few wooden hull (YMS type) minesweepers. In desperation, sweeps were improvised first using motor launches commandeered from ships in Japan. Even using lightweight sweeping gear with explosive cable cutters, the motor launches were under powered and unable to do the job. They had difficulty towing the gear, particularly against tidal currents, and the small overworked engines were burning out. The motor launches were soon replaced with LCVP landing craft that had more powerful engines but even they were inadequate for the task at hand. Ultimately, High Speed Minesweepers (DMS), Fleet Minesweepers (AM) and Auxiliary Motor Minesweepers (AMS) and support ships from the US arrived in Korea. Only then was the navy able to start systematically removing the mines.

Russia supplied the mines to North Korea and also supplied technicians to train the North Korean mine forces. Most of the mines were simple contact mines. These ball shaped devices contained a large amount of explosive and enough air to give them positive buoyancy. Several small detonator horns on the surface of the ball triggered the explosion. Normally a cable connected the mine to an anchor so that they floated 6 to 8 feet below the surface where they couldn't be seen. Storms often tore them loose from the anchor and they floated on the surface out to sea. In some cases where the North Koreans didn't control the coast, they released them in rivers to float freely out to sea. These mines were in violation of international law adopted at the Hague Convention, which stipulated that contact mines should disarm or destroy themselves if they broke loose.   The North Koreans improvised mine layers from barges and fishing boats and became quite adept at quickly laying large mine fields.   In some operations off Wonsan, Korea, U.S. forces were sweeping the mines during the day and the North Koreans were laying more at night.

A contact mine similar to 12,000 sown by the North Korean and Chinese in the waters around Korea.   When sown, they are usually moored about 6 to 8 feet below the surface. If they break loose, as this one has, they float on the surface and drift with wind and wave. (Wikimedia Commons Photo)

Simple as they may be, naval mines are powerful and effective and one can do enormous damage to a ship.   The ships trying to sweep the mines are in the greatest danger and being small are most susceptible to sinking.   Two U.S. minesweepers the Pirate (AM-275) and the Pledge (AM-277) hit mines within 20 minutes of one another while sweeping off Wosen on the east coast of Korea.   They both sank with 12 missing and 92 wounded.   Shelling from North Korean shore batteries complicated rescue.   One of the wounded later died.   The Magpie (AMS-25) struck a mine on its bow while sweeping off the East Coast of Korea.   Of the crew of 33 men, 21 were killed and the 12 survivors were all wounded.   Partridge (AMS-31) struck a mine while sweeping south of Wonsan and sank in ten minutes.   Eight were killed and 6 were seriously injured.   A U.S Navy Fleet Tug Sarsi (ATF-111) was sunk by a mine off Hungnam with loss of two men.

A South Korean wooden hulled minesweeper (YMS-516) hit a mine in Wonsan harbor and was literally reduced to toothpicks with a heavy loss of life.   A number of other South Korean patrol craft and mine sweepers were also lost to mines.

The first U.S. Navy ship to be mined in Korea was the Sumner class destroyer Brush (DD-745) on September 26, 1950. The incident occurred while hunting shore batteries off the northeast coast of Korea. The ship was severely damaged and 13 men were killed and 34 others seriously wounded. The ship was down by the bow six feet and almost did not make the 500 miles back to Sasebo. Another Sumner class destroyer Mansfield (DD-728) struck a mine several days after Brush leaving 28 wounded. The Gearing class 2250 ton destroyer Ernest G. Small (DD-838) struck a mine off Songjin Korea and lost 120 feet (165 tons) of its bow including the forward dual 5-inch gun mount. Nine men were killed and eighteen injured. Small had to back most of the way into Kure, Japan to prevent collapse of bulkheads and further flooding.

USS Ernest G. Small (DD-838) backing slowly toward Kure, Japan after losing 120-feet of her bow to a mine off the coast of Korea. Small was fitted with a blunt wooden bow and proceeded under her own power back to the U.S. where she was repaired with a bow cut off a mothballed Gearing class destroyer. (U.S. Navy Photo).

The Sumner class destroyer Walke (DD-723) hit a mine 65 miles east of Pusan, which blew its bow off. Twenty-six men were killed and seven injured. The Walke managed to limp back to Sasebo. There was a theory that if a destroyer didn't hit a floating mine with its bow, the bow wave would push it out of the way. That theory was demolished when the Sumner class Barton (DD-722) took a mine in the forward fireroom. Five men were missing and presumed lost to the sea and 6 wounded in that incident. Barton apparently hit a floating mine loosed by Typhoon Karen.

Most of this damage was done with simple contact mines! The US Navy was greatly concerned that the Russians would give their North Korean allies sophisticated magnetic, acoustic or pressure mines. They were so concerned about this threat that at one point a US Navy Lieutenant Commander who was a mine warfare expert was put ashore behind enemy lines in North Korea. He found the Russian built magnetic detonators hidden in a haystack and interrogated captured North Korean mine technicians. Knowing what they were up against certainly helped the U.S. mine forces in dealing with the magnetic mines they encountered.

Wren would sometimes anchor near a pair of old Liberty ships in the harbor in Yokosuka, Japan. We were curious about them because none of their booms were rigged to handle cargo; however, there were signs of activity on board. We later found out that their holds were filled with empty oil drums for buoyancy and they were at anchor in Yokosuka in case acoustic or pressure mines were encountered in Korea. The ships' engine controls had been remoted so they could be operated from the bridge. A layer of mattresses was placed on the bridge deck for the crew to stand on to absorb the shock of an exploding mine. The navy was prepared to steam these Liberty ships over the mines to detonate them. They had no other way to sweep pressure mines. One of these ships participated in the sweeping of the port of Chinnampo in December of 1950. It was vital to open this port near the North Korean capital of Pyongyang to provide logistical support for the US 8th Army driving north from Inchon. Mines were serious business and any ship steaming in Korean waters were well aware of the dangers.

One of the last tasks I did before the Wren left Norfolk for Korea was to install a modification to the sonar equipment to supposedly give it a mine detection mode. It was a "quick fix" designed to provide the search sonar with a short range, higher resolution capability. Normally, the sonar in 6000-yard range mode would emit a ping followed by reverberations every 7.5 seconds, a sound we all were accustomed to. When in the new mine detection mode that set it to 600-yard range, the sonar emitted a short bang every 0.75 seconds. The sound drove the sonarmen crazy. When we used the sonar in mine hunting mode, the other sonarmen made the operator use the headphones and turn off the loudspeaker. Better one guy crazy than all of us! In testing it we found that our modified sonar could sometimes pick up buoys (which were larger then mines) and some other deep draft small objects. On the occasion in Korea when we spotted a real mine and knew exactly where it was, we couldn't pick it up on our modified sonar. Maybe it worked better on mines that were moored and rode deeper in the water. Certainly none of us ever wanted to be in a position where we had to depend on the sonar to find out.

Once a mine was spotted on the surface, it was sunk with gunfire. The standard method was to fire at it with an M-1 30-06 Rifle. Using a 30-caliber rifle, firing multiple rounds would puncture the air cavity in the mine case and it would sink. Only rarely would one explode. If a 20-millimeter gun was fired at it, it was about a 50-50 chance it would blow. If a 40 millimeter gun was used it would certainly explode. Captain Green liked to shoot and he kept a 30 caliber M-1A Carbine in his sea cabin just aft of the bridge. He would occasionally hold mine-sinking drills from the bridge. A wooden box or empty oil drum would be thrown over the side and the ship would come about and approach it, as we would a mine (not too close). Several Gunners Mates with M-1 rifles would be summoned to the bridge and they and the old man would practice mine sinking. We were ready!

We were on our first deployment to Task Force 77 on October 22, 1953 when we had our first mine scare. I was working on some equipment in the lower sound room, which was not normally manned at sea. Lower sound was in the forward part of the ship three decks below the main deck right above the keel. Because it was in an isolated location at the bottom of the ship, we always notified the sonarman on duty when we were in lower sound. When I got to lower sound, I called the sonar shack, notified them I was there and went about my work. After a while I noticed that the ship was maneuvering and that it finally stopped. I didn't think much of it. I figured if something important was going on someone in the sonar shack would call me on the phone to tell me about it. After awhile when we still hadn't gotten underway, I got nervous and decided to call sonar. Whoever answered said "Oh yeah, we're shooting at a mine!" I immediately established a world record for coming up three decks. As I got to the main deck someone said, "Did you see that? We sank a mine." The thought went through my head "what would have happened if it had blown up?". I imagined that if it had the effect would have been rather exciting in the sonar room right down on the keel. The other sonarmen didn't seem to understand why I was so upset. It turned out that my informants were part of the "10% that didn't get the word". What we had sunk were some large floating tin cans. We did agree, however, that in the future if a mine was spotted we would make sure no one was in lower sound.

On another occasion, we spotted a steel cylinder floating in the water. It appeared that it could be a magnetic mine so we didn't want to get too close. Captain Green and the Gunners Mates took care of it!

Lookouts constantly scanned the air and sea around the ship. Each lookout was assigned a sector to monitor. Lookouts were the most likely persons to spot a mine. As an incentive to increase their concentration and vigilance, Lcdr. Baker, the executive officer (XO), offered a weekend liberty pass in Japan to any lookout spotting a mine.

Now offhand that doesn't seem like much of a prize except that liberty in Japan was rather limited. Also, sailors regarded Japan as having some of the best liberty ports in the world. Because of the large numbers of US Navy ships visiting Japan and the limited number of overnight facilities, sailors were limited to "Cinderella Liberty". Everyone had to return to the ship by midnight. If you didn't, you were Absent With Out Leave (AWOL) not a pumpkin. Each ship could grant a few overnight passes but that required filling out forms in duplicate and applying to the XO. Also a sailor usually didn't realize he wanted to stay overnight until he had been ashore awhile and had met an attractive young lady.

Of course there were segments of the Japanese economy that depended on overnight activity and had figured a way around the system. Almost all Japanese bordellos had an arrangement with local water taxis to surreptitiously return sailors to their ships anchored in the harbor early in the morning. For security reasons, no Japanese boats were allowed out in the harbor at night. A U.S. Navy Harbor Patrol enforced this rule. So at first light of dawn, as soon as they were legal, the water taxis shoved off with their cargo of smiling sailors. The sailors stayed out of sight in the water taxi cabin. The enlisted men on the destroyer 4 to 8 deck watch in the morning were well aware of the love boat connection and kept watch for water taxis right after dawn. If one was spotted approaching a destroyer from the stern, the Petty Officer of the Watch would lure the Officer Of The Deck to some place where he couldn't see the AWOL lotharios climbing aboard over the screw guard. With even overnight liberty scarce, a whole weekend in Japan was considered quite a prize and undoubtedly helped to increase the lookouts attention.

On January 16, 1954 we were with Task Force 77 in one of the "pouncer" positions in the rear of the task force. The aircraft carrier Oriskany (CV-34) was about 1000 yards off our port bow. It was a rather grey day with moderate seas. At 11:23AM, the port lookout on the flying bridge reported over the sound powered phones to the bridge, "Mine on the port bow 400 yards about 320 relative." Every pair of eyes on the bridge strained to see the mine.

U.S.S. Oriskany (CV-34) narrowly missed hitting a mine that was subsequently sunk by Wren. (US Navy Photo)

I was on the starboard wing of the bridge and strained unsuccessfully to pick up the mine. No one could see it but Washington, the lookout. Captain Green, who had been sitting in his chair on the starboard wing of the bridge, crossed through the pilothouse to the port side. He peered off the port bow through his binoculars but he couldn't find the mine. Finally he turned and looked up to the flying bridge. "Are you sure its a mine", he said to Washington. Seaman Washington, who was probably already planning his weekend in Japan, said, "Your f....g right it's a mine!" The captain stared at him for a moment and then turned around as Washington belatedly added, "Sir." As we got closer it indeed was a mine. It was a round horned M-Yam[10] type mine that could do enormous damage. The screen destroyers must have passed right around it and it went within 100 feet of the starboard side of the Oriskany. A very close call for all concerned. The captain, with his M1A Carbine, and the gunner's mates, with M1 Rifles, quickly sank the mine -- and Washington got his weekend in Japan.

---

[10]The M-Yam mine is still in use in the 21st century. Both the Iranians and the Iraquis have versions of the M-Yam that they have used in the Persian Gulf.

Domes Aweigh

SONAR (SOund Navigation and Ranging) locates submerged objects (including submarines) by transmitting high power sound pulses into the water and detecting the echoes from the submerged object. The time that it takes for the echo to return is used to determine how far away the object is because we know that sound travels at about 4800 feet-per-second in sea water. A Sonarman's job was to operate the sonar equipment. The "sonar shack, located on the bridge level just aft of the pilothouse, contained the Control and Display equipment for the entire system and was where the sonarmen stood their watches. There was another sonar space, the Lower Sound Room, down on the keel beneath the most forward berthing compartment. This space contained the high power sonar transmitters and sensitive receivers that were controlled from the "sonar shack". Directly under the Lower Sound Room was the transducer. The transducer actually transmits the sonar sound pulses into the water and detects the returning echoes and is mounted outside the hull. In the nineteen fifties, transducers were cylindrical devices about 2 feet in diameter and about 3 feet tall.[11] The cylinder was divided into 48 vertical segments each containing electro-mechanical devices that functioned like a loudspeaker when transmitting and a microphone when receiving. The transducer was mounted at the end of a 6-inch diameter stainless steel pipe so that it was in the water below the keel of the ship. For protection (particularly in shallow water), the pipe could be pulled up to retract the transducer into a cylindrical trunk in the hull. This whole mechanism was in the forward part of the ship close to the bow so that it was away from the noise of the screws and the engine room machinery.

As the ship moved through the water, turbulent water flow around the transducer and its mounting pipe would cause a roaring noise in the sonar equipment. This noise, which increases with ship speed, would obscure weak submarine echoes. To reduce the noise (and thus increase sonar range), the round transducer was enclosed in a streamlined, tear drop shaped sonar dome attached to a steel skirt on the hull. The dome was made of

---

[11] By contrast, the transducer for current naval sonars such as the AN/SQS-56 is about 16 feet in diameter, 7 feet high and the pressurized dome forms the bulbous bow structure of the ship.

rubber reinforced with thin steel rods so that sound could easily go through it. The water flowed smoothly around the dome and greatly reduced the water noise. The dome had a number of small holes in it at the top and bottom so that it would fill with water at the same pressure and temperature as the surrounding sea. It also had sound absorbing baffles in the aft part of the dome to screen the transducer from the propulsion noise in the stern of the ship. Needless to say something made of rubber and small rods could be damaged rather easily by striking a hard object. Occasionally a destroyer damaged one by hitting a large floating piece of wood or a whale or other large sea mammal. Unfortunately, the damage to Wren's sonar dome was self-inflicted.

We had been operating in the Straits of Korea doing gunnery and various other exercises for several days. There were no night exercises scheduled, so we were going to anchor overnight in a harbor in the Japanese Island of Tsushima. Tsu Tsu Wan harbor was small but well enclosed and sheltered. Although a Japanese possession, Tsushima was much closer to Korea than Japan. Archeologists had long thought that Tsushima had a part in the connection of Korean and Japanese culture. Legend holds that the Japanese Yamamoto royal family came from Tsushima. The island was very rocky with few trees and high cliffs surrounded the small harbor. As we approached we scanned the coast looking for signs of life. There was a small lighthouse, on the rocky eastern headland. It stood by itself and there wasn't anything that looked like a lighthouse keeper's home. There were no signs of any activity or inhabitants on the deserted beaches at the foot of the cliffs. From the Sailing Directions, we understood that some fishermen may have lived nearby but we could see no signs of life as we slowly proceeded toward our anchorage. It was a good, well-sheltered harbor with 21 fathoms of water and a sand bottom. We prepared to anchor.

The captain always wanted to be sure that the ship was dead in the water before letting go the anchor. He insisted that the quartermasters break up wooden potato boxes to make him a supply of wood chips. As we approached an anchorage he would tell the quartermaster to throw a wood chip over the side to see if we were still underway. If a chip drifted aft, we were still moving. Chips were thrown over until the captain was satisfied that we were dead-in-the-water or even drifting slightly astern and it was safe to drop anchor.

As we approached our anchorage at the island, the captain ordered "All back one". Both engines were reversed to slow the ship. Water boiled up around the stern as the screws worked against our forward motion. The quartermaster stood by with the supply of wood chips. "Throw in a chip" the captain ordered. The chip drifted briskly aft. A minute later he said "Another chip". It also drifted aft. The captain looked into the pilothouse and said "All stop". The engines stopped. "One more chip" he said. It drifted slowly aft. "Let go" the captain ordered. Forgerson, the Chief Quartermaster said, "He didn't say let go did he, we're still moving"? As if in answer there was the loud roar of anchor chain running out through the hawsepipe. The chain was stopped with the anchor windlass brake when we had 90 fathoms of chain out. The anchor detail prepared to lock the chain in place with the stopper when we came to rest. As the anchor took hold, the ships forward motion caused the anchor chain to pull back and down along the port side as the ship came to a stop. Some of the anchor detail were leaning over the side to see if the chain was dragging under the hull. It was! The stern started to swing to starboard as the chain tightened against the port side and we gradually came about as we swung on the anchor. As the ship settled in its anchorage, the sea detail secured and the anchor watch was set. None of us thought too much about the anchor problems (although the captain probably had second thoughts) and we passed a pleasant evening relieved from steaming watches and bobbing quietly in this protected harbor.

The next morning we got under way shortly after first light. We weighed anchor and started slowly out of the harbor. We were scheduled for more exercises and were proceeding to the operating area. As we cleared the harbor, we increased speed. I was on the sonar stack starting a beam-to-beam search for submarines as we left Tsushima and headed into deeper water. When we got to about 17 knots a bright line appeared on the sonar display radiating from the area of our port bow. The AN/SQS-10 sonar equipment had a round 9-inch cathode ray tube video display. The ship was in the center of the display and the greenish sweep spiraled out toward the edge at a rate corresponding to the speed of sound in seawater. Any noises or echoes caused a brightening of the sweep. I slewed the audio cursor over to the bright noise spoke so that I could listen to it and heard loud rushing water noises. As we increased speed, it got much worse and the bright area got wider and wider. By the time we reached 20 knots the noise spoke was brightening most of the screen, there was a roar coming from the loudspeaker and the sonar was useless. I reported to the bridge "The sonar is extremely noisy - I think we have a problem with the sonar dome". Mr. Davis the Division Officer poked his head in the door. He looked glumly at the bright display and the noise coming over the loudspeaker. If the dome was damaged, we would have to go into dry-dock in Japan. Davis looked like he didn't want to be the messenger bringing bad news to the captain particularly when it looked like the anchor chain could have been the culprit. Thinking of his own fitness report, I am sure the captain didn't want to notify Seventh Fleet that he had damaged his ship and had to return to port.

Not being of much use for submarine searches (one of our primary missions), we were detached from the task group and went back to Sasebo and tied up alongside the destroyer tender U.S.S. Prairie. Salvage divers from Prairie went under the ship and confirmed that there was a dent on the port after side of the sonar dome. The next morning we transferred electrical power to the emergency diesel generator and secured all of the boilers. With a Japanese pilot on-board, and towed and guided by three tugs, we got underway for an old Imperial Japanese Navy dry-dock facility on the west side of Sasebo harbor. Two dry-docks were located along an old stone seawall surrounded by open fields. There were none of he usual buildings or shipyard support services around the dry-docks. We assumed that they had been destroyed during the war and not yet been rebuilt. All support services for drydock repairs were provided by U.S. Navy tenders and repair ships. Although there was some welding and cutting equipment available at the dry-dock, the tender sailors had to bring all of the other required tools over by boat.

We entered the northernmost dock (Dry-dock 2) and the line handlers using capstans got the ship centered according to marks on the walls. The dry-dock gate was closed and pumps started draining the water. On the bottom of the dry-dock were a set of blocks about five feet tall that the ships keel sat on and sets of blocks on either side that the hull rested on. The blocks were set up for the particular type of ship to be docked and they had to be high enough so that the sonar dome cleared the dock floor. As the water went down and the ship came to rest on the keel blocks the pumps were stopped. This was a very old dock. In U.S. docks, even in the 1950's, chains controlled from the top of the dock were used to tighten the outer rows of blocks against the hull. Not here. A Japanese diver, in the oldest most decrepit hard hat diving rig I had ever seen, descended with a net bag full of wooden wedges and a sledge hammer. He was going to individually wedge each of the hull blocks! This was a slow job, and we could judge his progress by the location of his exhaust bubbles. But he wasn't the only holdup. A dry-dock located on the edge of the Pacific "Ring of Fire" also had to have earthquake protection.

The sides of the dry-dock were not straight. They descended in series of four-foot steps to the bottom of the dock. While the diver was wedging the hull blocks a crane was lifting 12-inch square timbers into place between one of the steps and the side of the hull. These timbers were placed about every ten feet along both sides of the ship. I had never seen braces used like that in a dry-dock before. And I guess I had never before been in a dry-dock where severe earthquakes were a definite possibility. If not braced, an earthquake jolt could throw the ship right off of the blocks causing serious hull damage. The Japanese honcho, or boss, stood on the Wren fantail with a megaphone. On either side at the end of the first beam was a burly Japanese worker with a large wooden maul. A wooden wedge had been placed between the end of the timber and the dock wall on both sides. The honcho picked up his megaphone and yelled "Ee-yo". And both men simultaneously drove in their wedge. After the first timbers were tight they moved to the next. As they moved forward the honcho kept going forward and higher on the superstructure. At the culmination of this procedure he was yelling "Ee-yo" from the top of the main battery gun director high above the bridge. It was quite a performance and we were now wedged in tightly against earthquakes.

Wren in Dry-dock 2 Sasebo, Japan to replace the sonar dome. Note the large timbers along the sides to prevent the ship from being shaken off the keel blocks by an earthquake. (Gordon R. Hipp Photo)

Once we were settled on the blocks, the crane lifted a long gangway in place from the starboard quarterdeck to the side of the dock. The pumping resumed and the water dropped in the dry-dock. The dock was almost empty, when suddenly all of the Japanese workmen dropped what they were doing and ran down the steps into the dock. We couldn't imagine what was causing this rush until we saw that they were gathered at the grates over the drydock water drains. All the fish that had been trapped in the dock were now being pulled toward the drains as the last of the water was pumped out. The Japanese workmen jumped into the shallow water and caught tonight's dinner as it approached the drain.

After the dock was drained, all of the sonarmen and the Mr. Davis and Mr. Bigelow went down to look at the dome. The dome was about five feet long and three feet high. On the after edge of the dome was a dent about the size of an anchor chain link. I ducked under the hull to take a look on the other side. On the port side of the hull were the unmistakable impressions made by the anchor chain in the plastic anti-rust coating. The link marks went diagonally down the hull right toward the sonar dome and there was a dent in the aft edge of the dome. The chain undoubtedly caused the damage as it tightened and pressed against the hull to stop our forward motion. No question how we got the dent. By this time it was late afternoon. The repair crew from the Prairie would be over first thing in the morning to replace the dome.

A starboard side view of a 60-inch sonar dome similar to the one installed on the keel line of Wren. The light line near the top of the dome structure is the interface between the rubber dome and the steel structure of the ship. The Wren's dome was dented slightly on the port side and had a big dent in the aft edge. (US Navy Photo)

They did in fact arrive first thing in the morning together with the civilian Philco TechRep who was to supervise the job. It was not a very good-looking group. The U.S.S. Prairie Christmas party had been the night before at a club in Sasebo and these guys looked like they had a really good time. They were all grumpy and red-eyed and there was a definite miasma of alcohol surrounding them. We all trudged down into the dock using the dock stairs on the starboard side of Wren. The Wren quarterdeck and OD were also on this side. We all moved forward to look at the dome -- or so I thought. I was looking at the dome and pointed out the dent to the TechRep. When I looked up not one of the Prairie guys were in sight. I ducked under the hull and looked around just in time to see them disappearing over the top of the port side stairs which were out of sight of the OD.   It turned out that Mama Sans Gin Mill was located about one hundred yards up the road from the dry-dock.   It appeared that the number one priority for the Prairie guys was getting their health back.   After that was accomplished they would consider replacing our sonar dome.

A crane lowered a large crate with the new dome to the bottom of the dry-dock near where we were working.   The Philco TechRep and a couple of Wrens were working to get the wood crate open.   Somewhere in the process a section of the crate dropped on the TechRep's foot followed by a loud yell and a lot of hopping around.   One of the Wren corpsman looked at the foot and decided he better go to the base sick bay.   Short day for him too.

While all this was going on, another little drama was unfolding up on the main deck. The First Lieutenant had decided that while we were out of the water in dry-dock, it would be a good opportunity to repaint the waterline black.   To do this would require the chippers and painters to go over the side in bosun's chairs and scaffolds.   The deck force didn't think this was such a great idea. It's one thing to be over the side when a fall only means getting wet – it's quite another thing to be suspended 25-feet above the concrete floor of a dry-dock.   Things were at an impasse. Mr. Harrison had ordered them over the side and they weren't going.   Harrison was just standing there.   The crew was standing around looking at their feet and contemplating the prospect of a mutiny court martial.   Finally, "Rocky" Stone a three-hashmark (12-year) seaman with a disciplinary record as long as his arm said "I'm not afraid, I'll go over with a lifeline".   That broke the impasse and with a lot of grumbling about a candyass lifer, everyone went over the side.   Stone had been as high as Boatswains Mate 1st Class and been busted down to Seamen twice and probably figured he could use a little good will before his next Captains Mast.

When the Prairie guys finally returned later in the morning they still didn't look very good but they certainly seemed to feel better.   They went to work and cut off the steel strip that streamlined the flange and covered up the connecting bolts. They then removed the many bolts holding the dome in place and we all helped them lower the old dome using pieces of timber as levers. We wrestled the old dome across the dry-dock to where the crane could pick it up and get it out of the dock. Before the ship went into dry dock we had hauled the sonar transducer up into the hull so that it wouldn't get damaged in case we hit something in the dock or in the process of taking off the dome. I went back up into the Lower Sound Room and told York to lower the transducer down so we could inspect it and clean off any marine growth. I told him that when we were finished, I would hammer on the hull and he could haul it back up using the chain falls. As I got back down by the dome, the transducer was coming down. We inspected and cleaned it and it seemed to be OK. Unbeknownst to me one of the Prairies had stuck his head up into the dome mounting skirt to look at the underwater telephone transducer. I picked up a small sledgehammer and hammered on the steel skirt about 5 times. The guy from the Prairie came out of the skirt with his eyes bulging. He looked as if he had just spent noon inside Big Ben. I had probably just negated all Mama Sans Gin Mills medicinal treatment for his hangover. All the Wrens thought it was pretty funny, however, he failed to see the humor in it and got downright belligerent. Fortunately Wrens outnumbered Prairies and the altercation didn't get beyond the shouting stage.

At that point everyone agreed that we all just wanted to get the job done and go on liberty. We turned to and got the new dome out of the crate, lifted into position and bolted onto the skirt. The only thing that remained to be done was to weld a strip of steel to cover streamline the flange of the skirt. But that was shipfitter work and not ours. A couple of Prairies finished that up as we showered got into "dress canvas" and hit the beach.

The next day the dock was flooded down, our earthquake bracing removed and we were towed back out to anchor. We were scheduled to be in Sasebo until December 27 when we would get underway again for Task Force 77. We were looking forward to Christmas and a brief respite from operations. While it wasn't exactly "visions of sugar plums" that were dancing through our heads, it was certainly the Wren Christmas Party on the 22nd and 23rd at the Jungle Club. Half the crew got to go each night – except for Arch who got to go both nights to play bass! I envisioned that we would probably look as bad after our Christmas Party as the Prairies looked after theirs.

Fruit Cocktail, PB&J and Saltines

Sailors have always been famous for drinking lots of coffee. If a sailor was sitting down or standing around talking, chances are that he was sipping coffee from a thick white cup with no handle. I guess the navy thought that there was less breakage and it was easier to wash cups without handles. If the coffee was really hot (which it usually was) not having a handle made it pretty hard to hold. In addition to being hot, Navy coffee was not that mild, aromatic just-ground stuff that Starbucks serves today. It was dark, strong and just a little rancid. The standard joke was that you shouldn't leave a spoon in the cup because the coffee would dissolve it.

In those days, the Navy didn't buy any of that sissified civilian coffee like Maxwell House or Chock Full o' Nuts. Navy coffee was roasted and ground at the Naval Clothing Factory in Philadelphia and sent to the fleet in double-weight 10-pound paper bags. As soon as the bag was open the already slightly stale coffee started to get even more rancid. To try to prevent this, the sonarmen devised a supposedly airtight storage container for our coffee. We took a 10-gallon snap-top dessiccant (air dryer) can, painted the inside white and dumped the coffee in. Unfortunately it didn't help much.

There were coffee messes all over the ship. Each "gang" has its' own coffeepot. Coffee was brewing twenty-four hours a day. Although we all loved coffee we also thought that it was nice to have a little something to go along with the coffee. Why just have coffee when you can have "coffee and"? Of course Navy health and sanitary regulations strictly forbid keeping food anywhere but in the official food storage and serving areas. The Chief Hospital Corpsman, who was responsible for public health among his other duties, would prowl the ship looking for unauthorized food caches particularly near the coffee messes. One day at sea, I was walking forward on the starboard side of the main deck. I saw the Chief Corpsman lowering himself through the Starboard Fireroom Hatch and down the vertical ladder into the Forward Fire Room. I continued forward and crossed to the other side at the forward passageway. I looked aft down the portside and saw two Boilermen passing food out the Port Fireroom Hatch. They were probably 10 seconds ahead of the Chief.

The sonarmen had a coffee mess on the little aluminum shelf that we had constructed between the Range Recorder and the Attack Plotter. The only problem was that the water required to make coffee was three decks below. There were not supposed to be any water taps in operations spaces. Someone noticed, however that the water line for the captain's sea cabin ran right through sonar. During the yard availability in 1953 in Charleston, one of the "yard bird" plumbers was bribed to install a brass faucet on the captain's water line. Before every inspection, the faucet was very carefully polished and buffed. Inevitably, one of the inspecting officers would comment favorably on our gleaming faucet - - forgetting, of course, that it was completely illegal.

On destroyers the ships galley was very small. As a result the bakers worked at night after the cooks cleaned up from dinner. When we were on watch at sea, one of us would go down to the galley at about 3:00 AM and see if we could talk the baker out of a loaf of bread and some butter. If you were lucky the baker would split a hot loaf in half and tuck a quarter-pound bar of butter in the middle. Hot buttered bread really hit the spot in the middle of the night. We were always sure to clean up the crumbs before the corpsman came poking around in the morning though. Of course the bread only lasted a short time. If we could get our hands on them, those delicacies of the naval supply system, peanut butter, jelly and saltine crackers would last for quite a while. The storekeepers kept all that stuff under lock and key. Once it was stored away, it was virtually impossible to get. The only way to steal the stuff was during provisioning when it was coming aboard and before it got inventoried and locked up.

Provisioning a ship, even an old 2100-ton Fletcher class destroyer, was a big job. There were dry stores like sugar and flour and canned goods, fresh vegetables and refrigerated and frozen things like meat and milk. Storage space aboard these old destroyers was in short supply. Storage was tucked into available space all over the ship. Some provisions were stored forward, some aft and potatoes were stored on the open upper level 01 deck. Getting all of these stores into all of the storage places on the ship is what the Navy calls an "all hands evolution." That means everybody gets to help. That also means that everyone got an opportunity to steal some goodies.

Provisioning in port was fairly straightforward. The truck loaded with provisions arrived on the pier. The duty Bosun's Mate piped All Hands and summoned the crew to the pier. The Masters-At-Arms (MA's) roamed the ship looking for slackers who might be trying to avoid this opportunity for aerobic exercise. A line of sailors streamed off the ship, to the back of the truck and back on to the ship. Each sailor got a case of something to carry back to the ship. Storekeepers were stationed at strategic locations to direct the cases to the correct storage location.   They were also there to assure that the Fruit Cocktail, Peanut Butter, Jelly and Saltine Crackers made it to their storage location and were not diverted to crew coffee messes. Although the crew was crafty, so were the storekeepers and most of the delicacies ended up in locked up in storage.

Replenishment at sea was an entirely different deal. Again it was an all-hands evolution. Everyone not directly involved in running the ship, helped in getting the stores aboard. Many manned the highline stations forward and aft where the stores came over in cargo nets on the highline from the supply ship.   Everyone else moved the stores from where they were dumped on deck to the storage areas.   There was a great deal of confusion and a demand for speed to get the stuff aboard and struck below as quickly as possible. If the weather was bad or the seas high, it became even more disorganized.   Being a crafty group, the sonarmen, radiomen, radarmen and fire control technicians (FT) organized a cooperative to insure a supply of PB, jelly, saltines and fruit cocktail to their respective coffee messes.   These four gangs' technical workspaces were in a vertical stack in the main superstructure. This made for convenient distribution of the spoils.   The Sonar Shack was on the 02 level.   Directly below sonar on the 01 level was the Radio Room and directly below that on the main deck was the Radar Room. The Plotting Room, where the FT's worked, was on the first deck right below the Radar Room.   A set of ladders (steep stairs), just outside each door, connected all four areas.   The route to the main food storage area up forward went right by the radar transmitter room.   The deal was that if during replenishment at sea any members of the co-op got a case of the top four (Fruit cocktail, PB, jelly or saltines), they would head for the forward storage.   As they passed the Radar Room, they would open the door and toss the case.   Hopefully there were no Storekeepers or MA's in the area to witness the deed.   They would then turn around and head empty handed back to the highline area for another load.   One of the radarmen would stash the loot under the workbench or in the darkened confines of the adjacent Combat Information Center (CIC) to await distribution.

As soon as replenishment was completed, there would be a meeting of the co-op in the radar room to divide the spoils.   A case of fruit cocktail, jelly or peanut butter contained four 1-gallon cans, which were distributed to the four gangs.   The saltines were also divided four ways.   All this may seem like a lot of trouble just to get some snacks to go with coffee. When you are at sea for long while, however, these little capers provide a break and some comic relief from the normal routine.   There is also deep in the heart of every "white hat" a strong need to beat the system whenever possible.   We all used to have a few chuckles over our "coffee and" thinking about the storekeepers trying to account for the missing fruit cocktail, PB&J and saltines.

By A Thread

During the Korean War period, most major naval ports in the United States (with the exception of Newport, Rhode Island) had sufficient pier space so that the majority of ships were "alongside", as sailors described it. Well, alongside something although not necessarily the pier. More often than not destroyers were nested 4 to 6 deep outboard of the pier. This meant that if you were in one of the outboard ships, you had to traverse the others to get ashore. It was more of a pain when the ship actually alongside the pier was a destroyer tender and you were in one of the destroyers moored outboard of it. The tenders were large ships and going through them meant going up and down a couple of decks in addition to crossing through it. So at eight o'clock at night when they passed the word "The Mobile Canteen is on the pier" you had to decide whether the trip was worth it. It was still a lot better than being anchored out away from shore. So even if we had to cross three or four other ships to get ashore – it was still much easier, drier and dependable than riding boats to go on liberty. Also there was Ramsour's Law to contend with. First Class Torpedoman Ramsour was my favorite "old salt", tin can sailor and deep-water philosopher. He was an old enough salt that his first ship had been a WW-I vintage "four piper" destroyer. He also looked very much like Popeye the Sailorman. Ramsour always contended that the main problem with anchoring out was that "You either had liberty and no boats or boats and no liberty". Very profound!

There were always some ships, of course, because of their size or cargo, that were moored "out in the stream". The main disadvantage of being anchored out of course was that (in addition to Ramsour's Law) liberty depended on the vagaries of the weather. If it was too rough to run small boats, you didn't get to go ashore. I said before that ships were alongside in most naval ports in the U.S. During the Korean War, the Naval Base at Newport, Rhode Island was the major exception to that rule. There was very little pier space available around Naragansett Bay and almost all of the destroyers "anchored out", usually in "nests" of four. Given the winter weather in the Northeast U.S. the Newport based tin can sailors missed a lot of liberty. Besides the inconvenience, boat transportation was also dangerous. On May 24, 1951 a navy liberty launch transporting sailors ashore capsized at Newport, killing 19.

Overseas, we rarely tied up alongside. Pier space was allotted to local shipping and all visitors (us) got to anchor out. The biggest problem we had when anchoring out overseas was lack of transportation. Most destroyers had only a single 26-foot whaleboat. Fletcher class destroyers carried a whaleboat and a gig. The gig was really another whaleboat that had been partly enclosed for protection against the weather and was reserved for the captain's use. He generally allowed the officers to use it for liberty runs so that left the whaleboat for the enlisted men. A whaleboat could only carry about 20 passengers so it would take a long while to ferry a liberty party of 125 ashore. If the ship was far from shore or if the number of passengers was reduced because of rough weather, it could take a long time.

The whaleboat being used as a liberty boat. Fortunately in most ports we didn't have to depend on these small craft. The nonchalant guy in front of the flag with his hand on the tiller is the coxswain. Note Wren on the horizon just to the right of the flag. (A.T. Miller Photo)

In Singapore, we were assigned to the man-o-war anchorage, which was so far out that Singapore seemed to be a blur on the distant horizon. We were pretty despondent about the prospects of ever getting ashore using only the whaleboat when lo and behold a Royal Navy landing craft appeared to take us ashore. Rule Britannia!

In many overseas ports frequented by U.S, ships there was a boat pool from which visiting naval vessels could borrow a steel-hulled Landing Craft Medium (LCM) or a plywood-hulled Landing Craft, Vehicle & Personnel (LCVP). Either one of these was a huge improvement over our whaleboat. Both of them were blunt-nosed, powerful, but slow, assault boats meant to transport troops and vehicles from a large transport to a beach while under fire. They were open to the weather and there were no seats but we usually didn't care as long as they got us ashore. The "M" boats were preferred because they were large enough to haul most of the liberty party in one trip. And of course there were in most overseas ports the civilian entrepreneurs operating "bum boats" that would transport sailors ashore for a small fee.

Whatever means of transportation was used, the trip over when everyone was sober was a lot better than the returning voyages when the boats were filled with bellicose and belligerent drunks. The "M" boats were particularly bad because the liberty party of 60 to 80 drunken sailors had to stand in the well deck which was a large space designed to transport a tank. A couple of guys thrown together by the boat's roll or an implied insult would set things off and fists would fly. The fight would surge back and forth over the length and breadth of the steel deck for the entire trip. Anyone who lost his footing and fell would awake the following morning wondering why the hell he was so sore and why were there footprints all over his uniform!

In Mediterranean ports there were not too many piers and to make maximum use of them, ships moored stern-first in to the seawall or mole – the famed Mediterranean Moor. It definitely beat anchoring out but it was kind of a tricky evolution – something like a K-turn with a car. The ship makes its approach parallel to the seawall, turns out so that its bow is pointing away from the wall and drops its anchor. Then the ship backs slowly while paying out anchor chain until the stern is close enough to the seawall to tie up. The slack is then taken out of the anchor chain so that the ship is moored pointed out and at a 90-degree angle to the seawall. That doesn't sound too hard – and it isn't if you have plenty of room to maneuver and there isn't much current or wind. In Naples we had to make a Mediterranean moor to the San Vincenza mole between two wooden-hulled Italian Navy minesweepers.   It took us three attempts; two anchor drops and at one point it looked as if we might reduce one of the sweeps to toothpicks.

On the French Riviera, DesDiv-61 anchored in the little fishing port of Villefranche. Fortunately, the harbor was quite deep and we were able to anchor close to the town.   It was not a big problem for Wren's whaleboat and gig to shuttle back and forth with the liberty party.   For Cone, Noa and Stribling it was a little slower because they only had a whaleboat (no gig).

DesDiv-61 anchored in Villefranche harbor.   The main, waterfront street of the town can be seen at the head of the harbor – a short boat ride from the ships. USS Wren is top right in the picture, closest to the landing! (A.T. Miller Photo)

The main street of this lovely town ran right along the waterfront. There were a number of sidewalk cafes along the street overlooking the harbor.   DesDiv-61 set up a fleet landing right in front of one of these cafes.   Boats from the destroyers had to swing a bit to the east to go around a buoy marking a line of underwater rocks and then proceed westward to the fleet landing.   I had liberty the first day that we were there.   About 10 PM Al Dodge, Al Berndt and I had come back from Nice and were knocking back a few cool ones at the Nautic´ café at the fleet landing.   We figured we could keep right on drinking up until the last boat was ready to leave.   Boats were coming and going returning sailors to the four ships.   We noticed that each time the Noa's whaleboat came in the coxswain popped into the café and threw down a quick drink.   We didn't think too much about it and when it got close to midnight we caught Wren's whaleboat (the gig was being used by the officers) back to the ship.

Noa's whaleboat enroute to Villefranche landing.   The 3-man crew consists of the bow hook, engineman and the coxswain at the tiller. Later that night, the whaleboat would be holed when a drunken coxswain decided to take a "shortcut". (A.T. Miller Photo)

The next morning we found out that the Noa's coxswain, evidently emboldened by the drinks, decided on his last trip to cut to the west of the buoy marking the rocks.   The Noa's whaleboat immediately hit the rocks and started to take on water.   The crew managed to get it off the rocks and headed back to Noa.   By the time they got alongside the ship, it was very low in the water and only its watertight flotation tanks were keeping it afloat.   It was quickly connected to the davits and hoisted aboard.   All the next day, we watched the beehive of activity on Noa.   There was much sawing, hammering and caulking around the whaleboat.   The crew, faced with loss of their transportation to the beach was giving the repair team a lot of gratuitous advice.   About 2 PM, as we watched through glasses, the whaleboat was lowered into the water. The whole liberty party was watching to see if it would float.   It wouldn't.   It sank more slowly than it had the night before but it was a long way from being seaworthy.   Even on Wren we could hear the angry shouts of the Noa liberty party berating the Noa boat crews and boat repairers. At that point, Captain Johnson felt sorry for the Noa's crew and had a blinker message sent that they could use Wren's gig for liberty.   I don't know what punishment was ultimately meted out to the drunken coxswain but I bet if it was up to the liberty party, they would have strung him from the yardarm.

The gig about to be lowered into the water.   The gig was basically another whaleboat with the forward section covered and decorated with a lot of "fancy work".   With the cover the capacity was lowered to about 15. (A.T. Miller Photo)

Although we sometimes "anchored out" by actually dropping our anchor, it was usually only done at little-used anchorages or unimproved ports.   Most times we anchored by connecting our anchor chain to a mooring buoy held in position by a large mushroom type anchor, a large concrete clump or similar immovable anchoring device. The mooring buoy is flat on top and has large steel eye or ring in its center. The flat top allowed the mooring party to stand on top of the buoy to handle the chain and to connect it to the eye with a large mooring shackle. As the ship approached the buoy, the mooring party went over to the buoy in the whaleboat. As the ship approached they passed a line over to the buoy that was reeved through the eye and passed back to the ship. That line was used to assist the mooring party by using the ships windlass to pull the very heavy anchor chain to the buoy from the ship. The bitter end of the anchor chain was shackled into the buoy, the pin in the shackle was tightened using a marlinspike and the pin wired in place with seizing wire. That should hold it – right? One stormy night in Yokosuka, Japan, it didn't and we only narrowly averted disaster.

Noa, Cone and Stribling moored to a buoy on a single anchor chain in Yokosuka as they await Wren to put her chain over to the buoy. Note that Stribling (867) has dropped her anchor temporarily until Wren moors and connects to the buoy. Also note the tender Bryce Canyon with destroyers moored alongside directly behind us. (A.T. Miller Photo)

It was the night of November 17, 1953 and the four ships of DesDiv-61 were moored in a nest to a buoy in the outer edge of Yokosuka harbor. Wren (which was the right outboard ship) and Stribling (which was between Noa and Cone) had their anchor chains shackled to the mooring buoy to hold all four ships. Noa and Cone were not attached to the buoy. A gale had been building all day and as the evening wore on there was some concern about whether the returning liberty boats would be able to make the side of Wren safely.   I had the duty and couldn't go ashore. After the nightly movie in the messdeck was over, I was tired ands hit the sack.   About 1:30 in the morning I heard the word passed "Now go to your stations all the special sea and anchor details".   I was only half-awake and pretty groggy and said to myself "Must be some drunk coming off liberty passed that word.   We aren't getting underway for a couple of days".   I rolled over and went back to sleep.   I was awakened again by the loud clanging of the general alarm and an announcement to go to General Quarters.   By that time I figured something was up and inasmuch as I had the duty I'd better report to my sea detail station.

When I arrived at the bridge level, things were pretty hectic.   It seems that I wasn't the only one that ignored the word to set the sea detail.   When not many folks showed up, Captain Green ordered the General Alarm sounded.   One look forward showed why. Stribling's anchor chain was no longer connected to the buoy and the whole nest was swinging on Wren's single chain.   All four ships were figuratively hanging by a thread in a gale.   There was a serious question of whether a single anchor chain could hold the load of four destroyers without parting under the best of circumstances.   With the gale wind and waves we were in imminent danger of breaking loose.   The captain kept looking downwind.   Directly downwind from us was the destroyer tender U.S.S. Bryce Canyon with four destroyers nested alongside!   If we broke loose, the four destroyers would drift right down on them and the collision would probably break them loose from their moor.

The only thing that could save us is if we could get up steam so that we could get underway or at least use our engines to stay away from the ships downwind of us.   We only had one of our four boilers on-line to provide energy for heat, electricity and a limited amount of propulsion power.   The snipes were trying mightily to get at least one more boiler on line.   Normally, a boiler is warmed up slowly to prevent damage to the boiler lining.   The number of burners and the size of the burner orifices are adjusted to gradually increase the heat in the boiler.   That night, the boilers were "lit off" from a cold start with all burners in with largest orifices and we got steam up in 28 minutes.   On inspection afterward, it was determined that some of the firebrick in the boiler was cracked from the sudden thermal expansion. It couldn't be helped; there was no other choice.

The mooring party from Stribling in foul weather gear and lifejackets was out on the buoy trying to reconnect their chain. It wasn't easy because the whole nest was swinging on the buoy held only by Wren's chain. Striblings bow wasn't even close to the mooring buoy. They had gotten a line over from Stribling to the buoy and were trying to drag the anchor chain across the open water. This caused a heavy strain on the mooring buoy pulling it over about 45 degrees and making it difficult for the mooring crew to stay on it let alone work. It was cold and rough and waves and spray were breaking over the buoy.

As if we didn't have enough trouble already, an LCM made our starboard side about this time and deposited our rather drunken liberty party back aboard. Of course, they all wanted to help. Pretty soon you could notice guys wearing dress blues and pea coats mixed into the foul weather clad sea detail. York, a Sonarman striker, was normally the phone talker on the foc'sle during sea detail. When he arrived back on board, he immediately went forward and demanded his phones in a loud voice. The talker relinquished the phones to York who put them on very deliberately over his rolled down white hat. His primary contact on that circuit was the phone talker on the bridge. The bridge phone talker had a special set of phones. In addition to the headset and mouthpiece used by the talker himself, there was a push-to-talk handset hanging on the talker's chest so that the OD or captain could pick up the handset to talk to another station themselves without going through the phone talker. By this time we had enough steam up for propulsion (as did Stribling) and we were trying to maneuver to take the strain off our chain and help restore Striblings moor. The Captain picked up the talkers handset and said "foc'sle, which way is the anchor chain tending?" York having had a full evening of partying and not realizing it was the captain replied "I'll play your silly f----ing game, which way is it tending?" At that Captain Green picked up the electric megaphone and screamed at the foc'sle "get that sonofabitch off the phone!" York

166

quickly disappeared below through the hatch to the bosun locker and we always thought he was lucky that he wasn't court martialed

After some tense times and tricky maneuvering, Striblings anchor chain was reconnected to the buoy. Because of the near impossibility of men working on the buoy itself, they used a line to pull the bitter end of the chain through the eye on the buoy and back up to Stribling's main deck. Wren slacked its chain from 15 to 19 fathoms to rebalance the load and everyone breathed a huge sigh of relief. There were also probably a few prayers of thanks from the ships downwind of us. Those of us who were sober through the whole evolution got quite a few laughs over the ensuing days listening to the wildly embellished versions of the incident (including the narrator's heroism) provided by our drunken helpers from the liberty party.

Homeward Bound

In early February 1954, Wren was alongside the destroyer tender Prairie (AD-15) in Sasebo, Japan along with Noa, Cone and Stribling preparing to go home. Wren had spent most of the last four and a half months at sea off the coasts of Korea. This would be the last tender availability for repairs until the ship was back in Norfolk, Virginia and there was a lot of steaming between here and there. We would stop at a number of ports on the way for several days each. These stops would be primarily to refuel and replenish food stores and for sightseeing for the crew. From Sasebo we would steam south to the British colony of Hong Kong. Leaving Hong Kong we would swing south to cross the equator before entering Singapore and then on to Colombo, Ceylon (now Sri Lanka). We would go 2000 miles out of our way to show the flag in Ras Tanura, Saudi Arabia then transit the Suez Canal and refuel in Port Said, Egypt. From there we would cross the Mediterranean, transit the straits of Messina between Sicily and Italy and arrive in Naples, Italy. After a few days in Naples (some of us would go to Rome), we would get underway for Villefranche on the French Riviera, on to Lisbon, Portugal, refuel in Santa Maria, Azores and home to Norfolk. It would be about a six-week trip and all departments were checking that everything was shipshape for the voyage. We would all hate to be dead-in-the-water in some isolated place like the middle of the Indian Ocean!

During the time we were in East Asia, we had operated either from Yokosuka or Sasebo Japan both basically "navy towns". When we finished our last operational commitments and before going alongside the Prairie, Wren was sent to Nagasaki, Japan for two days. This was an opportunity for us to see a historic Japanese city. Most Americans know that Nagasaki was the second city atom bombed in World War-II and that was certainly a very significant event. But Nagasaki was also the first Japanese port opened for trade with the west in the 16th Century. Portuguese from Macao began trading with Nagasaki merchants in 1570. Franciscan and Jesuit missionaries made many converts in Nagasaki and the oldest Catholic Church in Japan still stands there.

There was a strong anti-Christian movement in 1597 and 26 Christians were crucified. Because of its place in international trade, Nagasaki was also the setting for Puccini's famous opera Madam Butterfly.[12]   It was a very interesting and relaxing couple of days. It was also very sobering.   The hills around the city still had a burned stripe on them from the fiery blast of the atomic bomb.   Standing in the ruins of the Urakami Catholic Cathedral and seeing how the force of the bomb almost a mile away moved a three-foot thick stone wall is a very powerful message of its destructive force.

Wrens at the ruins of the atom-bombed Urakami Catholic Cathedral in Nagasaki.   The blast had slid those massive walls about 2-feet.   Sonarman Jim O'Connell is at the far left with jaunty white hat.   (A.T. Miller Photo)

There had been some discussion among the crew about making a "Homeward Bound" pennant to stream as we left Sasebo.   The practice of flying an especially long commission pennant on a ship's homeward voyage following an extended deployment is one of the long-standing traditions of the service.   It dates back to at least the early 19th century. Historically, such homeward voyages were invariably followed by an extended period of refit, during which the ship was "laid up in ordinary" and the crew was

---

[12] Puccini's popular opera Madame Butterfly takes place entirely within a house in Nagasaki, Japan.   Some enterprising Japanese had built "Madame Butterfly's House" in Nagasaki as a tourist attraction.   Of course all of the tours, including ours, had to see the house where this fictional character "lived".

discharged. For that reason, the extra-long pennant was also called the "paying off pennant," a term still in use in the Royal Navy. The pennant is flown from the time of the ships' departure for home until sunset of the day of its arrival in a United States port. It is then hauled down and divided among the members of the crew, the captain taking the blue portion and the remainder being cut into equal portions. Back in early October as we arrived in Japan, we observed a departing U.S. destroyer with a Homeward Bound pennant. We had just come across the Pacific and were steaming north in Sagami Wan inbound for Yokosuka. About a mile west of us was a southbound destroyer with a huge pennant streaming from her masthead. The tip of the pennant extended well beyond the stern of the ship. It was an impressive sight. Despite some enthusiastic discussion, we never streamed a Homeward Bound pennant. I don't know whether the project died for lack of enthusiasm or was killed by command.

On February 15th we and the other destroyers of DesDiv 61 slipped out of the nest alongside Prairie and got underway for Hong Kong. Sasebo is a large, very protected harbor with a long, narrow entrance. We steamed from the open inner harbor toward the relatively narrow outer harbor. Sasebo is in a very mountainous region of Kyushu and there are steep hills on both sides of the outer harbor channel. The hills to the west had been graded into large cultivated terraces. These terraces were always a beehive of activity. The Japanese farmers were busy cultivating and weeding the plots. Others carried buckets of water (and nightsoil) on shoulder bars hundreds of feet up the steep hills to their plots. As we steamed slowly by, whole families could be seen working together. For most of us this panorama, which we saw in our many trips in and out of Sasebo, was our first exposure to the very labor intensive methods of agriculture in a land that has very few flat fertile spots and a lot of people. "Sure doesn't look like Kansas".

Special Sea Detail piloting through Sasebo harbor. The pair of pointed mountains peeking over the ridgeline was identified for navigational purposes as "Jane Russell". (A.T. Miller Photo)

We proceeded outbound through the outer harbor at about ten knots (and without our Homeward Bound pennant) toward the sea. The entrance to the harbor from the sea was quite narrow, surrounded by high cliffs and heavily protected against submarine incursions. This was understandable because at any given time there was a substantial portion of the U.S. Seventh Fleet moored in Sasebo harbor (Remember Pearl Harbor!). Our enemies the Chinese clearly had operational submarines and we weren't sure about the North Korean submarine capability. The entrance to the harbor was sealed with anti-submarine nets extending from spherical floats on the surface to the seabed. There was a netted gate supported by floating pontoons that could be opened and closed by a small yard tugboat (YTL) to let ships through. The gate was closed at night and if there was danger of a submarine attack. It seemed that DesDiv-61 always timed its return from Korea so that we arrived off the submarine nets right at dawn as the gate was being opened for the day.

Farther out, on the seaward side of the nets, were a number of underwater acoustic and magnetic sensors on the bottom to detect approaching submarines. A radar on top of the cliff kept track of surface ship targets. The weapons for this system were carried by a pair of 42 foot plywood-hulled picket boats powered by two Gray Marine 225 HP diesels (basically a marine version of a GM bus engine) that gave them a top speed of about 22 to 24 knots. Although they were called picket boats, they were more often carried on capital ships as a captain's gig or an admiral's barge. They had pilothouse forward, engines amidships and a roomy cabin aft with upholstered benches and a table. I never quite pictured them as combat vessels. These picket boats had a short mast forward with a wire mesh radar reflector on it that allowed them to be tracked by the radar on the cliff. Each of these rather fragile plywood boats had four Mark 6 Depth Charges mounted in individual manual release racks; two on each side. The Mark 6 contained about 600 pounds of TNT that could cause a tremendous explosion, particularly in the shallow depths around a harbor entrance. The plan was that if the sonar sensors outside the harbor detected a submarine, the picket boats would be dispatched to kill it. They would be tracked by the radar and given directions by radio to steer over the suspected sub position to drop depth charges. I'm sure that someone had run the numbers and determined that the picket boat running full tilt could outrun the effects of the explosion from a shallow firing Mark 6 depth charge. I certainly wouldn't want to be the first to try it. I always felt that after the attack was over there would probably be a lot of small pieces of plywood in the water.

The shortest and most direct course from Sasebo to Hong Kong would have been due south through the Straits of Formosa. For a number of reasons, we took the longer route east of Formosa in the Pacific. It had only been five years since Chang Kai Chek and the Nationalist (Koumaintang) Chinese forces were driven from the mainland by Mao Tse Tung's Peoples Liberation Army (PLA) and had taken refuge in Formosa (renamed Taiwan). Now there were two Chinas; the Peoples Republic of China (PRC) on the mainland and the Republic of China (ROC) on Taiwan. The situation in the Straits of Formosa was very tense. The PRC's Peoples Liberation Army (PLA) did not (and still does not) have the amphibious forces to chase after Chang across the straits. The ROC forces were licking their wounds and trying to establish themselves on Taiwan. Hostilities between the two were limited to occasional seizure of fishing boats and shelling of outlying islands such as Quemoy and Matsu. The U.S. was supporting the ROC, and had been battling the PRC in Korea, until the truce was signed the previous July. They didn't want to antagonize the situation by injecting U.S military forces between the adversaries. As a result, we took the long way around.

Only a few weeks before, Wren had been involved in a very tense situation escorting some LST's (Landing Ship Tank) filled with PLA defectors being transported from South Korea to Taiwan as part of Operation Big Switch. In late1950 the United Nations forces were pushing the North Korean army northward and it was obvious that the North Koreans (despite massive aid from the Soviet Union) were losing the war. The Chinese felt that they couldn't afford to let that happen. In mid-October the Chinese Peoples Volunteers (a propaganda euphemism for the PLA) crossed the Yalu River into North Korea and joined the battle. The famous and very intense battles near the reservoirs ("the Frozen Chosin") and on the escape route to Hungnam followed and the UN was driven south in fierce fighting. Seoul fell to the Communists again as they advanced southward. Ultimately the UN forces regrouped and drove the North Koreans and the Chinese back over the 38th parallel and a truce was signed. United Nations forces captured over 60,000 Chinese troops during the three years of the Korean War. The Chinese and about 20,000 North Korean were imprisoned on the island of Koje Do off South Korea. One of the most contentious issues and ultimately one of the conditions of the truce that ended the war in July 1953 was that there would be prisoner exchanges controlled by the Neutral Nations Repatriation Committee. A major perturbation to that agreement, however, was that about 22,000 of the Chinese soldiers decided that they didn't want to go back to the joys of the Peoples Republic of China (PRC) but wanted to join friends and relatives in the Republic of China (ROC) in Taiwan. Needless to say, the PRC was furious over their decision and demanded the return of their soldiers. Mao Tse Tung accused the UN prison guards of the 190th Indian Infantry Brigade of coercing the PLA troops to defect and threatened retaliation. The United States and the UN were adamant that the PLA soldiers had the right to defect and seek asylum in Taiwan. The Chinese prisoners (including those wanting to go to Taiwan) had been moved from Koje-Do to Inchon, Korea in the fall of 1953. The bulk of the prisoners in Big Switch were exchanged in October 1953. Wren stood off Inchon in January 1954 at battle stations on a drizzly cold day as the last of the defectors were loaded into the landing vessels. We were within range of Chinese aircraft and didn't know whether Mao's air force would try to stop the transfer. The Chinese knew precisely when the ships would move out because Inchon's 26-foot tides severely limit ship movements. When the ships were loaded, we escorted them slowly (the only way an LST can go) toward Taiwan. Fortunately there were no problems and the former PLA troops are probably even now enjoying their grandchildren in Taiwan.

We arrived off Hong Kong early on the morning of February 15. Cool winter northeast monsoon air over the warm waters of the South China Sea resulted in a dense fog. Using radar and with a pilot on board we proceeded inbound very slowly up the West Lamma Channel. We were using the radar reflector buoys and the many islands (235 in the Hong Kong colony) to navigate toward our anchorage in Victoria Harbor. Little did I know, as I stood at my sea detail station on the bridge, that 41 years later my wife and I would be living in Hong Kong and would take ferries through these same waters. As we proceeded up the channel, the VD radar repeater on the bridge showed Lamma Island about three miles off our starboard beam. This is one of the larger islands in the colony and lies just south of Hong Kong Island. Forty some years later Catherine and I would have a long and pleasant Sunday afternoon seafood lunch at a waterfront restaurant in the So Kwu Wan fishing village on Lamma. We came over on the ferry from Hong Kong Island where we lived in Happy Valley. Our table at the restaurant was right above the water and we could look out at the Tanka water people paddling about tending the floating fish farms in the harbor. Fish farming is a lucrative business so each of the fish farms had "junkyard dogs" patrolling the floats that supported the net fish pens to discourage fish thieves. In 1954 there were no fish farms (and no fancy restaurants that accepted American Express) on Lamma Island and the native Tankas made their living fishing the waters around Lamma for the markets of Hong Kong.

As we passed Lamma on the starboard side, we held Cheng Chau Island on the radar off to our port side. There was no mistaking Cheng Chau's distinctive dumbbell shape on the radar. Cheng Chau had at one time been two, separate islands. They were later joined by a thin sandbar, thus giving it its distinctive shape. Actually, the township on the sandbar is the most densely populated area of the island because of its central location adjacent to the typhoon shelter harbor. In the spring of 1996 Catherine and I spent a pleasant Saturday on Cheng Chau. I am an avid windsurfer and wanted to investigate the possibility of windsurfing at Cheng Chau. Cheng Chau was the home of the 1996 Olympic Women's Windsurfing Gold Medalist Lee Lai Shan and had become a center for Hong Kong windsurfing activities. After leaving the ferry, we walked across the narrow isthmus past the rental beach cottages to the west side of the island. We walked along the beach (protected by shark nets) looking at the water. The waters around Hong Kong Island are severely polluted but I had thought that Cheng Chau being out in the South China Sea would be clean. It was a lot cleaner than the waters around Hong Kong Island but not clean enough for me (toilet paper in the water just makes me suspicious). In addition, the windsurfers were sailing outside the shark nets! I decided to take a pass on windsurfing and Catherine and I repaired to the patio restaurant of the Warwick Hotel, which overlooks the windsurfers in Cheng Chau Wan.

We had a nice lunch and got lost wending our way through the narrow back streets to get back to Tung Wan harbor and the ferry home. On this Saturday afternoon the main noise in these quiet alleys was the clacking of mah-jong tiles – obviously a popular pastime in Cheng Chau.

Lantau Island is the largest island (about three times the size of Hong Kong Island) in Hong Kong. It provided a radar backdrop to Cheng Chau, Hei Leng Chau and Peng Chau as we proceeded slowly northeastward toward Victoria Harbor. About the time

Discovery Bay on Lantau was on our port beam, we started to swing further east. In 1954 the land around Discovery Bay looked like grassy California hillsides. When Catherine and I lived in Hong Kong, the shores of "Disco" Bay were covered with condos, apartments and a golf course and was an enclave of western expatriates.

Although we couldn't see it in the fog, Kennedy Town on Hong Kong Island was on our starboard beam as we swung toward the harbor. Suddenly, as if a veil had been lifted, we broke out of the fog. The mountains of Hong Kong Island soared off of our starboard side. The nine mountains of Kowloon (Kowloon means 9 dragons) peaked above the fog in the distance to our port. Wispy tendrils of fog clung to some of the hills. The valleys were still filled with fog and it appeared like the fog was streaming down the hills and into the harbor where a thin layer still lay on the water. A weak sun was breaking through the overcast giving the whole scene a rather ethereal appearance. Welcome to Hong Kong!

Cone and Noa moored to a buoy off Causeway Bay, Hong Kong. The morning fog still clings to the hillsides. (A.T. Miller Photo)

We proceeded slowly east through the harbor toward our mooring buoy off of Causeway Bay. We adjusted our course to pass between the Star Ferryboats shuttling back and forth on their short trip (less than a thousand yards) between Central on Hong Kong Island and Tsim-Sha-Tsui in Kowloon. As we came closer in we could see that there were few trees on the steep slopes above the city on Hong Kong Island. During their World War II occupation the Japanese had cut down almost all of the trees and shipped the lumber to Japan. Many squatters' huts could be seen in the hills. In 1954, Hong Kong was seriously overcrowded. Thousands of Chinese refugees had fled the new Communist regime to the safety of the British colony. We weren't allowed to go on liberty to the Kowloon side mainly because of the dangerous conditions caused by the many refugees jammed into the infamous Kowloon City. The refugees continued to escape from China and pour into Hong Kong depending on the political climate and repression in the PRC. There was a great exodus during the "Great Leap Forward" starting in 1958 when millions in China starved to death and again during the excesses and persecution of the ten years of the "Cultural Revolution" from 1966 to 1976.

DesDiv-61 anchored out off the Causeway Bay Typhoon Shelter, Hong Kong on a rainy February 16, 1954. Wren is the ship to the left. This photo was taken from Tiger Balm Gardens. The large open area in the center of the picture would later become Victoria Park. Today this view is entirely blocked by high rise apartment buildings. (A.T.Miller Photo)

The four ships of DesDiv-61 tied up to buoys off the Causeway Bay typhoon shelter. The ships were circled by a large number of "bum boats" filled with various entrepreneurs awaiting an opportunity to come aboard. The honchos for the different groups of these tradesmen were allowed to come aboard to pitch their deals to Lt. Commander Baker, the executive officer. As was usual with U.S. Navy ships in Hong Kong, Mary Soo won! Mary Soo's Side Cleaners were famous throughout the U.S. Navy. In return for allowing her crew (all women) to collect waste food from the mess trays and sell Cokes on the fantail they would scrub down the side of the ship and cut in and paint the black waterline. What a deal! Mary Soo's girls came alongside in small boats with their cleaning supplies and long handled brushes and started to work. After scrubbing down the whole ship, they snapped a chalk line to get a straight edge and proceeded to paint a new black waterline. We ended up with the waterline neater and straighter than it had been since we left the yard.

Mary Soo's Side Cleaners scrubbing the port side of Wren adjacent to the gangway in Victoria Harbor, Hong Kong. (A.T. Miller Photo)

Some of the young women's little brothers were also in the boats and would dive for coin thrown into the filthy water by the sailors.

Young Cantonese boys offering to dive for coins thrown overboard by sailors (A.T. Miller Photo)

Liberty boats ran from the DesDiv-61ships moored off Causeway Bay, to Fenwick Pier in the Admiralty section of Hong Kong. The wives in the small Hong Kong American expatriate colony had formed the Servicemen's Guides Volunteers to welcome American servicemen on leave in Hong Kong. They manned an information desk on Fenwick Pier and hosted sailors to dinners with their families. Some Wrens participated in that program. Over the years, as the number of Americans grew that small women's organization joined with two others and became the American Women's Association (AWA).   When Catherine belonged to the AWA in 1995 and 96, there were 38,000 Americans in Hong Kong and the AWA had become a very large and effective organization.   They published a glossy monthly magazine, fielded two 20-woman teams in the Dragon Boat Races and thought nothing of oversubscribing a 1500 seat charity luncheon. Each year they donated about $HK1.5 million to charity

An American Franciscan priest stationed in Hong Kong also met the liberty parties at Fenwick Pier to warn them of some of the dangers in the city.   His primary message was "do not ride in the rickshaws". It seems the rickshaw drivers would detour into an alley where accomplices would relieve the sailors of their wallets.   Proving that there was some honor among thieves, however, they would drop the American sailors ID card in one of the red Royal Mailboxes and it would be returned to the U.S. Consulate!

There was lots to see in Hong Kong.   We went up the tram to "The Peak", lunched in a nice restaurant at Repulse Bay, went to see the floating fishing villages in Aberdeen and took pictures of Ah Boon Haw's tasteless extravagance, Tiger Balm Gardens.   Many of the crew took advantage of cheap tailoring prices to buy custom made suits or uniforms. The local tailors were geared up to turn out suits in the few days that the sailors were in Hong Kong. Two fittings and a suit in less than three days! The price was right and the suits really looked good.   The problem turned out to be that the thread used to tailor the suits was inferior and in a few months the suits fell apart!   Fortunately, I didn't buy any. Forty some years later when I was living on Hong Kong, quality had improved markedly. The pace was more leisurely too.   A couple of fittings and tailoring took a few weeks. I had a suit, cashmere jacket and some slacks tailored quite reasonably by Hollywood Tailors in Tsim Sha Tsui, Kowloon.

As we departed Hong Kong, we headed south toward Singapore.   Shortly after leaving, rumors flew through the ship that we might be diverted to help extract some Americans from French Indochina (later called Vietnam).   The Communist Viet Minh insurgents had been battling the French for control of Indochina for several years. On November 20, 1953, while Wren was departing Yokosuka for Korean waters, General Henri Navarre, the new French commander in Indochina launched Operation Castor. His objective was to occupy the Dien Bien Phu valley in northwest Indochina, engage the Viet Minh in a pitched battle and destroy them. He seriously underestimated the Viet Minh and Operation Castor was to prove his and the French's undoing. The Viet Minh surrounded the French forces in the valley and rained destruction on them with their artillery. Navarre had thought the Viet Minh could never move those heavy guns through the jungle and up to the surrounding hills. By February of 1954 as we proceeded South off the Indochina coast, the French military effort was collapsing in disarray. About two months later, on May 8, 1954, Dien Bien Phu would fall and the French would accede to the Viet Minh peace demands and abandon Indo China.

The story we heard was that a U.S. Navy Destroyer Transport (APD) was standing by off the mouth of the Red River to evacuate Americans. It was thought that there might be a requirement for a destroyer to support them. Although the U.S. had refused to aid the French with combat forces, they had given them a large number of twin engine B-26B bombers. U.S. Air Force ground support people were also sent to French Indo China to help the French maintain the planes. I have always assumed that the APD's mission was to remove the Air Force technicians from the French airfields near Hanoi and Haiphong plus any U.S. civilians that wanted to get out. At that point the French were using a fleet of U.S. supplied landing craft[13] converted to gunboats to fight their way up and down the Red River and were meeting increasingly heavy and better armed opposition. Most of the crew thought that this would be an exciting and interesting diversion on our peaceful trip home. Fortunately or unfortunately nothing ever came of the rumors and we proceeded on our way southward to cross the equator and visit Singapore.

---

[13] These small ships were LSSL's, the same type of fire support ship that the US had given to the South Korean Navy. It was one of these (LSSL-108) that almost collided with Wren about a month earlier off the coast of North Korea.

East Of Suez

In the heyday of the British Empire in the late 19th Century and up to World War-II, the British used to refer to the Middle and Far Eastern portions of their empire as being "East Of Suez". And there was a lot of the British Empire east of Suez. Several areas of East Africa, Aden, Bahrain in the Persian Gulf, India, Pakistan (including what is now Bangladesh), Burma, Ceylon (now Sri Lanka), Malaya, Brunei, Papua, Singapore and Hong Kong all were British Crown Colonies or Protectorates. In addition Australia and New Zealand were part of the British Commonwealth of Nations. In those days, the primary business of the Pacific and Orient (P&O) Steamship Line was carrying British expatriates to the eastern extremes of this far-flung empire. There were, of course, no air-conditioned passenger ships and the sun was brutal in the Red Sea and the Indian Ocean. The choice staterooms were those on the side of the ship that would generally be facing north during the voyage. These turned out to be "Port Out, Starboard Home" or POSH. And so an acronym that described the preferred way to travel "East of Suez" became the common word for smart and fashionable.

When I was "East of Suez" the shipboard accommodations were neither smart nor fashionable. Like the old P&O steamships, U.S.S. Wren was not air-conditioned. Unlike the P&O steamships there were no portholes to let in cooling breezes from the north or any other side of the ship. The berthing compartments, which were very crowded with bunks stacked three-high, were ventilated with noisy forced air and exhaust blowers. In hot climates it often got pretty beastly below decks. Many sailors would sleep on deck when it really got bad. Fortunately Wren transited this area in late February and early March and except for pretty severe heat in the Strait of Malacca and later in the Persian Gulf, it wasn't too bad.

After leaving Hong Kong, Wren was bound for Singapore. Singapore is less than 100 miles north of the Equator so naval vessels usually take the opportunity to "cross the line" and convert their "slimy pollywogs" into "trusty shellbacks". So instead of proceeding direct to Singapore, Wren swung southward and anchored on the equator at 105 degrees E. Latitude just west of the Lingga Islands on February 21, 1954. The shellbacks had been planning the initiation ceremonies in secret for weeks. They had also been trumping up charges against all the pollywogs and preparing their summonses. Although there were a sizeable number of shellbacks on board, there were many more pollywogs including Captain Johnson and the oldest man on the ship Chief Radioman Ketchie

The morning of the crossing, the shellbacks were up early setting up the facilities. A "dunking tank" was constructed on the fantail using shoring timbers and tarpaulins. The "hell tunnel" was a canvas tube about three feet in diameter and twenty feet long filled with several days worth of the ships garbage. A group of thrones for King Neptune and his court was set up on the starboard quarterdeck.

SUBPŒNA AND SUMMONS EXTRAORDINARY.
THE ROYAL HIGH COURT OF THE RAGING MAIN.

REGION OF THE SOUTH SEAS }
 }ss.
DOMAIN OF NEPTUNE REX }

To All Who Shall See These Presents.

GREETINGS:

WHEREAS, The Good Ship WREN bound southward, is about to enter our domain; and whereas the aforesaid ship carries a large and loathsome cargo of landlubbers, beach-combers, guardo-rats, sea-lawyers, lounge-lizards, parlor-dunnigans, plow-deserters, chicken chasers, four-flushers, dance-hall sheiks, drugstore cowboys, asphalt arabs, and other living creatures of the land, masquerading as seamen of which low scum you are a member, having never appeared before us; and

WHEREAS, THE ROYAL HIGHCOURT OF THE RAGING MAIN will convene on board the Good Ship WREN on the _21st_ day of _Feb_, 1964 in Latitude 0°0'00", and Long _105_ whereas, an inspection of our ROYAL ROSTER shows that it is high time your sad and wandering nautical soul appeared before Our August Presence;

BE IT KNOWN, that we hereby summon and command you _Miller,_ _Archie T. 503 #24 21 50_ U. S. Navy to appear before the ROYAL HIGHCOURT to be examined as to your fitness to be taken into the citizenship of the deep and to hear your defence on the following charges:

CHARGE I: In that you have hitherto wilfully and maliciously failed to show reverence and allegiance to our ROYAL PERSON, and are therein and thereby a vile landlubber and pollywog.

CHARGE II: Big bearded whalebanger caused all hands to lose half nites sleepchasing a whale.

Given under our hand and seal.

[signature] BMC
NEPTUNUS REX,
Supreme Ruler.

DAVY JONES,
Scribe.
[signature]

The author's pollywog summons before the royal court. You can see that the crew didn't quickly forget the whalebanger fiasco.

Captain Johnson (a pollywog) and Davy Jones inspecting a group of Slimy Pollywogs on the f'ocsle. (A.T. Miller Photo)

Fire hoses were broken out all over because copious amounts of water are always a big part of the ceremony (particularly after transiting the hell tunnel). A royal barber administered haircuts to the pollywogs. Pollywogs also had to kiss the belly of the "royal baby". The baby was not only the most rotund shellback on board but his belly was also liberally coated with graphite grease. Although it seemed like some of the shenanigans were a bit extreme, strict safety rules were established, published in the Plan of the Day and enforced by the Masters at Arms.

King Neptune's court as the initiation started. (C.C. Powell Photo)

The royal barber about to initiate a pollywog. (C.C. Powell Photo)

Neptunis Rex's court in session with royal baby on foreground. (C.C. Powell Photo)

Singapore was a relatively small city and flat as a pancake. After coming from the rugged mountainous terrain of Japan, Korea and Hong Kong, it was quite a contrast. There were many broad boulevards and parks and it was generally a pretty place. When we got ashore of course the first thing we had to do was to have a beer in the famous Raffles Hotel[14]. It was named after Sir Thomas Stamford Raffles, who established a fort in Singapore in 1819 to protect British shipping. He became the first governor of the new British colony of Singapore. The hotel was very nice and we enjoyed ourselves in the posh surroundings. At the prices they charged for beers, however, we didn't stay too long.

There were many "snake charmers" along the streets who would demonstrate their talents for a small fee. They each had a cobra in a woven covered basket about a foot in diameter. They also had a small wooden flute that they would play while sitting in front of the cobra. It must have been pretty cozy in the basket because when they

---

[14] The Raffles, The Peninsula in Hong Kong and The Raj in Bombay were the posh and most famous British colonial hotels in Asia. We didn't get to the Peninsula when Wren was in Hong Kong because in 1954 U.S. sailors were not allowed to cross the harbor to Kowloon. Forty-one years later when we were living in Hong Kong, Catherine and I had high tea one fine Saturday afternoon at the Peninsula.

removed the cover to start their act the cobra appeared to be sound asleep.   They would play the flute and the cobra would ignore them and keep on sleeping.   Finally they would take the basket cover and smack the cobra.   That got its attention and it popped up about a foot and extended its hood.   They then went into their act of playing music for the cobra who appeared to care less.   When the act was over they just dropped the cover back on the basket and I guess the cobra went back to sleep.

The Royal Navy had very nice enlisted men's club in Singapore called the Britannia Club.   Being a bit short of money, one afternoon a bunch of us went swimming in the huge pool there.   Afterwards we attended a tea dance at the club.   We danced with some of the local Malay and Chinese girls under the steely-eyed gaze of their mothers and chaperones.   We decided very shortly that this wasn't going to be very productive and moved on to the American Club.   This was another low budget liberty stop.   Any U.S. servicemen passing through Singapore was welcome at the club located on the top floor of one of the high rise office buildings.   Drinks were cheap and there were usually plenty of American expats around willing to set up rounds for the "boys from home".   Most of the expats were in the rubber business with such U.S. companies as U.S. Rubber, Firestone and Goodyear.   Raw rubber was Malaya's largest export at that time.   We played pool with the expats, drank beer and had a good time.

We departed Singapore and proceeded through the Straits of Malacca. It was hot enough there that I finally shaved off a rather luxurious black beard.   That solved a problem for Lcdr. Baker our Executive Officer.   When we left Hawaii on our way to Korea, Captain Green said that we could grow beards.   One of the first things that Captain Johnson said after he took command in February was that he didn't like beards.   He allowed however that we could keep the beards until we crossed the equator. At that time there would be a "best beard" contest.   The two winners could keep their beards - - everyone else had to shave them off.   A guy with a bright red beard and I had won the contest.   He immediately shaved his off so I was the only guy on board that still had a beard.   Despite his promise, the captain wasn't happy.   He didn't want us to arrive back in Norfolk with me still having a beard.   He had told the XO that it was his job to get rid of my beard. That was why there was a smile on the XO's face when I appeared on the bridge sans beard.   I didn't really care.   All I knew was that it was hot and the beard was itchy so it had to go.

We continued across the Indian Ocean to Colombo, Ceylon which turned out not to be the greatest liberty port in the world.   I have previously related the tale of our partying with HMS Wrens at the Mount Lavina Hotel.

Bumboat selling carved wooden elephants alongside Wren in Colombo, Ceylon. These entrepreneurs later learned that it is not a good idea to cheat sailors with access to a mooring shackle. (A.T. Miller Photo)

One other short anecdote is worth the telling.   We were moored between two buoys in the harbor.   As soon as were tied up, an assortment of bumboats came alongside with various trinkets and souvenirs to sell.   Up near the bow one of the small boats had some rather attractive carved and polished wooden elephants for sale.   The vendors had thrown up a line with a small basket attached that was used to consummate the transactions. This had worked pretty well and a number of sailors had bought elephants. Late in the day, after sales had slowed down, the vendors appeared to be going to leave after getting a seamen's' money but before delivering the elephant and a substantial amount of change. A loud and rather animated discussion ensued until the boat actually started to leave. The seaman dashed down the nearby ladder to the boatswain's locker and returned with a large mooring shackle that weighed several pounds. As the elephant boat started to move away, he heaved the shackle into the boat. It was about 15 feet down to the boat and the shackle had picked up sufficient speed that when it hit the thin bottom of the small boat, it went right through. The boat quickly sunk. I doubt that the guy ever got his elephant or change but I guess he got some satisfaction seeing the two entrepreneurs floundering around in the water surrounded by their, now floating, wooden elephants.

The next day we left Colombo, proceeded around the southern tip of India and headed northward toward the Persian Gulf. The crew was not very happy about this. We were going about 2000 miles out of our way to make a show of force in Saudi Arabia. Wren's and Noa's "liberty port" was Ras Tanura, Saudi Arabia which being a strict Muslim country was "dry". The only refreshments available were milk shakes in the Arabian-American Oil Company (ARAMCO) canteen. To add insult to injury we found out that Cone and Stribling were going to Bahrain about forty miles south, which was a British Protectorate and "wet". Oh well!

The Ras Tanura Arabian American Oil Company refinery in the Saudi Arabia desert circa early 1950's. The oil refinery itself is north of the pier (and the main road) and the expatriate employee homes and recreation facilities are south of the pier. The author stood at the end of the pier watching the famous poisonous water snakes. Great liberty port! (John C. Tarvin Collection)

We had secured the sonar after we left Singapore and the Sonarmen were now alternately standing Quartermaster or Radar watches. I had the 4 to 8AM Quartermaster watch on the bridge as we approached Ras Tanura. From 20 miles at sea, it was pretty eerie. It was still dark and the whole western horizon was aglow with a flickering yellow light. As we got closer the tops of the refinery cracking towers appeared over the horizon with huge flames streaming downwind from them. The ARAMCO refinery evidently burned off all their unwanted refinery byproducts. Aside from pollution considerations, it was a terrible waste of valuable natural resources. Now almost 50 years later almost every refinery byproduct is used. If nothing else there are electric power plants collocated with the refineries that burn the waste gas. In 1954, however, there was not very much concern about air pollution or that there might be a finite limit to natural resources especially if the resources were in a foreign country.

We went ashore but there wasn't anything to see but the refinery and the ARAMCO compound all sitting in a sea of sand. In the expatriate compound there was a pitiful golf course that looked like one big sand trap. Today, of course, they use surplus heat from refineries and nuclear power plants to desalinate water and there are lawns everywhere - -

but not in 1954. There was a beautiful air-conditioned movie theater, which was a nice place to spend the afternoon.   We found out that the ARAMCO employees got around the Saudi liquor prohibition by making their own booze.   Makes sense. After all, for a bunch of engineers running a refinery, building a moonshine still should be a piece of cake.   So we had our milk shake in the gedunk and went back to the pier to wait for the whaleboat.   Looking in the water we saw quite a few of the famous Persian Gulf poisonous sea snakes.   Nobody stood very near the edge of the pier.   The only good news about stopping in Ras Tanura was that we got a huge delivery of mail that had been flown in to the U.S. Air Force Base in Dharan.

"So", as they used to say in the movie travelogues, "we bid a fond farewell to Ras Tanurra". Right!   We couldn't get out of there fast enough.   Our next liberty port was Naples, Italy and we had a lot of steaming to do to get there.   As I have noted before, Wren was the only 2100-ton Fletcher Class destroyer in DesDiv-61.   The three other cans were 2250-ton Gearings that could carry more fuel than Wren.   Normally, Fletcher Class destroyers going from the Bahrain area of the Persian Gulf to Port Said on the north end of the Suez Canal stopped and refueled in Aden at the south end of the Red Sea.   It was decided that with careful fuel management, Wren could make it to Port Said without refueling at Aden.   So instead of Cone, the flagship, being the guide, Wren was made guide and steamed for maximum fuel economy on the shortest course while the other three followed our lead.

As we proceeded south through the Persian Gulf it was dead calm and the sea was glassy and pink.   No one had ever seen a pink ocean before.   One of the boatswain mates threw over a bucket on a line to collect some of the water. It turned out that the water was very warm and filled with pink plankton.   I guess in these dead calm conditions the plankton had come to the surface.   We also saw enormous schools of porpoises. There were hundreds of them.   They were rather lethargic and just laid on the surface unlike their cold water relatives.   We all agreed that the Persian Gulf was not one of our favorite places.   We had some discussions about the poor bastards that were out here in the US Navy Persian Gulf Station ships.   Their official name was the Middle East Force and they operated out of the British base HMS Juffair in Bahrain.   No permanent flagship was assigned, so duty rotated between three former seaplane tenders: U.S.S. Duxbury Bay, U.S.S. Greenwich Bay and U.S.S. Valcour.   Fortunately with three ships they rotated out pretty frequently.   The ships were converted Barnegat class Seaplane Tenders (Small). They had been painted white to reflect the intense sun and had been air-conditioned. Air-conditioned or not, none of us thought we wanted a transfer.

U.S.S Valcour (AVP-55) one of the three converted seaplane tenders serving as Persian Gulf Station Ships in 1954. (US Navy Photo)

While transiting the Persian Gulf we took advantage of the calm sea to do the periodically required tests of our VT (proximity) fused ammunition for the 5-inch, 38-caliber guns.   Nowadays (after the Gulf War, Yugoslavia, Iraq and Afghanistan) we are all generally familiar with various kinds of "smart munitions".   In the Korean War period, proximity fuses were the only smart thing we had.   These anti-aircraft fuses transmitted a radio signal in front of them and when they received some of the signal reflected back from a target, they exploded the shell.   The principle was that you didn't necessarily have to hit the plane, only get near it.   The problem with VT fuses was that long before the invention of solid-state electronics and microchips the electronics were crude and fragile.   Each fuse contained tiny miniaturized vacuum tubes powered by a battery that was activated by a vial of chemical being broken open by the concussion of the gun firing. Experience had shown that older lots of fuses had high failure rates (probably from battery failure).   So the test was to fire a certain number of rounds selected from each lot of fuses to find out the percentage of failures. To do this we fired rounds on a high looping trajectory that would have them fall into the calm sea near enough to see the results. If the VT fuse worked correctly, the radio signal would be reflected back from the flat sea and the round would explode in the air. If not, it would splash in the ocean. It was kind of neat watching the air bursts and counting the splashes. Unfortunately after almost 50 years I don't remember the results - - nor do I care!

Through most of this trip we were close to land. Our course around the Arabian Peninsula was basically U-shaped and, in order to save fuel, we steamed close to the coast to make the trip as short as possible. The scenery was mostly desolate and barren desert. In the Arabian Sea along the coast of Oman it was much like a huge beach. As we proceeded westward in the Gulf of Aden off Yemen it became more rugged. In many places there were cliffs along the coast. Great rivers of sand had cascaded down ravines in the cliffs from the desert on top. It was desolate but beautiful.

As we proceeded westward we passed Aden to starboard. Normally we would have stopped there to refuel.[15] Aden is a natural port and has been used by seafarers since ancient times because of its convenient location on the most important sea route between India and Europe. Because of its strategic location, it has been fought over many times. Aden's last foreign rulers were the British, who conquered it in 1839, when it became known as the Aden Protectorate.

We turned northward and proceeded through the Bab el Mandeb and into the Red Sea. I had the midnight to 4 AM watch as a radarman in the Combat Information Center (CIC) on the morning that we were scheduled to arrive in Suez. In those days, the Suez Canal was only wide enough for one way traffic. Northbound traffic went through at night and southbound during the day. As we proceeded north through the Red Sea we began to encounter the day traffic that had exited the canal and was proceeding south from Suez.

---

[15] Forty-six years later, the U.S.S Cole, an Arleigh Burke class Aegis destroyer, in transit to the Persian Gulf would stop in Aden to refuel and be severely damaged in a terrorist suicide bomb attack. The terrorists drove a motorboat laden with explosives into the port side of Cole.

One of the functions of the CIC is to acquire and track all surface radar targets (Skunks) and determine their closest point of approach (CPA) to the ship. If it appeared that they would pass dangerously close, CIC would recommend a course change to avoid the other ship. When I went on watch, I was assigned to track skunks. As I relieved the radarman and sat down at the VK Radar Display, there were four skunks being tracked. Because we were four ships traveling together, when a new skunk was acquired, DesDiv-61 would assign only one ship to track and report on it. This cut down the CIC workload on each ship. DesDiv-61 also assigned a tracking letter to each target. Starting at midnight, targets were assigned Skunk Able, Skunk Baker etc. In a normal day, you might get up to the middle of the alphabet. This wasn't to be a normal day. By the end of my 4-hour watch we were halfway through the second alphabet (Skunk Able Able, Able Baker, Able Charlie etc.). We were so busy it made the watch go fast though. Between plotting CPA's and recommending course changes we had a lot to do. Normally we reported CPA's as "Bearing 090, Range 2500 yards". When I would get a collision CPA, I would tell the bridge "CPA is port side in the Chief's Quarters". Fortunately the OD was one of the Annapolis guys with a sense of humor and I could get away with it.

We anchored in the port of Suez in the afternoon to wait for the southbound convoy to clear the canal. About 5PM, a barge came out to bring us our "headlight". It consisted of an 18" searchlight in a large wooden box with a big eye ring on top. We passed a line out our bullnose and hauled up the light on our bow. The electricians connected the 220-volt power and we were ready for our night transit of the Suez Canal.

French engineers of the Universal Company of the Maritime Suez Canal built the Suez Canal in the 1860's. It is a 101-mile canal connecting the Red Sea to the Mediterranean across the Egyptian desert. It is a sea level canal with no locks. It passes through three lakes; Lake Manzala in the north, Lake Timsah in the middle and the Bitter Lakes further south. The northern end of the canal is at Port Said that is named for Sa`id Pasha the Viceroy of Egypt who gave permission for the canal to be built. Ownership of the canal was to be held by the French/Egyptian Company for 100 years and then pass to the Egyptian government. In 1875 the British government purchased Egypt's shares in the company and in 1936 they signed an agreement that gave Britain the right to maintain defense forces in the Suez Canal Zone. A new agreement, signed in 1954, called for the removal of British troops by June of 1956.   At the time Wren went through the canal in March 1954 Egypt was in political turmoil. Two years earlier the army had staged a coup and overthrown the monarchy of King Farouk and put General Naguib in power.   In February 1954, just before we arrived, Col. Gamal Abdal Nasser deposed General Naguib and took over.   All was quiet and there were no signs of any problems either during our transit of the canal or during refueling in Port Said.   At that point, it was certainly in Egypt's interest to keep the canal running smoothly and bringing in revenue.

As darkness approached we weighed anchor and started north through the canal.   We had an Egyptian Suez Canal pilot Mr. G. Alvar on board.   Unlike the Panama Canal, the captain retained responsibility for the ship and the pilot's role was advisory.   Actually it was pretty straightforward.   Stay in the middle of the canal and follow the buoys going through the lakes.   As usual we had movie call at 8PM.   Wren had a large canvas movie screen that was set up across the stern.   We all sat on the fantail facing aft to watch the movie.   Occasionally during the movie we would look over on the bank of the canal and see an armed sentry on a camel!   Surreal!

The next morning, I had the 4 to 8 quartermaster watch on the bridge.   As it got light a strange sight presented itself?   Except for the strip of water forward and aft of the ship, all I could see was desert.   There was this vast sea of sand extending from horizon to horizon.   Although it is a name applied to camels, I couldn't help thinking that Wren was a "ship of the desert".

Looking aft from the bridge of Wren while transiting the Suez Canal. An Egyptian sailing dhow is behind us in the canal. (A.T. Miller Photo)

As we approached Port Said, signs of civilization appeared along the canal. The canal widened into a harbor and we headed for the fueling pier. Wren was just about running on fumes. We were the first Fletcher-class destroyer to go from the Persian Gulf to Port Said without fueling. The crew was happy and ready for us to get underway again. The Mediterranean beckoned in the distance. Our next stop, only two days away, was Naples, Italy and many of us had arranged for a couple of days in Rome. After that we were on to Villafranche on the Riviera and finally Lisbon, Portugal before heading home. We certainly weren't "East of Suez" anymore.

Fire At Sea

The SS Empire Windrush ploughed slowly through the glassy calm seas of the western Mediterranean Sea in late March 1954. The Union Jack flapped listlessly from its mast for there was no wind and not much generated by Windrush's sluggish pace. The Windrush was an old and tired ship approaching the end of a long voyage that had covered half the world through many seas. Originally built in Hamburg, Germany in 1930, the 14,561-ton troopship had been used during World War II to move troops of the Third Reich to many Axis battlefronts. After the war, it was transferred to the British from Germany as war reparations. It had been used by its new owners for many non-urgent tasks involving transfer of Her Majesty's subjects from the far-flung outposts of the British Empire. It plodded the worlds' oceans transporting army and air force troops and their dependents to and from posts in the empire on which, at that time, the sun still never set. It had also been used by the British Government to bring subjects from the colonies back to "Old Blighty". In 1948, it earned a special place in history by carrying 492 Trinidadians and Jamaicans to Great Britain in the first emigration of black subjects from the colonies to the motherland. The date of that voyage is remembered today as the beginning of the civil rights movement in Britain.

Empire Windrush in 1954 as a British troopship.

Her current voyage had originated in Kure, Japan in the late winter of 1954.   Her passengers were some of Her Majesty's troops and their dependents that had completed overseas assignments and were returning home.   In its meandering voyage, it had stopped at Crown Colonies in Hong Kong, Singapore, Colombo, Aden and the newly independent Port Said, Egypt.   At each port, it picked up more homeward bound troops and dependents.   The final destination was England.

Coincidentally, Wren had followed a similar path across the oceans as Empire Windrush. In fact, because of a different itinerary and our detour through the Persian Gulf, we probably overtook Windrush twice between Japan and the Med.   Wren left Japan and then stopped at Hong Kong, Singapore and Colombo.   DesDiv-61, including Wren, then went into the Persian Gulf in a show of force in support of American oil interests.

Ordinarily a Fletcher class destroyer leaving the Ras-Tanura/Bahrain area of the gulf for Port Said, Egypt would have stopped at the British port of Aden (another Windrush stop) at the southern end of the Red Sea to take on fuel.   We didn't, however, and we steamed right past Aden on our starboard side and into the Red Sea without stopping again passing Windrush.   As Empire Windrush also did, we stopped briefly in Port Said, Egypt to fuel.   Empire Windrush was behind us at this point and while she transited the canal and started west in the Mediterranean, we proceeded northwest across the Med.   We steamed through the Straits of Messina and stopped at Naples, Italy and VilleFranche on the French Riviera.   While Wrens were sightseeing in Rome, Pompeii, Nice, Cannes, Grasse and Monaco, Empire Windrush was slowly sailing from Port Said westward along the North African coast.

Wren's sightseeing in Saint Peters Square Vatican City, March 1954. (A.T. Miller Photo)

In the early morning of March 28, 1954, the Empire Windrush was about 50 miles off the coast of Algiers headed for Gibraltar, the Atlantic and, at long last, home. There was little or no wind, there was a bright hazy sun and the sea was a glassy calm. By that time, after its many stops, the human cargo had swelled to 1286 active duty troops, 17 military retirees, 125 women and 87 children. At about the same time Wren, in company with the other DD's of DesDiv-61, sortied from Villefranche bound for Lisbon, Portugal. It was a beautiful day. The crew was upbeat about getting to Lisbon, the last stop before going home to the U.S. after having been gone for eight months.

Shortly before 7:00 AM there was a violent explosion in the Empire Windrush's engine room. Four engine room personnel were immediately killed. Flames roared out of the engine room and started to spread through the ship. The Empire Windrush transmitted an SOS and its position as Lat. 37° 4′ N and Lon. 2° 24′ E on the international distress frequency. Although there was little or no wind, the fire spread at an alarming rate. Over the years, very little old paint had ever been chipped off the ship. New paint was applied over old and thick, highly flammable paint layers had built up over the hull and superstructure. The fire spread very quickly through the ship fueled by the paint and many flammable furnishings. Despite the intensity of the fire, everyone remained calm and the abandonment was conducted in a disciplined manner. All of the dependents and the injured plus some troops were loaded into lifeboats. Other troops went over the side in rafts and floats. The fire spread so rapidly that about 300 troops were cut off from their boats and rafts and had to jump into the sea. Other troops and crew threw wood and other floatable material to them. Amazingly, except for those killed in the initial blast, everyone got off the ship and ultimately into a boat or raft. It was most fortunate that the sea was calm and warm. If the abandon ship operation had been conducted in heavy seas and colder weather, it would undoubtedly not have been as successful. Now they had to sit and wait for rescue as Empire Windrush was consumed by flames before their eyes. Fortunately, help was on the way.

The Empire Windrush on fire of the coast of Algeria. (A.T. Miller Photo)

The Mediterranean is heavily traveled and there are always many ships underway across its length and breadth. Because of the large number of ships in the area, it was not long before aid began to arrive at the scene of the disaster. About an hour after the SOS the Dutch freighter Mentor arrived on the scene. It was followed shortly by the Italian tanker Taigete, the British steamer Socoria and the Norwegian freighter Hemspefgell. They went from boat to boat and raft to raft picking up the survivors.   By 10:10AM, all of the survivors had been rescued and the four ships were headed for Algiers.

When Wren received the SOS from Empire Windrush, we were less then 100 miles away. We immediately put all four boilers on line and went to the maximum speed possible for that distance which just over 29 knots.   At that speed, the whole ship vibrated from the beat of the screws. Standing on the fantail right over the screws, the four-blade screw beat vibrated me slowly across the deck.   Electric light bulbs in the after compartments were failing because of the vibration. Standing on the fantail, I could not see the horizon for the wall of water on either side of the ship.   As the ship increased speed, the stern set down more deeply in the water. When dead in the water, Wren drew about 14 feet aft and at 25 knots about 24 feet.   At 30 knots, it probably drew close to 30 feet and the main deck was well below the sea surface.   Astern, water leapt into the air in a huge "rooster tail". Noa, Cone and Stribling also went to max speed but they were nowhere near as fast as we were.   We soon left them behind.   While Empire Windrush was still below the horizon we could see an enormous plume of black and white smoke rising high in the still air.   This was obviously a very serious fire.   As we sped toward Windrush we were making fire-fighting preparations.   Two and a half inch hoses were broken out on deck and connected to the fire mains.   Some of the hoses were led topside to the upper decks so that they could spray water onto the upper levels of the burning transport. "Handy Billy" and P500 portable fire fighting pumps were loaded into the whaleboat and the gig together with hoses, nozzles and foam applicators. Cans of fire fighting foam were loaded in the boats. Wren was prepared to do whatever was necessary to save the ship.

Empire Windrush being consumed by flames. The thick coating of paint melted and slid down the sides into the water. (A.T. Miller Photo)

Wren arrived at the Empire Windrush shortly after the four other rescue ships had departed for Algiers with the survivors. As we got closer, it was apparent that the ship was totally engulfed in flames and no one was going to go aboard to fight the fire. It was amazing that in a little over three hours the fire had spread to all parts of the ship. Wren's deck log entry stated "Burning fiercely in midships section from the stacks down as far as the 3rd deck. No survivors apparent." The blazing hulk floated quietly in the calm waters surrounded by wreckage, debris, lifeboats and rafts. Her funnel had collapsed and flames were roaring out of the top of the superstructure near where the funnel had been. A large and dense column of smoke rose a thousand feet in the still air. Black smoke poured from the after part of the ship. White smoke billowed out of various openings from the bow back to amidships. The ship had about a 10 or 15 degree starboard list, probably from hull damage suffered in the initial explosion. The most dramatic thing was what was happening to the 20-year accumulation of paint. The hull was so hot that enormous slabs of paint, 20 or 30 feet wide and probably over a quarter of an inch thick, slid slowly down the ships side and into the water as it melted away from the steel. In other places, it bubbled and smoked and ultimately burst into flames. The way the thick slabs of paint slid off her indicated that no paint was ever chipped before new was applied. One of the First Class Bosun Mates used the inferno in Windrush to bring home to the Wren deck force why he always demanded that old paint be chipped off before applying new. It was a rather dramatic lesson.

The first thing we did was to inspect all of the lifeboats and rafts to be sure that there was no one aboard any of them. The lifeboats were scattered over several miles of ocean. We came alongside each boat and made sure they were empty. Some of the boats were filled with water but it was soon obvious that all of the survivors had been picked up. Then we swung back to take another look at Empire Windrush.

Empty swamped lifeboats. The huge smoke plume from Empire Windrush can be seen on the horizon. Another DesDiv-61 destroyer is standing by. (A.T. Miller Photo)

As we neared Windrush, some of the junior officers on the bridge were discussing whether we could go alongside and fight the fire with hoses from our upper decks. Captain Johnson quickly ended that discussion. "No way are we going alongside! . . Remember the Birmingham!" In October of 1944, the light cruiser Birmingham (CL-62) went alongside the aircraft carrier Princeton (CVL-23) which had been heavily damaged by Japanese Kamikaze suicide aircraft and was on fire. Birmingham was alongside pouring water into Princeton's fires when Princeton's torpedo magazine blew up. Birmingham was severely damaged and suffered 237 crew dead and 426 injured. I think that all the crew concurred in the captain's assessment. None of us in a relatively small ship wanted to be within hosing distance of a large ship burning as ferociously as Empire Windrush.

While we were on scene, a French B-24 bomber modified for Air-Sea Rescue overflew us and circled the scene. The B-24 had a lifeboat fastened to the underside of the aircraft that could be dropped by parachute. There was obviously no need for that capability. As they circled us, we communicated with them by blinker light. The quartermaster on the port side would work the aircraft as long as he could and then pass it to the QM on the starboard side. As there seemed nothing more that we could do, we informed them that we were proceeding on to Lisbon.

As we were leaving, we spotted several ships on the horizon coming out from Algiers. One of them, the French destroyer Saintes took Empire Windrush in tow. We heard later that it sunk while in tow at about 1:00 that afternoon. The fact that a ship that large sunk in only six hours after the fire started says something about the force of the initial explosion and the ferocity of the fire. There were some theories that the ship had been sabotaged by those at odds with British Suez Canal policy. This was never proved and seems rather unlikely. She was an old ship; probably not too well maintained that had a serious accident.

From Algiers, the British aircraft carrier H.M.S. Triumph picked up the survivors of the Empire Windrush and took them to Gibraltar from where they were flown home to England.

As we approached Gibraltar, we observed several British and French destroyers maneuvering several miles north of us closer to the Gibraltar harbor entrance. They were obviously conducting some kind of a NATO exercise. The quartermasters on the bridge were watching the ships through binoculars and long glasses. One of them reported "They're all flying black pennants at-the-dip". We knew that this meant that they were looking for a submarine but didn't have contact. Since leaving Singapore, our sonar had been secured and I was standing quartermaster watches on the bridge. I said "I'll just duck into sonar, fire up the SQS-10 and see if we can find their submarine for them." It didn't take long. As soon as the sonar warmed up, I picked up a submarine-like contact off our port bow. I returned to the bridge and suggested sending a blinker message that their sub was about 3000 yards off our port bow. Shortly a couple of the DD's headed in our direction and as they approached, their black pennants went "close-up" indicating they had contact. We got a "Thank You" blinker message from the leader. Bet the submarine guys were wondering who the hell blew their cover.

We cleared Gibraltar and proceeded northwestward through the waters off Cape Trafalgar where Admiral Horatio Viscount Nelson resoundingly defeated a larger French and Spanish fleet on October 21, 1805. This defeat effectively ended Napoleons' plans to invade England. Admiral Nelson was killed at the height of the battle while his flagship Victory was locked alongside the French ship Redoubtable repulsing a French boarding attack. The stunning British victory not only doomed Napoleons' dreams but also laid the foundation for British dominance of the seas for the next 150 years.

We turned northward from Cape St. Vincent (the site of another Nelson victory in 1797) and proceeded up the Tagus River. We arrived in Lisbon on April 1 ("April in Portugal") and wonder of wonders we tied up to a pier right in the center of town. Lisbon was a beautiful city and we had a good time. While we were crossing the Pacific in September 1953, Hollywood had gone wide-screen with the release of "The Robe" in Cinemascope. Al Dodge and I saw The Robe in Lisbon. What a change from the small screen in the mess deck – and the seats were softer too. We were only in Lisbon for a couple of days, which was good because we were really getting anxious to get home.

A dhow loaded with cargo sails across Lisbon harbor as Stribling prepares to get underway for the U.S.in the background. (A.T. Miller Photo)

We left Lisbon, refueled in the Azores on April 3rd and headed into the Atlantic. The crossing was brutal. We were going head on into a storm out of the northwest most of the way across the Atlantic. The engines were making turns for 18 knots but we were only making 12 knots good. The ship was being battered as tons of water rolled over the decks. Between the heavy rolling and pitching and the noise, no one was getting much sleep. Whenever the seas were this rough, the midships lifeguard watches were movedfrom their normal station on the main deck up to the 01 level in the steel tubs surrounding the Quad 40mm Gun Mounts. In mid-Atlantic, a huge wave roared over the main deck, over the 01 deck and smashed in the side of the port 40mm gun tub. The steel splinter shield was collapsed and bent down. The lifeguard watch was knocked to the deck. When he recovered, the first thing he reported over the sound powered phone to the bridge was that 40mm ammunition had been thrown out of the ready-service racks and live rounds were rolling all over the deck. He was afraid of an imminent explosion and was crawling around on the deck trying to corral the loose rounds.   Help arrived shortly and the ammunition was quickly collected and safely stowed.

Stribling was steaming parallel to Wren as we crossed the Atlantic.   Her bow had just been under water and now is almost completely out of water as tons of water pour off the foc'sle and back overboard.   Of course Wren was doing the exact same thing. (A.T. Miller Photo)

As we neared the East Coast the weather improved and we kicked up our speed to try to make up for lost time.   We still arrived in Norfolk over twelve hours late but we were home – better late etc.   We had been gone for over seven months, had circumnavigated the globe and had logged over 55,000 miles in most of the major seas of the world. Truly a fantastic voyage.

Late as we were, we had a great homecoming.   They did in fact have the fireboats out spraying red, white and blue streams of water in the air to welcome us back to the United States.   We tied up alongside the destroyer tender U.S.S. Grand Canyon (AD-28) for some much-needed maintenance. It had been about six-weeks and many thousands of miles since we pulled away from the destroyer tender Prairie in Sasebo, Japan.   A large number of family and friends were gathered on the tender to greet us.   I had leave coming and Everly and I hustled over to the Grand Canyon as soon as we got our leave papers.   Everly's parents had come down from Alexandria to meet the ship and they were going to give me a ride home.   It was good to get home.   Sleeping in a nice soft bed that didn't roll and pitch and not getting up 'til mid-morning was a real pleasure.   It was also nice to be able to be a civilian for awhile. I renewed acquaintance with some old girlfriends, and generally had a relaxing ten days.   Finally, I boarded a Greyhound in Washington and headed back to Norfolk.   Knowing the reputation of destroyers as "haze grey and underway" I expected that, despite our recent long trip, we would be back to a heavy operations schedule shortly.   I was right.   The Monday after I reported back on board, we got underway for a week of "Chesapeake Raider".   And for the next six months there were few weeks that we weren't steaming somewhere.

Blockade

It was a Sunday afternoon in early June 1954 and Al Dodge and I were in our bathing suits catching a few rays on the foc'sle.   It was very hot, extremely humid and there was no wind. We were more interested in keeping cool than in getting a tan but we couldn't think of any really cool place on the ship (no air conditioning on these old cans) so we settled for trying to find a breeze up on deck.   The heat down below in the berthing compartments was unbearable, which was the primary reason we were out on deck.   The sea was glassy calm and the jungle coast of Honduras shimmered faintly on the hazy western horizon.   Wren with only one of its four boilers on line cross-connected to both engines was going about 10 knots northeastward in the Gulf of Honduras.   We were hardly even leaving a wake and certainly not creating much of a breeze. Why was this man-o-war that had done 38.6 knots on the measured mile at Gitmo limping along and barely moving off the coast of Central America?

Depending on your viewpoint, we were either saving the Western Hemisphere from a communist menace by blockading the only Guatemalan port on the Caribbean or we were overthrowing the democratically elected government of Guatemala for the benefit of the stockholders of the United Fruit Company.   The fact was that for whatever reason, we were blockading Puerto Barrios to support a Central Intelligence Agency (CIA) operation to replace the government of Guatemala.   To carry out this operation, the CIA had dispatched an old hand and a rising star to Guatemala.   U.S. Ambassador John Emil Peurifoy was sent to Guatemala to implement the CIA's Operation PBSUCCESS. E. Howard Hunt was to manage the propaganda and psychological warfare in Guatemala. Jack Peurifoy had been ambassador to Greece during the Communist insurgency and was generally credited with an important role in U.S efforts to help crush it.   He would only be in Guatemala long enough to complete PBSUCCESS and then on to his next CIA assignment.   After Guatemala he became ambassador to Thailand and was killed in a jeep accident near Hua Hin in 1955.   Hunt was in charge of the political and propaganda campaign, which included air, dropped leaflets and extensive radio broadcasts.   Most of the radio programs were taped at a CIA facility in Opa–Locka Florida. They were then broadcast from a station that said it was at a secret hideout in Guatemala but was really safely located in neighboring Nicaragua. To further support the ruse, the radio actors staged an on-air supposed raid by Guatemalan government forces complete with shouting and sounds of the door being broken down. Hunt's post Guatemala activities included planning the CIA's Bay Of Pigs invasion of Cuba and being one of Nixon's "plumbers" in the Watergate affair. Hunt served 32 months in prison for burglary, wiretapping and conspiracy in connection with Watergate.[16] The 1953/54 Peurifoy-Hunt CIA team was charged with replacing the Guatemalan government of President Jacobo Arbenz with one to be led by Castillo Armas.

John Peurifoy (Right) and CIA agent Eno Hobbing in Guatemala, 1954. Hobbing had worked for Time Inc. and was supposed to write a new Constitution for Guatemala as soon as the coup was complete. (LatinAmericaStudies.org Photo)

Guatemalan President Jacobo Arbenz had been a thorn in the side of the United Fruit Company (UFCO) since he was elected president in 1951. Besides growing bananas (and exporting them duty-free), UFCO had over the years gained control of the railroads, ports, electric utilities and sizable land and water concessions. Arbenz enjoyed wide popular support in Guatemala and had been elected with 65% of the popular vote in an open and free election. UFCO contended that Arbenz was a communist. There was no

---

[16] Hunt's wife Dorothy was killed in the crash of United Flight 533 in Chicago shortly after her husband was indicted. Found in the wreckage was her handbag containing $10,585 in mostly $100 bills that was widely believed to have been from the Nixon "slush fund". This led to subsequently disproved theories that the flight was sabotaged.

definitive proof of that, but he certainly was a land reformer. He courted the communists for political support, but there was never proof of any ties to international communism. The single Russian that had visited Guatemala during the Arbenz regime was trying to buy bananas.

Arbenz was carrying on a tradition of land reform (albeit more aggressively) started in 1944 with Guatemala's first democratically elected government led by Juan Jose Arevalo. At that time Arevalo was appalled by the fact that 2.2% of the population owned 70% of the land. He also felt that it was unjust that 94% of UFCO's land was not even being used while the majority of the peasants had no land at all. The laws Arevalo put in place were the basis for Arbenz's land reform. Arbenz had appropriated thousands of acres of uncultivated, unimproved land, owned but not being used by United Fruit Co., and given it to the peasants in small plots of 20 to 30 acres. United Fruit claimed Guatemala owed it $19,355,000 for the land. The Arbenz government offered $1,185,000, the amount that United Fruit had claimed the land was worth for tax purposes. United Fruit was furious.

President Truman approved a CIA plan to topple Arbenz in 1952 but Secretary of State Dean Acheson persuaded him to abandon it. Acheson believed that the Guatemalan military was fiercely anti-Communist, that Arbenz was not a communist and had to court the communists only for internal political reasons. Soon after Eisenhower became President, the plan was dusted off and reinstated. The primary UFCO lobbyist Thomas (Tommy the Cork) Corcoran had been pressing Eisenhower heavily to do something about Arbenz. There were a number of people in the Eisenhower administration strongly advocating Arbenz' overthrow. Not the least of these was Allen Dulles the head of the CIA (and a UFCO shareholder) and brother of Secretary of State John Foster Dulles. John Foster Dulles while a senior partner of the New York law firm Sullivan & Cromwell[17] had represented UFCO (and their Guatemalan railroad IRCA) in the 1930 and 1935 contracts with the Guatemalan government. Walter Bedell Smith,

---

[17] Attorneys from Sullivan & Cromwell represented William Jefferson Clinton in his February 1999 impeachment trial before the U.S. Senate

Undersecretary of State (and former CIA chief) was planning the coup while at the same time seeking an executive position with UFCO. He wanted to be UFCO President but later settled for a place on its board of directors.

There were some dissenters. Kermit Roosevelt, (Teddy's grandson) had directed the successful overthrow of Iran's Premier Muhammad Mussadegh and the installation of Shah Reza Pahlevi to the Peacock Throne in August 1953. As a reward for his success in Iran, he was offered the opportunity to head the CIA operation in Guatemala and he turned it down. He felt that in order for covert operations to be successful you must replace the old leadership with a better one that can take control and you should have the people behind you. He didn't think that the Guatemalan operation met either of those criteria.

Eisenhower approved the plan to overthrow Arbenz and Colonel Albert Haney was assigned by John Foster Dulles to organize and run the operation. The CIA headquarters for what ultimately would become operation PBSUCCESS were set up in the abandoned Marine Air Station at Opa Locka, Florida. The plan was to use Guatemala's' neighbors as bases for the operation.

There had been several U.S instigated threats against Guatemala from neighboring Nicaragua and Honduras. The U.S. had signed mutual security treaties with both countries and had conspicuously shipped them large quantities of arms. As recently as late January of 1954, Guatemala had charged the Somoza regime in Nicaragua of plotting an invasion with support from El Salvador, the Dominican Republic, Venezuela and the "Government Of The North" (U.S.A.). Arbenz had repeatedly requested U.S. help in obtaining weapons to defend Guatemala but had been rebuffed not only by the U.S but also by all of its western allies.

The relations between the United States and Guatemala reached a crisis point in the spring of 1954 when the CIA determined that Arbenz had secretly arranged to obtain the arms he felt he needed from Eastern Bloc communist countries. The Swedish ship Alfhem, a 4900-ton freighter under charter by a British company, had loaded Czech arms in Stettin Poland and departed for Guatemala. It changed course and intended destination four times during its passage to try to mask its true intentions. Initially it filed its destination as Dakar, French West Africa. When in the Bay of Biscay off France, the destination changed to Curacao, Dutch East Indies. While in the mid-Atlantic heading westward, a new destination of Puerto Cortes, Honduras was filed and when just south of Cuba, Puerto Barrios, Guatemala was finally revealed as the true destination. When the Alfhem arrived in Puerto Barrios on May 17, 1954, the CIA confirmed the arms shipment and estimated its size at 2000 tons. On May 20th the CIA tried to blow up the 10 car freight train carrying the Czech weapons near Castañeda, a small village located 20Km from Puerto Barrios. Torrential rains soaked the explosive detonators and they never went off. The CIA agents engaged in a brief firefight with guards on the train as it proceeded westward. One guard and one CIA agent were killed in the exchange. CIA agents made further attempts to stop the movement of the weapons on the 24th and 25th, but again failed.

To try to prevent further introduction of arms into Guatemala, Eisenhower ordered the stopping of "suspicious foreign-flag vessels on the high seas off Guatemala to examine cargo". State Department international law experts advised in no uncertain terms that "Such action would constitute a violation of international law". They also pointed out that British boarding of our ships on the high seas was one of the reasons we went to war in 1812. The British notified the U.S. that no one was going to board any of their ships no matter what. Nevertheless, the decision was made to proceed and Dutch and French ships were stopped and searched in short order. It was at this point that the U.S. Navy (and ultimately Wren) became involved in the effort to prevent additional communist arms shipments from arriving in Guatemala.

The 49,000 ton Swedish freighter SS Alfhem that transported the Czech arms for Guatemala from Stettin, Poland to Puerto Barrios

While all of this Top Secret activity was going on in Washington, Wren was in Key West in company with Cone, Noa and Bristol (DD-859) replacing Stribling. Wren had always been the anomaly in DesDiv-61 as the only Fletcher class can among three Gearing class destroyers. Bristol as the last Sumner class destroyer ever built made DesDiv-61 a real motley array of two Gearings, a Fletcher and a Sumner. We supposedly were in Key West for training and went out each day for exercises with a submarine and came back to Key West each evening. It was pretty routine stuff and in retrospect we had probably been sortied to Key West in anticipation of possible service in Guatemala.

The crew actually thought this was pretty good duty. Out in the morning, a day of easy steaming in calm weather and then back to the fleshpots of Key West in the evening. Although Key West had been "cleaned up" since I had last been there in '51 and '52, there was still quite a bit of action in the joints on Duval Street. The 1953 Navy Relief carnival held on the Naval Air Station had employed some of the local young ladies for entertainment and had occasioned the "cleaning up". One of the attendees had provided a rather graphic description of the festivities in a letter to his mother who forwarded it to her congressman. The resultant flap had caused the admiral in Key West to be relieved and the Navy to threaten the town fathers and mothers with bussing liberty parties to Miami if the town wasn't cleaned up.

U.S.S. Bristol (DD-857). Bristol was the last Sumner class destroyer built. It had the exact same 376-foot long hull as Wren but a completely different superstructure and armament. This is a classic "destroyer underway" picture. (US Navy Photo)

In 1954 things were about the way they were when Harry Truman would vacation here in '51 and '52 when the town was wide open. I was going to the Fleet Sonar School, Key West at that time and most of the sailors rued the fact that Harry's vacation put a damper on a lot of the local recreation activities. As soon as the president would arrive, most of the illegal activities would close down and the girls at the Habana Madrid and the Mardi Gras would keep a few more clothes on. The reason of course, as we finally figured out, was the large number of news persons that had accompanied Harry to Key West with very little to write about. Obviously the movers and shakers in town didn't want them to discover (and report on) the vice and corruption in Key West. The day after Harry left everything was back to normal.

While Wren was in Key West, it became evident that something was afoot in Guatemala. There was quite a bit in the papers and on the radio about the Arbenz government, communist conspiracies and arms shipments. On May 25 the New York Times reported that two more arms shipments were underway to Guatemala from "undisclosed Baltic ports". Also reported on May 25 was that the U.S. was airlifting 25 tons of small arms from a base in Mobile, Alabama to Nicaragua. To further increase the pressure on Guatemala, the U.S. Air Force announced that three B-36 nuclear bombers would make a "goodwill visit" to Nicaragua. There were many rumors flying about the possible involvement of the U.S. Navy in stopping ships at sea in the Caribbean. On May 26 the French Line freighter Wyoming was detained in the Panama Canal Zone on suspicion of carrying arms. The Wyoming's Manifest listed "General Cargo, machinery and 25 boxes of Belgian Sporting Rifles". After a thorough search by U.S. Customs, no military arms were found and Wyoming was allowed to proceed.

About 7:00 AM on May 28, while it was returning from Puerto Barrios after delivering the arms, the SS Alfhem was forced into Key West by the U.S. Coast Guard for inspection. It was anchored-out off Fort Taylor about a half-mile from Wren. There were no visible flag displays on the yardarm to indicate that the ship was under inspection by customs or immigration officials. Locally, the incident had caused quite a stir and we could see Coast Guard boats busily trying to keep the swarm of news boats and sightseers away from Alfhem. The Key West Citizen described Alfhem as a "big dirty freighter" and reported that the Coast Guard cutter CG-52303D repeatedly warned the newsmen's boat to "stay at least100 yards away".

Wren crewmembers used all available optics, including gun directors, to scan Alfhem and try to find out what all the fuss was about. It just looked like a somewhat rusty old freighter with crewmembers lounging around on the decks. There wasn't much to inspect on the Alfhem, of course, because the guns had already been delivered to Guatemala. The Citizen speculated that "the cargo of arms had been picked up at a port behind the Iron Curtain". The real reason for the stop was so that a contingent of CIA personnel who had flown down from Washington could interrogate Captain Johan Henry Lind and the crew. Secretary of State John Foster Dulles had declared the Alfhems voyage to be under "conditions far from normal". It turned out that neither the captain nor the crew was anxious to discuss their escapade and very little was learned by the CIA interrogators. The Alfhem was eventually released and we watched her proceed slowly out of Key West and on her way.

On May 28, as we returned to Key West from our daily ASW ops, we were ordered to refuel and take on provisions for 30 days. Something was up! Wren was moored on the seaward side of the mole surrounding the submarine harbor. Directly ahead of us across the entrance to the harbor was the submarine tender U.S.S Gilmore (AS-16). There were several subs nested alongside. Over the weekend from our location we could see a lot of activity on the submarines alongside Gilmore. A steady stream of sailors came across the gangway from Gilmore carrying boxes and equipment on to the submarines. I was watching the loading operations through binoculars from Wren's bridge. I had previously been stationed at a torpedo testing range and it was clear to me that the submarines alongside Gilmore were loading war-shot, high explosive torpedoes. They had black warheads with the small red panel where the detonator was installed. The two submarines passed Wren on their way to sea. The Key West Citizen reported that they had left so unexpectedly "that some crew members who were on leave in Miami were left behind". It was impossible to identify the subs because their names and all identifying numbers had been painted out! Wherever they were going they didn't want anyone to know who they were and, as we had observed, they were loaded for bear. When questioned about the submarines by newsmen in Washington, the Navy would only acknowledge that they were "going south". Later, when we were in the Bay of Honduras, we would meet these subs again.

We finally departed Key West under sealed orders in company with Cone, Noa and Bristol. Commander Carribean Sea Frontier (ComCaribSeaFron) Op Order 8-4 established the Honduras Patrol Group to blockade Puerto Barrios, Guatemala. Commander Destroyer Division-61 was in Officer in Tactical Command (OTC) of the group and issued Op Order 001-54 defining ship interdiction procedures. After we were at sea, Captain Johnson announced to the crew that we were on a secret mission to prevent communist ships from delivering arms to Guatemala. (Unbeknown to us, the

CIA referred to this mission as Operation Hardrock Baker.)   If necessary, we would board ships to determine if they had the guns which were supposedly being shipped to Puerto Barrios labeled as optical goods and laboratory equipment.   We were all sworn to secrecy.   There was a high level of excitement and anticipation throughout the ship. The landing force was cleaning and checking their weapons and boarding equipment was loaded into the whaleboat and the gig.   Because I was qualified on the Browning Automatic Rifle (BAR), I volunteered for the boarding party.   The Gunners Mates told me that they had all the help that they needed but thanks anyway.   Five-inch target projectiles filled with sand were moved up into the ammunition handling rooms under the 5-inch gun mounts.   We could fire one of these across the bow of a reluctant ship to show we meant business without much danger of serious damage.   We also had some high explosive rounds ready in case the sand loads didn't achieve the desired results.

As we arrived in the Gulf of Honduras, each of the four ships was assigned a patrol sector about 60 miles long.   Puerto Barrios is located at the head of the V-shaped Gulf of Honduras in the middle of the very short east coastline of Guatemala.   The limited coastline and the surrounding geography made it very easy to blockade.   Noa was assigned Station 1 extending from the coast of Belize southeastward.   Cone and Bristol were assigned respectively Stations 2 and 3 across the center of the Gulf of Honduras. Wren was assigned Station 4 extending to the coast of Honduras and just off Cabo Camaron.   Given that our quarry was slow and our radar range was about 20 miles, Wren and the other three ships effectively sealed off the entrance to the gulf.   The two submarines we had seen leaving Key West were inside our blockade line and were prepared to sink any ship carrying arms that got past us.   Although we never saw it, we understood that there was also a High Speed Transport (a converted destroyer escort) in close to Puerto Barrios to evacuate American civilians if things got really bad.   We shut down one of the two boilers we had on line and cross-connected so that the one boiler could feed both engines and both generators.   The reason for the fuel-efficient engineering configuration was so that we could stay on the blockade station as long as possible. The freighters that we were trying to intercept couldn't go more then 12 or 13 knots. Even with only one boiler, we could get to 18 or 19 knots if needed.

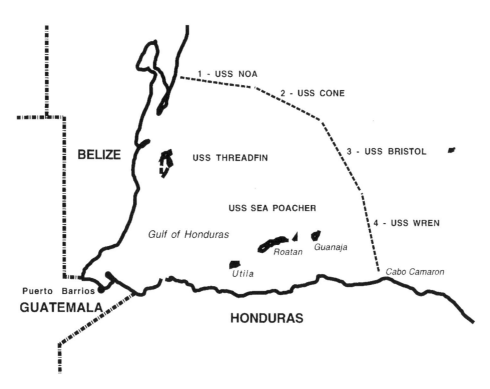

The broken lines show the blockade patrol stations for the destroyers Noa, Cone, Bristol and Wren across the Gulf of Honduras. The two submarines Threadfin and Sea Poacher patrolled inside the blockade line. (A.T. Miller Map)

Our orders were to identify all shipping in our patrol zone and determine their ports of origin, cargo and destination. If the ship was on our list of suspects we could try to make them stop but we could only board and search them if approved by Washington. On May 30th as we approached our station at about 1:00AM we overtook a fishing boat in tow and decided it was of no interest. About 4:00AM we picked up a surface radar contact. We turned to intercept and identify it. The standard procedure was to approach ships from astern so that we could read the ship name and homeport off the stern transom. As we overtook the contact we identified it as the Greek freighter Evanthsa. She was outbound from Puerto Barrios headed for Jamaica. Evanthsa was not on our list and it was leaving not heading for Puerto Barrios so we continued southward.

We continued to investigate and challenge ships in our zone. The larger ships were easy. We challenged them by blinker light and their radioman would respond with a hand held signal light in Morse code. In a few minutes, we would have the information we needed and they would continue on their way. The small "banana boats" were something else. They didn't have very competent radio operators and didn't understand English. Although we were sure they weren't of interest, we had to get the information and it sometimes took the better part of an hour.

In the Gulf of Honduras on May 30, Cone had surfaced the submarine USS Sea Poacher (SS-406) to highline them some supplies. At 6:46AM Wren went to lifeguard station astern Cone during this operation. We now knew the identity of one of the unmarked subs! As soon as the highline was complete, Sea Poacher quickly submerged. As we arrived on Station 4, we rendezvoused with the USS Gatling (DD-671) at 8:10AM. Gatling and three other destroyers had been hurriedly sent to Guatemala after the Alfhem incident. Gatling put her whaleboat in the water and brought over orders and data on their intercepts. Wren relieved Gatling and took up patrol duties 8:50AM.

The next morning at 2:15AM, lookouts sighted a ship bearing 266 at a range of 2000 yards. We turned and closed it at 19 knots and then slowed as we came up astern. Other then the required running lights, there were no other lights on the ship. There was no sign of activity about the decks. As usual, we were challenging the ship by blinker light as we approached. There was no response, which was unusual for a ship of that size and made everyone a little nervous. As we approached the port quarter, we were shining signal lights on the transom of the ship trying to read the name and homeport. It appeared to be a German ship, named Pegasus. As we got closer, there was still no response. Suddenly the ship became ablaze with light. All of the cargo lights came on clearly illuminating us. Everyone jumped about two feet when the lights came on wondering what was going to happen next. As soon as the captain saw that we were a U.S. man-of-war he acknowledged the blinker and supplied us the required information. He explained that he had been pulled in to San Juan for inspection while inbound to

Puerto Barrios and had been stopped twice since. He was getting nervous about what was going on and was reluctant to answer challenges. He was advised to quickly answer any further challenges because ships were prepared to shoot if ignored. The Pegasus was outbound from Puerto Barrios for Santo Masta, Colombia.

At 4:40AM radar picked up a contact at bearing 355 at a range of 10 miles. At 5:15AM Wren determined contact to be the Honduran merchant ship SS Ganflo, a small coastal freighter not capable of carrying the guns.

At 7:03AM radar picked up a contact bearing 235 and 10 miles. Evidently because of its location and intelligence information, the contact was considered suspicious. We had 5-inch and 40-millimeter gun mounts manned with life-jacketed and helmeted crews so that the target ship could see that we meant business.   The ship turned out to be a large German freighter SS Heidburg.   We approached on their port quarter. Not knowing what to expect, everyone was very nervous. Every eye on the ship was straining to see something on the freighter -- including the lookouts who should have been scanning all of the sectors around the ship.   All of a sudden there was a great roar as two U.S. Navy P-2V Neptune Patrol Bombers zoomed right over our mast top.   As we looked up, we could see that they had a full load of rockets under the wings. Captain Johnson almost had apoplexy.   Everyone had been so busy watching the freighter that no one had seen the bombers coming across the water at practically wavetop level and below radar coverage.   The captain was threatening to court martial the lookouts and everyone else in sight. "If those had been enemy planes we would have been a smoking hulk right now" he screamed.   The P-2V's flying out of NAS Coco Solo in the Panama Canal Zone had picked up the freighter on radar and decided to take a low-level look at it.   Seeing the amount of armament on the planes impressed us that this was serious business.

A P2V5 Neptune Patrol Bomber. This was the view that we had as the bombers out of Panama roared over our mast except that the wing racks that are empty in this picture were filled with war-shot rockets. (US Navy Photo)

A little after 9:00AM, we were notified by DesDiv-61 that one of the submarines, USS Threadfin (SS-410) had an air conditioning problem. It needed Freon refrigerant to recharge the system. Wren had plenty of Freon and we were given orders to rendezvous with Threadfin. As we approached the rendezvous point we picked up Threadfin on sonar and used the sonar Underwater Telephone to establish communications and prepare to bring her to the surface. We were not allowed to surface the sub and transfer the refrigerant, however, until we had aircraft cover from Panama. As soon as the P-2V Patrol Bombers arrived from Coco Solo we brought Threadfin to the surface and highlined over the Freon. As soon as the highline was cleared, Threadfin quickly submerged. The brass wanted to be sure that an unmarked U.S. sub would not be caught on the surface in Guatemalan waters. I always figured that was to give everyone in Washington deniability in case a merchant ship full of arms mysteriously blew up off Puerto Barrios.

USS Threadfin (SS-410) receiving Freon refrigerant by highline from Wren in the Gulf of Honduras June 1, 1954. Note that the white hull number 410 normally painted in large white numbers on the submarine sail has been painted out. (A.T. Miller Photo)

On June 1st at 1:20PM we picked up surface radar contact bearing 245 at a range of 23,400 yards. We intercepted the contact about 20 miles east of Guanaja Island. The ship was the Norwegian merchant ship SS Freden V bound from Puerto Cortes, Honduras to Curacao, Netherlands East Indies. No interest to us.

On June 2nd at 1:45AM we were overtaking a large well-lighted ship that turned out to be the SS Yuisqeya. We were in our usual challenge configuration with gun mounts manned, the armed boarding party standing by and everyone looking rather grim and warlike. As we came alongside, it became obvious that it was a freighter that also carried first-class passengers. A group of late-partying passengers in their tuxedos and long dresses were waving to us as we went by. What else could we do -- we waved back!

On June 2nd at about 11:30PM, we came up astern of a large freighter and identified it as a German ship SSWulfbrook that was on our list of suspects.   The captain acknowledged that he was bound from Kingston, Jamaica to Puerto Barrios and that the ship's homeport was Kiel, Germany.   Wren immediately radioed an Operational Immediate (Highest Priority) message to the Chief of Naval Operations (CNO) in the Pentagon saying that we had a suspect ship and asked permission to board.   Although still in international waters, the ship was getting close to the Honduran territorial limits.   We sent a blinker message asking Wulfbrook to stop and lay to until we advised him to proceed.   He replied that he had no intention of stopping or obeying any U.S. ships order while in international waters.   We tried to cut Wulfbrook off and get her to turn so that she would stay in international waters.   No luck!   She wouldn't give and was much bigger then us.   We had to play chicken of the sea and veer off.   We trailed Wulfbrook as she headed toward Puerto Barrios waiting to hear back from the CNO.   At about 2:17AM we left Wulfbrook to intercept a radar contact designated Skunk Able.   We came up astern and identified Skunk Able as the SS Eros, out of Belfast and enroute from Caiba to New Orleans with a cargo of bananas.   At 2:40AM we resumed trailing Wulfbrook which was now well within Honduran waters near Utila Island.   Finally, at 5:50AM we got a message from CNO saying our friend didn't have the guns anymore.   Chagrined that it had taken so long for a response to an Operational Immediate message and disappointed that we didn't get to board, we broke off from Wulfbrook and returned to our patrol station.

For several days things were quiet and we had no contacts.   We did man overboard drills and drilled at General Quarters a couple of times.   The captain held personnel inspection on Saturday morning.   On June 6 at 5:51AM we proceeded to investigate a surface radar contact bearing 151 at a range of 5 miles.   Contact turned out to be SS Marcella enroute to Trinidad from Puerto Barrios.

As with so many of these cold war incidents, it ended not in a bang but a whimper.   On June 6 at 6:34AM Wren was routinely relieved by the USS Borie (DD-704).   The Borie's captain came over in their whaleboat and had a transition conference with Captain

Johnson and picked up our orders. Borie and the three other ships that relieved DesDiv-61 also brought a tanker with them so they got to stay a lot longer off Puerto Barrios than we did. They were evidently no more successful than we were in finding the guns. I'm convinced that the arms delivery by the Alfhem was a one shot deal and despite all the rumors, there were no other arms smugglers in the Caribbean.

The Zacapa Team, part of the ragtag "army" that the CIA had assembled to overthrow Arbenz. (LatinAmericaStudies.org Photo)

The air attacks on Guatemala City, heavy radio propaganda attacks directed by Howard Hunt and the CIA 150-man invasion force from Honduras ultimately caused Arbenz to resign on June 27, 1954. According to veteran CIA operative Richard Drain, "PBSUCCESS was a success through dumb luck more than anything else". The ragtag invasion force refused to fight, however, the psychological warfare (and probably the presence of Wren et al off the coast) convinced Arbenz that the U.S. wouldn't give up until he stepped down.[18] Castillo Armas, who was installed as President by the CIA to succeed Arbenz, was later elected president in a free election and was assassinated by one of his presidential bodyguards in 1958.

---

[18] While all of this was going on, Ernesto "Che" Guevera, a young Argentine doctor, sought refuge from the conflict in the Argentine Embassy in Guatemala City. Supposedly his observation of the CIA's "couterrevolutionary" coup convinced him that armed revolution was the only path for communist takeover. He fled from Guatemala to Mexico where he met the Cuban exiles Fidel and Raul Castro and the rest, as they say, is history.

The climate of frenzy over communism that prevailed in Washington in the spring of 1954 seems difficult to understand today. It has to be seen in the context of the political debate and finger pointing over who had "lost China to Communism" that had raged in the early '50's. Earlier in May just before Wren went to Guatemala, the French Indochina stronghold of Dien Bien Phu had just fallen to the Communist Viet Minh and the French hold on what was to become Vietnam was doomed. In the U.S. Senate, Joseph McCarthy's committee was on a witch hunt for communists in government. In fact while Wren was in Guatemala the hearings were coming to a dramatic end with the confrontation between McCarthy and the Army's counsel Joseph Welch.

It is also obvious in all of this that the United Fruit Company was very powerful and had many friends in Washington including some of those very close to the seat of power. I am convinced that this whole operation was mounted for the benefit of UFCO and its powerful stockholders and had little if anything to do with Communism. Unfortunately the overthrow of its freely elected government started Guatemala on a path of dictatorships, violence and human rights abuses that would continue for forty years.

The success in overthrowing governments in Iran and then in Guatemala gave the covert operators within the CIA the power base to continue these operations. Kermit Roosevelt's admonitions about the requirements for better leadership and popular support were quickly forgotten in the flush of victory. In 1955, the CIA engineered the election that made NgoDinh Diem the first president of the Republic of Vietnam and started the U.S. on its long and tragic intervention in that troubled country. It also set the precedent for the CIA's ill-starred invasion of Cuba at the Bay of Pigs in April 1961.

Rum and Coke

In December of 1951 I was about half way through the six-month course at the Fleet Sonar School in Key West.   Although it may sound like an exotic tropical paradise, most sailors regarded Key West as a hole.   In 1951 Key West was a small town of about 10,000 (what is now called "Old Town").   Its main industry was the Navy and the entertainment thereof.   There was also a sizeable number of commercial fishermen (shrimp) and some Cuban cigar makers.   Key West's biggest problem was that it was 120 miles at sea and 160 miles from the nearest real city, Miami.   The few towns like Marathon and Islamorada along the Overseas Highway between Key West and the mainland at Homestead were little more then fishing camps.   The water in both the ocean and the Key West swimming pools was so warm (eighties) for most of the year that it was hardly refreshing -- more like a bath.   The other major recreation was fishing. If you didn't like to fish of course you could always enjoy the local nightspots. Key West was wide open at that time and had many bars, loads of strip joints, B-Girls and gambling in addition to the famous Mom's bordello on Stock Island.   Duval Street was one long strip of bars many with gambling rooms in the back.   A popular sailor's recreation was to drink your way from the Gulf Of Mexico to the Atlantic Ocean.   Even at one beer each, that was an ambitious project given the number of joints on Duval Street.   The time a group of us did it, we ended up standing on the sea wall congratulating ourselves on having made it when the guy next to me fell into the Atlantic.   To try to prevent sailors from getting in trouble in town the navy provided as many on-base recreation facilities as possible including a couple of nice clubs with cheap drinks.   They also tried to provide opportunities for the sailors to get away from Key West for weekends.

When any of the ships in the Sonar School Squadron were going somewhere for weekend R&R they would notify the sonar school as to how many empty bunks were available. The spaces were made available to students on a first come basis as long as your grades were OK.   This is how I got to go to Havana on the U.S.S. Damato (DDE-871).

Postcard of U.S.S. Damato entering Havana harbor early December 1951. The author was in the groups on deck. The Morro Castle is in the left background.

Early Friday morning I went down and picked up Damato at the SURASDEVDET piers. Damato was a Gearing, 2250-ton class specially modified for antisubmarine warfare and was classified as an escort destroyer. We got underway and the students on board worked with the submarine all morning. In the early afternoon, we laid to, put the whaleboat over the side and transferred the students to one of the ships going back to Key West. We then got underway for Havana. On the way, a sheet was handed out to each member of the crew and passengers like myself, outlining expected standards of behavior in Cuba. Damato was the first U.S. Navy ship allowed to go into Havana in a couple of years. It seemed that a sailor from the last US Navy ship to call at Havana had urinated on the statue of Jose Marti, the revered poet, martyr, hero of the Cuban revolution against Spain. In the diplomatic incident resulting from this indiscretion, U.S. Navy ships were banned from Havana. Damato was the first ship to return to Havana after the ban was lifted. We were all admonished to avoid the statue of Jose Marti and to behave ourselves. We were also cautioned that an election campaign was in progress and not to discuss politics.

We tied up to the United Fruit Company pier that was covered by a large warehouse building. As we walked through the warehouse toward the front entrance, we could hear a great deal of yelling and screaming. Not knowing what to expect, in what was for most of us our first experience in a foreign land, we approached the entrance cautiously. Caution didn't help. The tumult was caused by a large and enterprising group of kids who worked for the individual cab drivers parked along the street near the pier. As soon as we ventured through the entrance, kids jerked our blue overnight bags out of our hands and ran for the line of cabs. Not knowing what was going on we started off in hot pursuit of the blue bag thieves. The kids opened the back door of a cab and threw the bag in the back seat. No sooner did you follow your bag into the cab then the kid slammed the door and the cab was on its way. The driver immediately started into his broken English pitch of what a fine cab driver he was and how he could take care of all our needs during our weekend in Havana. Tour of the city? -- Restaurants? -- Bars? -- Girls? -- he could take care of us during our entire stay. Actually, our plan was to do a bit of bar hopping (including the famous Sloppy Joe's) Friday night and tour the city on Saturday. Every time we got into a cab on Friday night we got the same spiel. Each driver assured us he gave the absolute best and most comprehensive tour of Havana. We told each of them to be at our hotel at nine o'clock the next morning.

Saturday morning as we descended the stairs into the small lobby of our hotel, somewhat the worse for wear from our evening in Havana, we could hear quite a hubbub. All of the cab drivers we had seen the night before were waiting for us in the lobby ready to start the tour. We immediately held an impromptu auction and gave the tour to the low bidder.

The low bidder had brought his brother along to translate at no additional charge. My two buddies and I were complimenting ourselves on our wise choice as, at our guide's suggestion, we headed for breakfast. Our guides were well known in the little restaurant they took us to and we had a great breakfast. Our guides wouldn't tell us where we were going next, but we knew they were a discerning pair when we turned into the grounds of the Cristal Brewery. Other relatives of our guides were loading trucks and as we pulled alongside the truck, they passed in beers for all of us. Talk about something hitting the spot. There were two major beers in Cuba, Cristal and Hatuey. The previous evening we had been drinking Hatuey, which was brewed by the rum distiller Bacardi. The label on the bottles of Hatuey contained a profile view of an American Indian. Hatuey was known as the "one eyed Indian" and there was a widely held theory among sailors that when the one eyed Indian winked at you it was time to quit. The previous evening I think we either missed or were unable to see the wink! As we all sipped our beers we set off to see Havana.

Our Havana tour guides. One drove the 1941 Ford and the other guided and translated. (A.T. Miller Photo)

Havana in 1951 was a beautiful and interesting city. It was also one of the most wide open cities in the Western Hemisphere. There were bars of all kinds, prostitution and sex shows. There were many gambling casinos. The most elegant of these was in the Hotel Nacional. The Russian-born, American gangster Meyer Lansky made enormous payoffs to the Cuban politicians to maintain his control of gambling in Cuban casinos. We didn't get to do any gambling, however, because all of the gambling facilities were off limits to American servicemen.

Our guides drove us along the Malecon, the beautiful boulevard on the oceanfront. One of the sights we passed was the famous statue of Jose Marti. We only got close enough to take a picture. They took us to the zoo and through the beautiful suburb of Miramar where wealthy Cubans lived. They also took us to a Jai-Alai game, which was one of the fastest sports any of us had seen. It is played with a ball (pelota) about as hard as a baseball that is thrown so hard with the wicket (cesta) that the walls have to be made of granite to withstand the impact. One of the players got hit in the stomach by the ball and was carried off curled up in a ball. We decided that, for us, jai alai was just a spectator sport.

Two fellow sonar school students and our cabdriver in front of the famous Jose Marti statue. Note the sign in the background for the also famous "one-eye Indian beer". (A.T. Miller Photo)

They showed us the huge (by 1951 standards), new Sports Palace, which was used for everything from basketball to boxing. Little did I know that thirteen years later in 1964 I would be helping a Cuban who had become a political refugee because of what he had tried to do in this same Sports Palace. I was living in Northern Virginia at that time. Rafael had escaped from Castro's Cuba after discovery of his part in a plot to assassinate Fidel Castro's right hand man Che Guevera. Evidently Che was a big fight fan and always sat in the front row for the boxing events at the Sports Palace. Rafael, and his co-conspirators planned to shoot him at ringside. Unfortunately, a mole in the group who turned them in to the Castro government betrayed them.

The Havana Sports Palace in December 1951. It was here at a boxing match that Che Guevera was to be assassinated. To this day, it is still used for boxing matches (A.T. Miller Photo)

Rafael, who had previously gotten his wife and children out of Havana to Miami, barely escaped to the U.S. Rafael was an interesting man. He had worked in the underground to overthrow the dictator Batista and install Castro. After the overthrow of Batista, Rafael and his friends realized that Castro was a hard line Communist and not the Socialist reformer he had professed to be. Rafael and his brother had a profitable construction business, which the Castro government promptly nationalized. After that, Rafael went back underground against Castro and got involved in the plot to kill Che Guevera. After escaping to Miami, he couldn't find work in Florida and took a job as a bookkeeper in a sawmill in South Carolina while his family remained in Miami. The CIA tracked him down and recruited him for the CIA-organized Cuban Brigade 2506. He trained as an infantryman in Guatemala and landed at Playa Giron in the Bay of Pigs. When the invasion failed for lack of air support[19], he was one of those few who got off the beach and back to the ships. When he got back to Miami, there were many Cuban refugees and no jobs to be found. I met him after Catholic Relief Services had moved he and his family to Northern Virginia to make a new home. "I've had it as a revolutionary" he told me. Small wonder. My part in this project was to find Rafael a job. Although an experienced bookkeeper, Rafael was willing to take almost any kind of job to support his family. Our biggest problems were that his English was not conversationally good. He was also having a hard time explaining to potential employers the gaps in his resume for the periods when he was working for the CIA. The CIA had sworn him to secrecy about both the Che Guevera and the Bay of Pigs affairs so he couldn't discuss what he was doing during those times. Rafael kept telling me that "Bobby Kennedy promised us jobs when he addressed the Cuban Brigade at the Orange Bowl in Florida". "Just call his office", he said, "he will take care of us". I kept telling him that we ought to hold off on that until we had exhausted all other possibilities. Nothing turned up so I finally called Attorney General Robert Kennedy's office. An assistant assured me that the Attorney General would be happy to talk to Rafael, however, she explained that Mr. Califano was handling Cuban matters. I told her that would be fine and was transferred to Joseph Califano[20] who assured me that they were committed to finding jobs for Cuban Brigade veterans. He said that they had set up a special office in the Pentagon and gave me a number to call. The contact was Lieutenant Colonel Alexander Haig[21]. Colonel Haig outlined their program which would involve Rafael going to the King Ranch in Texas for training and then on to the Belgian Congo to help Moise Tshombe defeat the Simba rebels. Thanks a lot colonel! I told Haig that I doubted that Rafael was interested but would convey the offer to him. Rafael was furious and disappointed when I told him

---

[19] In the fall of 1960 I was working for RCA Service Co. in Alexandria, VA. I worked on a project to build a transportable ground –to-air communication and navigation system contained in eight easily interconnected fiberglass boxes. This system was built for a customer who was known only as the "United States Government" (read CIA). The system ultimately ended up at the Retalhuleu, Guatemala airfield where it provided communications to the ill-fated B-26C bombers involved in the Bay of Pigs.

[20] Joseph Califano Jr. had various responsibilities in the Kennedy and Johnson administrations and went on to become Secretary of the Department of Health, Education and Welfare under President Jimmy Carter.

[21] Colonel Haig went on to be a decorated combat hero in Vietnam, White House Chief of staff under Nixon, Supreme Allied Commander Europe (NATO) and Secretary of State in the Reagan administration. Who can forget his statement to reporters after Reagan was shot "I'm in charge here"?

what the deal was. Fortunately, I was ultimately able to find him a job as a bookkeeper with US Gypsum in Alexandria. Our parish got the family an apartment and furnished it and the Franchi family prospered in their new homeland.

Back to December 1951. As we were driving down one of Havana's main streets, our driver looked in the rear view mirror and swerved suddenly to the curb. As he did, a calvacade of three cars roared by. The middle car was an open touring car with two very official looking personages in the back. Our guides were quite impressed and had an excited conversation in Spanish. It turned out that one of the personages was Fulgencio Batista. He had been head of government from 1940 for a number of years but in December of 1951 out of office and running for president in the upcoming election. Our guides were seemingly in awe of the "strongman". We figured that if the "little people" in Havana were so impressed, he was a shoe in for election. I guess Batista didn't share that confidence. Early one morning shortly before the election, he and some of his military supporters executed a quick coup at Camp Columbia and installed himself as Presidente. When I was back in Havana in August of 1954, elections were again in progress. The city was plastered with posters for the various candidates for the legislature. No matter who the candidate or for which party, the bottom of every poster said "Presidente Batista". There were apparently limitations on the democratic process and Batista was not about to take any chances on the will of the electorate. Ultimately it was the dissatisfaction with the brutal and corrupt Batista government that fostered the support for the Castro revolution.

By the middle of the afternoon, our guides announced that it was time to hit the rum distilleries. Sounded like a plan to us. Havana had many "mom and pop" distilleries. Many of them were in what appeared to be storefronts. They were really most hospitable considering that they knew that sailors couldn't bring booze back on board the ship. As we entered they gave each of us a frozen daiquiri which we sipped as we "toured" the distillery. Basically it was just a bunch of vats, barrels and plumbing. Then we went back up to the front room where there was a long table with bottles of all of the products and shot glasses to sample them. There was the usual light and dark rum in addition to such exotic things as pineapple, mango and banana brandy. Our standard practice was to sample everything. After a few of these places we were feeling not much pain and the tour was over. We were feeling so good we lavishly tipped our guides, which was probably why the distilleries were included at the end of the tour. Nah.... we really did have a good day.

El Capitolio, the Cuban National Capitol on Del Prado in Havana. It was modeled after the U.S. Capitol. (A.T. Miller Photo)

We spent the rest of the evening in the sidewalk cafes on del Prado. The Cuban Capitol building (El Capitolio) is on del Prado a broad street running through the downtown Havana. It was copied from the U.S Capitol so it all looked quite familiar to us.

Directly across the street from El Capitolio were about two blocks of sidewalk cafes. They were very nice. Having had such a good start on free rum we continued with rum and coke. We had some dinner and were entertained by the strolling musicians and singers.   One thing that made us all a bit nervous was the fact that all of the Cuban Army officers carried their sidearm even when off duty.

Del Prado viewed from the steps of El Capitolo. The large awnings are over the sidewalk cafes where we consumed a few rum and cokes. (A.T. Miller Photo)

We were having a great time that evening but kept an eye on a number of these guys who were proceeding to get pretty drunk with these huge horse pistols on their hips. We had some discussions about where we were going to go for cover when the shooting started. Fortunately everyone remained mellow and we didn't have to execute Plan B.

In August of 1954 Wren visited Havana while on a midshipman cruise.   We tied up across the ship channel from downtown Havana.   There were several other destroyers and the Light Cruiser Juneau (CLAA-145) over there so a fleet landing was set up across the harbor in the park in front of the Presidential Place. The harbor was only a couple of hundred yards wide at this point and it only took our boats a few minutes to make the fleet landing.   We noticed as we debarked that Wren was operating the landing on this watch. There was an ensign, two petty officer shore patrol and a Quartermaster striker signalman. We waved, made some smart remarks about them having the duty and headed for the bars.

Wren entering Havana harbor August 1954. Wren proceeded to the turning basin at the end of the harbor, turned around and moored to the seawall on the far side.

Batista had been back in power a little over two years at this point. It was a rather repressive regime and he used the army as enforcers. I had been concerned about gun toting army officers when I had been in Havana in 1951. It was worse in 1954. There were many soldiers with guns walking the streets and every public building had a soldier with an M1 rifle standing in front of it. The Presidential Palace had guys with Thompson Submachine Guns at each corner. Al Dodge, Gene Staunton and I came across in the whaleboat and flagged a cab at the fleet landing. The cab driver was a wild man. He put the accelerator to the floor and started up the wide one-way boulevard alongside the park in front of the Presidential Palace. There were three lanes of traffic plus cars parked on each side. As we approached the palace, traffic had started to back up. Didn't daunt our driver. He changed lanes, gunned it and aimed for the short traffic line in the leftmost lane. He almost made it. Another kamikaze cab changed lanes at the same time and slammed into our right side and drove us into the parked cars on our left tearing up both sides of the cab with a great crash. That got the attention of the palace guards who came running toward us brandishing their Tommy Guns. The cab driver was yelling to us "No pay!... No pay". We weren't about to pay but our primary concern was to distance ourselves from the guys with the Tommy Guns. We ducked over and around the sea of cars as a very loud discussion commenced between the drivers and the guards.

As we got up to the next corner we quickly grabbed a cab and headed uptown. The cab driver immediately started the spiel about how he could take us to the best spots in town. Been there – done that! We were wandering around town hitting bars as we went. At one point, we realized that we had gotten pretty far from downtown and got on a streetcar that seemed to be going in the right direction. The driver didn't speak English and my rudimentary Spanish didn't seem to be working. Some people came up from the back of the car to help - - and then some more. Eventually it seemed if everyone was huddled behind us near the driver waving his or her arms and talking. Finally, we recognized some landmarks and got off the streetcar. We walked a bit and found ourselves on the boulevard going along the west side of the harbor. We could see Juneau right across the harbor and Wren a little further North. There were a group of Wrens in one of the open-air cafes and we joined them. We were drinking Hatuey cervueza but some of the others were drinking rum and shots of Cuban dark rum kept turning up in front of me. I noticed that the Shore Patrol and Seaman Deamiches, the signalman from the Fleet Landing, were also drinking with us. The SP's guard belt, brassard and billy clubs were stashed under the table, as was the signalman's signal lamp. It turned out that the officer in charge at the landing had released them at the end of their watches and just told them not to go too far. Deamiches was getting worried because he had the 8 to 12 watch on the bridge and he didn't want to go back to the ship. He also wasn't in any shape to assume the watch. He decided that the thing to do was to signal back to the ship with his signal lamp and get someone to take his watch. The signal lamp had a barrel about 4 inches in diameter and 2 feet long mounted on a gunstock. The trigger operated the battery-powered signal light. Now you have to remember that this was Havana in 1954 with a dictator in charge as result of an armed coup. People were nervous enough with all the army guys carrying around guns and now this sailor brings out something that looks like a sawed-off bazooka and starts pointing it around. He steadied himself against the support for the awning and pointed this gun-like thing toward the Wren and pulled the trigger.   Some of the Cubans ran down the street and others crouched under the tables. At first we thought it was pretty funny.   Then we started to look around to see if there were any of those guys with the big horse pistols in the neighborhood.   We decided a firefight between .38 caliber pistols and a signal lamp was definitely an uneven contest. Fortunately there weren't any pistoleros in sight so we beat a hasty retreat to another bar around the corner.   From there on the memories fade but we all apparently got back to the ship safely and on time.

Sunday morning I awoke with the granddaddy of all hangovers.   The combination of Hatuey and rum was lethal.   My head was pounding and my mouth tasted like the Russian Army had marched through.   I rolled out of my bunk and went aft to the next compartment where the scuttlebutts (water fountains) were located.   I was gulping down huge amounts of water.   When I came up for air I saw that the guy at the other scuttlebutt had been with us the night before and was in no better shape than I.   He told me that when he arrived back aboard there was a guy passed out on the deck with a bottle of rum in his hand.   Not wanting him to get in trouble for bringing liquor aboard, he had relieved him of the bottle and stashed it in the machine shop just two compartments forward.   We immediately decided that something was needed to get our health back and proceeded to the machine shop still dressed only in our skivvies. Although I had the duty that day, I figured I could get away with drinking because I didn't have a watch until eight o'clock that night.   We passed the bottle around our small party in the machine shop.   In our shape, however, the rum quickly took its toll and a couple of the guys threw me into my bunk completely passed out at about 8 AM.   Now under ordinary circumstances, I could have slept straight through until I had to go on watch at 8 PM. Unfortunately for me, the XO decided to give the Sunday liberty party a couple of extra hours and called away liberty at 10 AM instead of noon.   So at about quarter to ten, the duty messenger came down and after some difficulty awakened me and told me to relieve the morning 8 to 12 Petty Officer of the Watch on the quarterdeck.   With some difficulty I got up and pulled on the whites that I had worn the night before despite the fact that they showed quite a bit of wear and tear from the previous days adventures.   I went up to the head splashed some water on my face, combed my hair, adjusted my white hat to the regulation angle and proceeded to the quarterdeck. Mr. Tiffin, the Officer of the Deck was watching me as I proceeded forward, somewhat unsteadily, toward the quarterdeck. He had this puzzled expression on his face. I guess he couldn't figure out why I was so drunk when they had just awakened me. At first he wasn't going to let me relieve the watch but then relented because he didn't really want to write me up for drunk on duty. He told me though that if I was going to stand the watch I at least had to put on a clean set of whites. I thought that was a deal and proceeded to below to make myself presentable. That accomplished, I returned to the quarterdeck, relieved the Petty Officer of the Watch and strapped on the Colt 45. I stood up straight, tried to look sober and not breathe on the OD. They were serving brunch on Sunday morning and the OD let me go up to the galley and get a steak sandwich which I washed down with lots of tomato juice. That enabled me to make it to noon when I was relieved. I promptly returned to my bunk and crashed for seven hours. That was my last experience with rum. I decided that inasmuch I escaped without even a captain's mast no less a court martial; I had better stick to beer.

In recent years when I see pictures on the TV news of Havana in its current rundown and decrepit condition, it makes me sad. I remember the beautiful and vital Havana that I knew and can hardly recognize in today's pictures. The streets are filled with the same cars that I saw there 45 to 50 years ago. The buildings are falling apart and the people appear dispirited. As badly as I feel, I can only imagine how my friend Rafael feels. He was willing to risk his life to rid Cuba of communism and now over 40 years later Castro is still in power in the ruins of Rafael's beloved country.

Hurricanes

It starts as a low-pressure area traveling slowly westward across the equatorial Atlantic Ocean. The low pressure deepens and ultimately becomes what the weather people classify as a tropical depression. As the winds around its center increase and it builds in size, it is classified as a tropical storm. Eventually as it proceeds westward and gathers energy from the tropical seas its winds exceed 75 miles-per-hour and it becomes a full-fledged hurricane. As these powerful storms approach North America they usually head either into the Gulf of Mexico (sometimes going across Florida in the process) or turn northward up the eastern coast of the United States. In 1953 and particularly in 1954 some very powerful and devastating hurricanes came up the eastern seaboard. Riding them out in an old Fletcher class destroyer was an exciting experience to say the least.

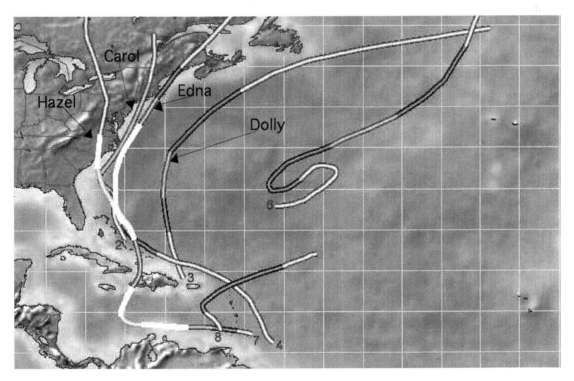

The tracks of the 1954 Atlantic Hurricanes. Carol, Edna and Hazel battered the US East Coast and Wren. (Map by University of Maryland, Baltimore County; NOAA Data)

Strange as it may seem to landlubbers, ships are much safer riding out a bad storm at anchor in protected waters then they would be tied alongside a pier. Alongside a pier getting pounded into the wood and concrete structure may damage the ship. At sea, particularly in a protected anchorage, the ship is in no danger of smashing into anything. They can also put out multiple anchors and use their engines to help hold position in the anchorage. The primary US Navy Atlantic Fleet hurricane anchorage is in the Chesapeake Bay just south of Tangier Island. Each ship is given an assigned location in the anchorage. There are hurricane anchorage charts with numbered circles on them indicating the location for one ship. The ship approaches its assigned location and drops its anchor(s) at the center of the circle. The circle is large enough that they can let out a lot of anchor chain to reduce the probability of dragging and not be in danger of hitting a neighboring ship. The circles also vary in size for different classes (battleships, cruisers, destroyers, etc.).). Obviously a destroyer like the Wren got assigned to one of the smaller circles.

I reported on board Wren in early August 1953. I had only been aboard a short time when on August 13 it appeared that the Norfolk area would be hit by hurricane Barbara. Over on the Grand Canyon, the flagship of Destroyer Flotilla Four (DesFlot4), the signal flags Prep - Easy - Victor - One - Four were snapping briskly from both yardarms in an increasingly strong wind. Their message was "Prepare to get underway at 1400" (2:00PM). Wren actually got underway from the Convoy Escort (CE) Piers at 4:16 PM and joined the long parade of ships going through Hampton Roads toward the Chesapeake Bay. As we entered the bay the ships fanned out to go to their assigned location. We proceeded to Anchorage George among a large group of destroyers.

As we arrived in the center of the anchorage just before sunset, we put out our starboard anchor with about 50 fathoms (300-feet) of chain. A small can buoy attached to the anchor with light line marked its actual position on the bottom. The anchor windless, which is used to pull it up and the windless brake, which is used to stop the chain when it is running out, control the anchor chain. As soon as the chain is stopped, a large pelican hook fastened to the deck forward of the windless is snapped over the anchor chain and secured with a locking pin. This stopper as it is called is connected directly to the main structure of the ship with a short piece of chain and holds the anchor chain securely in place independent of the windless.

The windless can only control one of the two anchor chains at a time. To change over from one anchor to the other is a long and complicated procedure. It involves using the windless to pull the chain up out of the chain locker until there is enough slack to slip it off the wildcat and over the top of the windless. The chain is very heavy and it takes a number of men with special hooks to heave it off while a chain compressor bar in the hawse pipe down to the chain locker is pulled tight to prevent the chain from slipping back down the pipe. Getting the other anchor chain on the windless is even more complicated. A line with a hook on the end is hooked into the chain for the other anchor and wrapped around the capstan. The capstan is then used to pull the line up and the chain out of the chain locker. The chain compressor is pulled tight to hold the chain from sliding back into the chain locker. This operation is repeated several times until there is enough slack chain topside for the crew to heave it over the windless and position it on the wildcat. I once asked an old bosun mate why it was called a "wildcat". He looked at me with one of those looks reserved for dumb boots and said "You'd be wild too if you had an anchor chain running out your ass." Sounds reasonable to me. This extended dissertation about the anchor equipment or ground tackle (tay-kle), as it is correctly called, is a prelude to how Wren got in big trouble during Barbara.

When we anchored, the Normal Steaming Watch was set and the seas were still relatively calm. After midnight the wind increased and the seas started to rise. By dawn it was blowing a gale. The wind was out of the southeast and all of the ships were riding on their anchors with their bow into the wind. We still had the Normal Steaming Watch set, however. I was ordered to monitor the NMC depth sounder. The Chesapeake Bay is not very deep in that area. Where we were anchored it was only about 40 feet to the bottom. Never having been in a hurricane before, I was concerned that as the seas became higher (and the troughs lower) the depth sounder showed that the keel of the ship was at times within six feet or less of the bottom. I pointed this out to the Officer Of The Deck but he didn't seem concerned. If he wasn't worried, neither was I. It turns out he had more important problems on his mind then the possibility of us kissing the bottom.

As the storm intensified we were having more and more trouble holding position in our mooring circle. At 7:05AM on the morning of the 14th we started to drag our anchor. By 7:15AM the OD was using engines one at a time and in combination fore and aft trying to hold our position without putting a heavy strain on the anchor. We could drive forward into the wind but the sea and gusts would set us over to one side or the other. Eventually we would use up all the slack in the anchor chain with it tending out to the beam and we would have to let the Wren drift back. After drifting back the OD would use the engines to try to come forward toward where he thought the anchor was planted. Engine speed was adjusted to try to hold us dead-in-the-water but the wind and sea made it very difficult. Despite these efforts, we continued to drag our anchor away from the center of the circle. By 7:25 the spray and rain had become so heavy that it reduced visibility to the point that we were ringing our bell as a fog signal.

The captain wanted to get the other anchor out abeam of the wind so that the two anchor chains would be in a big Vee with the wind down the center of the Vee. As you have probably guessed by now, the problem in getting this done was that the chain for the starboard anchor that was out was still on the windless. The First Lieutenant, Mr. Larson, estimated a half-hour to switch the other anchor chain to the windless. Besides the basic time consuming problems in changing over, it was very windy, extremely rough and green water was coming over the foc'sle. It would be very dangerous for all those working on the foc'sle. Captain Green insisted he had to have the other anchor out. Mr. Larson came up with a scheme to drop the anchor without getting the chain on the windless. They would drop the port anchor by knocking the stopper pelican hook loose. Then they would use the chain compressor in the chain locker hawse pipe to stop the chain from running out. As soon as they got it stopped, the guys on deck would immediately get the stopper pelican hook on the chain and locked. Although not unanimous, there was general agreement that this approach seemed reasonable under the circumstances.   A couple of the strongest guys were put on the block and tackle used to pull the chain compressor bar against the chain.   They braced their feet against the hawse pipe to gain the maximum leverage.   Three men with sledge hammers and marlinespikes huddled in the bow near the pelican hook on the anchor stopper.   During all of this the bow was pitching violently and green water was coming over the foc'sle.

The ship was maneuvered forward to where the captain wanted the other anchor dropped and at 7:28AM the order was given to let go.   The crew on deck removed the locking pin and then sledge hammered the pelican hook free.   The half-ton anchor dropped into the water with a great splash and the chain started to run out with a roar. So far so good. When the Mr. Larson decided we had enough chain out he yelled, "Stop it"! The guys down below laid their backs into the line on the block and tackle and pulled the chain compressor against the chain screaming through the hawse pipe.   The moving chain links vibrated the bar and those pulling on it until they thought their tooth fillings would come loose. The chain gradually slowed down.   "Heave" the bosun screamed and they all pulled even harder.   The guys on deck were poised with the pelican hook waiting for the chain links to stop. The chain finally stopped and they pounced on it trying to close the large and heavy pelican hook around a link. Unfortunately as they tried to maneuver the pelican hook around the chain, a gust surged the ship over and chain started to move again.   The crew trying to close the pelican hook jumped to get their hands out of harms way. "Heave on the son of a bitch" the bosun yelled and all down below pulled the compressor bar with their last ounce of strength.   It wasn't enough.   "Oh shit," yelled someone at the stopper. The last fifty feet of the anchor chain is painted bright red. When red links started screaming across the deck Larson yelled "Clear the foc'sle". Everybody started running aft.   The weak link that connected the end of the chain to the chain locker bulkhead parted with a loud bang.   The end of the chain flew out of hawse pipe, into the air and slammed across the bow tearing down the jackstaff and the lifelines before disappearing over the side.

To put it mildly, Captain Green was not pleased. Larson, probably contemplating his next fitness report, had a very long face. At 7:48AM the captain decided it would be better if the first team was running the ship and he ordered the Special Sea and Anchor Detail set. Over the next few hours using engines we managed to hold our position reasonably well and not run into anyone else. That night as Barbara headed north, we steamed back to Norfolk. We tied up in one of the berths at the end of the pier closest to the sea wall.

A few days later, a fleet tug towing a barge went out to Chesapeake Bay and divers retrieved our anchor and all its chain. Our position at the land end of the pier insured that the barge delivering our anchor and chain back to us got the maximum visibility from the maximum number of ships at CE piers. There was a loud chorus of catcalls from the other ships and smart remarks about seamen who lost their anchors as the barge wended its way to our port side. A red faced Mr. Larson supervised the retrieval, repainting and stowing of the anchor chain -- using the windless.

The 1954 Hurricane season was marked by several severe storms that battered the East Coast of the US. Carol and Edna moved up along the Mid-Atlantic States crossed over Long Island and smashed into New England. Hazel came ashore in South Carolina and devastated the Mid-Atlantic States, New England and even caused damage in Canada.

Wren was returning from Cuba in late August. We had come through the Windward Passage and were heading north when we ran into a stormy area in the Bahamas that would eventually be Carol. We would pass through a severe rainsquall and then a few minutes later we were in bright sunshine. The winds were very humid, gusty and disorganized. At one point I saw two waterspouts off to our northeast. We passed through this tropical disturbance and proceeded northward. We were no sooner back in Norfolk when we had to get underway for the hurricane anchorage. Carol, that we had passed in the Bahamas in its formative stage was now a Category 3 hurricane heading north with a vengeance and was going to overrun us. Needless to say we moored in our spot in the hurricane anchorage south of Tangier using both anchors.   Carol passed about 50 miles east of Wren traveling northward at 40 miles an hour with winds of 100 knots.   Although we got blown around quite a bit in heavy seas we didn't have too much trouble. Carol was moving so fast that it was all over in a short while.   Unfortunately New England caught the brunt of it.   Carol roared across Long Island and came ashore in Rhode Island forcing a 8 to 12 feet above mean tide storm surge ahead of it.   It was the worst storm to hit New England since the 1938 hurricane.   Damage was estimated at over $400,000,000.

The Edgewood Yacht Club in Rhode Island is submerged by Hurricane Carol's storm surge in 1954. (Wikimedia Commons Photo)

Following closely on the heels of Hurricane Carol was Hurricane Edna. Edna followed a track up the East Coast that was slightly east of Carol's track. Edna raced towards southern New England at over 45 mph, but veered about 100 miles further east. Edna made landfall during the morning of September 11, passing over Martha's Vineyard and Nantucket, then across the eastern tip of Cape Cod, Massachusetts.   Wren went to the Chesapeake Bay hurricane anchorage for Edna and rode it out without any major incident. Our experience during hurricane Hazel was something else, however.

On October 13, 1954 hurricane Hazel crossed the island of Haiti and headed northward. Winds in Haiti were measured at 110 miles per hour. Thirty-six people were killed and there was an enormous amount of damage. As Hazel proceeded northward through the Bahamas it gained energy and power. It ultimately became a Category 4 hurricane – a very violent storm.

As Hazel was roaring through Haiti, Wren was alongside Pier 23 at the Convoy Escort piers in Norfolk. The crew hated Pier 23. It was the westernmost of the CE piers right next to the Norfolk and Western Railroad coal pier. The N&W pier was long and coal cars were pushed right onto the pier to be unloaded. There was a huge mechanism on the pier that picked up the railroad coal cars and turned them upside down to dump the coal into the ships. Although this was a quick and efficient way to load the ships, it resulted in great clouds of coal dust boiling into the air and descending on the navy ships at pier 23. The damned stuff came down and coated everything on the ship. Whenever we got assigned to Pier 23, we figured Wren had done something to piss off DesFlot4 and this was our punishment.

On October 14 we were at the very end of pier 23 on the west side (toward the coal pier). In order to fit more ships at these piers a large group of pilings had been driven into the harbor bottom about 75 feet beyond the end of the pier. Only about the forward 200 feet of the ship was actually alongside the pier. The aft part of the ship extended beyond the end of the pier and the after mooring lines were tied to the cluster of pilings.

Hazel was starting to take a more westward track and it appeared that it would come ashore in South Carolina. Preparations were being made for the 80 or so ships in Norfolk to get underway for the hurricane anchorage in Chesapeake Bay. I was really upset. I had the long weekend liberty which meant I could get off the ship by 10AM on Friday the 15th and would not have to be back until Monday morning. I had been planning to go home to Arlington, Virginia for the weekend. My buddy Everly, who was in the same watch section, was going to give me a ride home. There would be no liberty if we had a hurricane on Friday.   Sure enough, Thursday afternoon at 2:00PM all ships were placed on two-hour notice to get underway and weekend liberty was canceled.   At 4:13PM USS Green (DDR-711) got underway from Wren's port side.   The USS Everglades (AD-24) got underway from Pier 23 in front of us.   One by one ships were clearing the CE Piers.

Wren, however, wasn't going anywhere. We could not get underway.   We were in the middle of what was called a Survey Inspection in preparation for going into the Norfolk Naval Shipyard for a major overhaul in early 1955.   The whole engineering plant was torn apart so that it could be inspected to determine what work had to be done in the yard. We effectively didn't have any engines.   As the other ships were leaving, Wren started making preparations to ride out Hazel alongside pier 23.   By 6:51PM Wren was able to light off Boiler No. 1 and at 7:50PM we had steam up and could disconnect the steam line from the pier.   By 8:40PM we were able to bring a generator on line and disconnect shore power.   The "black gang" worked all night trying to get the engines back together before Hazel blew us away from the pier.

Hazel was reported as a fast moving very strong and concentrated hurricane. All of the engineering force was feverishly working to get the engineering plant back together. The deck force was working securing all loose gear and battening down all topside areas. They doubled up all the mooring lines.   In addition they doubled them up again with steel cables. About thirty of us were directed to go out onto the pier up near the bow.   A line connected to our port anchor chain had been passed through the bullnose and over to the pier. All of us grabbed onto the line and we started to haul the chain to the pier.   It was heavy going. As the chain was let out at the windless, we dragged it over to the pier and tried to drag it as far forward as we could get it.   The chain was very heavy and did not come over gracefully.   At one point, I was leaning over at about a 45-degree angle. When we finally got it as far forward as our combined strength could drag it, the bitter end of the chain was shackled into one of the bits on the pier.   The slack in the chain was adjusted from the windless so that it would be a backup if the mooring lines broke.

Friday morning the sonarmen were given the assignment of rigging another set of manila mooring lines all the way across the pier to the bits and bollards on the far (east) side of the pier. It was late morning and although there were high clouds, a hazy sun was still out and a light warm humid breeze was blowing. It was rather pleasant on the pier. Most of the other ships were gone by this time and there was no one on the pier except the half dozen of us sonarmen working on the lines. Everybody was in fairly good humor even though a destructive hurricane was bearing down on us. All of the regular mooring lines were already in use so we were working with brand new lengths of six-inch (circumference) manila line. Regular mooring lines had an eye spliced in the end of the line, but we didn't have enough time to do anything that fancy. The solution was to put a bowline in the end of each line that was to go on a bit or bollard. There was discussion among the sonarmen about who remembered how to tie bowlines. Mr. Bigelow our division officer who was an Annapolis graduate came down on the pier to see how we were doing. He looked at the lines and said, "Even I can do a bowline". We dropped the lines and Staunton said, "OK, do it". Bigelow started wrestling with the end of the heavy stiff line. He was getting a lot of coaching from us. "The squirrel comes out of his hole, goes around the tree and back down the hole" which was boot camp trick to remember how to make a bowline. Each time he went to pull it tight the knot fell apart. He finally gave up. I took the line, flipped a loop in it and quickly tied a bowline. Although I won one for the enlisted guys over the Trade School guys, we all laughingly agreed we should have gotten Bigelow[22] to put some money on it before we started. While we were disporting ourselves on Pier 23, Hazel was coming ashore at Myrtle Beach, South Carolina that was being devastated by high winds and heavy seas. Over 270 homes were destroyed in Myrtle Beach representing 80% of the waterfront development.

---

[22] David Skinner Bigelow was an excellent officer admired and respected by all of the sonarmen. He handled the men well, made decisions easily and generally exhibited the characteristics of a true leader. After retiring from the navy in 1960 as Lieutenant Commander, he went on to an impressive career in business. He was an executive with a number of international companies including CEO of a large French company owned by Tenneco. He died in 1998 at the age of 67.

Beach homes wrecked by Hurricane Hazel in Carolina Beach, NC. (ncdcr.gov Photo)

As we were finishing the cross pier moor, the deck force had been working a long shot of chain up out of the anchor chain locker. As we came back on board we were each given a two-foot piece of 21-thread manila line which we put through the chain to use as a handle to lift it. The individual links of the chain were about four inches long and the chain was very heavy. We were spaced at three-foot intervals along the length of the chain. We slowly started aft straining to carry the chain. As more chain came up out of the locker more sailors were tied into it to carry it. It took a large portion of the crew to finally move the chain aft. The deck force petty officers were stationed along the deck to see that we didn't drag the chain and scrape up their painted deck or deck treads. We were literally a chain gang. It was very slow going -- we kind of shuffled along. As the chain reached the fantail it was led around the huge forged base of the aft five-inch gun mount 55. A large mooring shackle was used to close the loop of chain around the gun mount. Lines were passed over to sailors on the mooring pilings and the bitter end of the chain was hauled over to the pilings with a lot of grunting, groaning and colorful language. The chain was wrapped a couple of times around the pilings and shackled into place by 2:30PM. By the time we were finished, it was getting darker, the wind was picking up and it was raining intermittently.

The plan was that the heavy manila lines were the primary moor. They would stretch and act as shock absorbers as we were buffeted by wind and sea. The 5/8-inch and 7/8-

251

inch steel wires would back them up and if all else failed, the anchor chains shackled into the pier would hold us. Unfortunately, it didn't work out quite that way.

The skies were getting darker and a gusty moist wind was blowing with increasing strength from the east. The piers where normally there would be two large destroyer tenders, a submarine tender and fifty or more destroyers and submarines were deserted. Normally the piers would be filled with people and vehicles and now there was nothing. Only a couple of ships and no people. The parking lots and ball fields at the foot of the piers were deserted. There was no sign of life on the shore anywhere. Everyone had gone for cover. I had never seen it like this. It was an eerie feeling. It felt as if we had been left alone at the end of this pier with our stern sticking out into the stream, no engines to propel us and helpless before the oncoming storm. It wasn't a pleasant feeling.

The wind was increasing and blowing across pier 23 pushing Wren away from the pier. At the land end of pier 23, a football field or more from where we were, there were two Gearing class destroyers one on either side of the pier. They couldn't get underway either. They were more sheltered there and the windward destroyer tended to protect the destroyer on the leeward side of the pier. We waved down the pier to a few of their crew that were doing just what we were -- checking the lines one more time. To our east, across from Navy Pier 20 there was an old merchant freighter tied up at the civilian grain elevator pier. They were checking and doubling up their lines. With a last look around we went on board as the skies darkened, the wind rose and it began to rain.

Hazel was moving fast and conditions deteriorated quickly during the early afternoon. At 3:25PM the Normal Steaming Watch was set as the engineers tightened down the last bolts on our engines. The rain became torrential at times and the skies got very dark. The wind screamed around the ship and the waves were bigger then any of us had ever seen in Hampton Roads. By this time all of us had put on waterproof foul weather pants and hooded jackets. We had pulled the hood laces as tight as we could to keep the water from running down our neck.   We put on steel helmets over the hood and tightened the chinstrap. All of us had our lifejackets on. All of the sonarmen were in the sonar shack or the gun director area, which is between sonar the pilothouse. Our instructions were to standby and be prepared to help out on deck where needed.   The pilothouse door was open and we could hear what was going on the bridge. As the ships plunging and rolling increased, the Bridge Phone Talker called out " Engine room reports one boiler and one engine now on line. Prepared to answer bells at 3:30PM".   The captain said to the OD "At least if we get blown away from the pier, we'll be able to back out into the stream clear of the coal pier".   I thought to myself "That's nice but what the hell would we do out in Hampton Roads in a hurricane with only a fraction of our propulsion power"?

The wind continued to increase and by 3:42PM visibility was down to 1000 yards. I went around to the sheltered port side of the bridge.   The rain was torrential.   The ship was plunging and rolling. The two destroyers at the head of the pier weren't getting it as bad as we were and did not seem to be in trouble.   Ashore, the wooden light poles for the ballfields were swinging in a crazy top-heavy rhythm.   The wind had snapped all of the steel guy cables leaving them free to blow in the wind. I waited to see them snap and they never did -- they just swung in crazy circles.   Debris and junk, some of it quite large, was blowing all through the pier area and the parking lots.   As I was watching, something (probably a metal garbage can) blew into the electrical power transformer vault at the head of pier 23.   There was a huge blinding flash followed by an enormous explosion and the few remaining lights on shore went out.

I got back around to the director room as the storm intensified. The phone talker reported "The wires on lines two and four have parted and a manila line on two has parted".   The wind was stretching the manila lines and pushing us further and further from the pier. The ship was rolling quite heavily now and everyone was rolling with it. All of a sudden there was a pounding noise and we all lost our footing.   "What the hell was that" someone said as we tried to keep from falling. The phone talker said "Foc'sle reports we are coming up hard on the bow anchor chain".   Everyone had a hand hold on something now.   The ships motion stopped and it shuddered every time it came up hard on the chain.   The noise was getting louder.   We all knew the chain couldn't take that for very long.   The captain told the OD 'Tell the engine room to stand by to back down with all the power we've got.   If we get torn loose we'll back out in the stream and try to anchor".   As we braced for the next hit on the chain, there was a loud noise and only a small jolt and the ship resumed normal rolling.   The phone talker said "Foc'sle reports the anchor chain has parted ".   Somebody said "Oh shit, we're in it now".   Suddenly the XO stuck his head through the pilothouse door and yelled "All you ping jockeys (sonarmen) lay down to the foc'sle on the double".

As we went up the port side of the main deck to the foc'sle we could see that crew of the USS Hank (DD-702) at the head of the pier were pouring off their ship.   They were pulling the 1-inch diameter steel towing cable from Hank down the pier to us.   The cable was very heavy and there was a man about every three feet along its length.   They were leaning into the wind and trying to keep their footing as they fought their way down the pier.   At times it looked like they were holding on the cable for dear life rather then pulling it.

I fought my way across the foc'sle to the starboard side and then lost my footing.   The wind blew me straight across the deck to the port side.   For a minute I was afraid I was going over the side but the ratlines on the bottom of the lifeline stopped me.   As I crawled on hands and knees over to the starboard side I could see something moving over at the grain elevators through the downpour.   The merchant freighter had been blown away from its moorings at the grain pier, went sailing across the open water and finally stopped hard up against Navy CE Pier 20.   The freighter crew quickly got some lines over to the pier and moored themselves fast. Any port in a storm.

As the Hank's towing wire was being hauled down the pier, the bosun mates were trying to get a light line over to us to haul in the towing cable.   The wind kept blowing heaving lines away but finally they got one to us. This light line was used to haul over a manila line which would be used to haul in the cable.   When they got the cable rigged to the line all of us grabbed on to it and pulled.   It was slow work. The cable was very heavy and very stiff. The ship was rolling heavily, the wind was almost blowing us over and the rainwater ran across the deck in great deep streams. We kept falling but we kept pulling. Finally the cable end was on board. With a great deal of effort an eye was made in the cable, shackled in and the eye worked over a cleat.   The guys on the pier finally managed to get the cable secured around a pair of bollards.   With a great deal of additional work the cable was doubled up. The towing cable saved us.   If we hadn't gotten it we could well have blown away from the pier.   All of us leaning into the wind on the foc'sle breathed a little easier.   We really hadn't noticed while we had been working so hard, but water had blown into even the tiniest openings in our foul weather gear and we were soaked – and exhausted!

I hadn't noticed it before but as we rested I noticed that our main deck was now below the pier level.   The wind was blowing the water out of Hampton Roads!   Gradually as the storm moved on the winds became less and the rain abated. The eye of the storm passed inland of Norfolk about 3:30 PM.   At that point Hazel was moving north at an incredible 55 miles per hour. By five PM the worst was over.   The winds had pushed us 10 to 12 feet away from the pier.   The manila lines had been stretched so much that they were about half their original diameter.   No one had ever seen that before.   All the steel cables had broken. Both the fore and aft anchor chains had broken. Later we would find out that five-inch gun mount 55 had been pulled out of alignment by the chain jerking on it.   The wind had in fact blown the water out of Hampton Roads.   The main deck was about seven or eight feet below the pier. It was a wonder we weren't aground.   We were so far down that even if we hauled the lines in to get us closer to the pier, we couldn't possibly get the gangway over. No liberty tonight. The good news was that Mr. Baker, the executive officer, broke out the medicinal brandy. All of us who had been working out on deck got to "splice the main brace".   An old and cherished tradition of the Royal Navy comes to Wren.

Hazel was a Category 4 hurricane and the most powerful storm to hit the East Coast until Hurricane Hugo in 1989. The winds had unofficially been clocked at 130 miles per hour in Hampton about 10 miles from Wren. Gusts well in excess of 100 miles an hour had certainly hit Wren. The Norfolk barometer dropped to 28.99. The hull of the battleship Kentucky anchored out in Hampton Roads had been ripped from its moorings and it was aground in the James River. A commercial tug had sunk in the James River and four men were missing. Seventy-five percent of Tidewater Virginia was without electric power. As far inland as Richmond, Hazel had torn off the steeple of the Trinity Methodist Church. Along the East Coast 39 people had been killed. Hazel was a very violent storm but fortunately for Wren it moved quite fast. The peak of the storm at CE piers was at about 3:30 PM. By 6 PM Hazel was in Washington and by 8 PM it was approaching New York.

It certainly was a humbling and somewhat frightening experience. The amount of energy and power in a major hurricane such as this is awe-inspiring. Having been through riding out one at the pier, I certainly understand why the fleet goes to sea in the face of a hurricane. We were very close to a serious problem at the height of the storm. If the Hank hadn't passed us their towing wire we may well have blown away from the pier. If the storm had lasted longer our moorings may not have held. If we had ended up out in Hampton Roads with only one engine and one boiler we could have been in serious trouble. There was little danger that we would have foundered, however, we could easily have been driven aground or pounded against structures along the shore. It was a close thing.

By eight o'clock Saturday morning the sun was out, the sky was blue and the tide had returned. We had pulled ourselves into the pier and the XO called away the liberty party. I was off for home no worse for wear. Better late then never.

Grand Theft At Sea

In the 1950's all naval personnel were paid in cash. Payday was twice a month, at sea or in port. A day or so before payday, a list was posted containing the amount of money each person was eligible to draw. You didn't have to draw all of it. You could "let some ride" on the books. Not that any of us were receiving huge amounts of cash. In 1954 as a Second Class Petty Officer, my base pay was $147 a month plus $16 sea-pay for a grand total of $163 a month plus a small clothing allowance. Of course we also had a clean place to sleep and "three squares a day". And in the 1954 economy a cup of coffee was a nickel, a draught beer fifteen cents and a gallon of gas a quarter!

In order to get paid we filled out a Navy Pay Receipt with our name and Service Number; the amount requested and signed it. In the presence of the Paying Officer you affixed your Right Index fingerprint to the box in the lower left corner of the receipt. You then received your pay in greenbacks.[23] Now in order to be able to pay a couple of hundred crew members required that the Paymaster maintain a large amount of cash in his safe. A couple of times a month; a Disbursing Clerk and the Paymaster strapped on 45-caliber pistols and went ashore to draw cash. The money was carried in large, square, leather "litigator case". Attached to the case by a long line was a wooden buoy just in case the money accidentally got dropped over the side. The money was deposited in the safe in the Paymasters' stateroom and the safe locked. This story revolves around one time that the safe didn't get locked.

When you are in the military, there is always a little petty theft going on. Clothing and personal items and occasionally something more valuable disappear if not kept in a secure place. Given the cramped living conditions and the homogeneous makeup of a ships crew, that is not surprising. Given the security and accountability on a naval vessel, however, it is pretty hard to believe that anyone would try to rob the paymasters' safe. It is almost impossible to believe that someone would steal cash from the paymasters safe

---

[23] There were not many two-dollar bills in circulation in those days. The Navy always included two-dollar bills in sailor's pay. The theory was that the appearance of these bills in the hands of merchants was a constant reminder of the navy's contribution to the local; economy. .

in a destroyer 100 miles at sea. And would you believe that with all the possible hiding places on a destroyer, the thief would stash the loot in his own locker? What kind of a nut would do a thing like this – and think he could get away with it? McCarthy would!

Robert P. McCarthy was a Seaman Apprentice Storekeeper striker -- a supply clerk. He worked in the Wren's Supply Department disbursing stores and keeping inventories. But he always acted like he was on a different level than the rest of the crew. He came from a well-off family in upstate New York. His father was a medical doctor and surgeon. He seemed to feel that he was a higher class and didn't necessarily have to abide by all the rules. I didn't know him very well, but he once boasted to me that he had a liberty card for each duty section. That technically meant that he could have liberty every day if he wished. I don't think he used the illegal cards very often but I always thought that he had to show that he had the power to beat the system. There was an entry in the Wren Deck Log, however, that stated "McCarthy returned to ship by Shore Patrol for having two liberty cards in his possession". Maybe that was why he was only a Seaman Apprentice. So how did he go from illegal liberty cards to grand theft?

It was the fall of 1954 and Wren was scheduled to participate in the Lantflex exercises off the U.S. East Coast. These were full-scale exercises involving large numbers of all types of naval vessels operating under simulated wartime conditions. We had been preparing for the exercises by insuring that all of our equipment was in top condition and that we were completely familiar with all of the applicable procedures. As so often happens (and maybe it was done to simulate wartime conditions), we were ordered to sea a day earlier than anticipated and had left some of the crew on shore. I was particularly concerned because we left about a quarter of the sonarmen ashore. Shorthanded as we were it meant that it would be very difficult to cover Condition 3 (Wartime) watches. The only way we could do it was to stand what is called "watch and watch". That meant that each man stood a four-hour watch, had four hours off and then came back on watch again. Even sleeping between watches no one got enough rest. In addition, if General Quarters

(GQ) were called away, everyone had to go to their battle station even if it was your time to sleep.

On the morning of October 31, 1954, I had the 4 to 8 morning watch in sonar. There had been some excitement because the destroyers Lind and English had been in collision just before dawn. English had lost her bow and Lind was badly damaged and flooded up forward and was riding down by the bow. At 5:22 in the morning Wren was ordered to standby Lind and English in case they needed assistance. As Wren stood by them, I had been out on the bridge looking at the damaged ships through the long glass. As interesting as it was, however, as soon as I got off watch, I gulped down some breakfast and went below to get some sleep. Shortly thereafter General Quarters was called away for a gunnery exercise. I rolled over and went back to sleep because the off-duty sonarmen had permission to sleep in during this exercise. A short time later I was awakened by Mr. Arnason the Supply Officer. He asked me what I had been doing and why I wasn't at GQ. I told him we had permission to sleep in but he said that he didn't care and that I had to go up to sonar. He seemed to be quite upset and dashed off looking for other persons in the berthing spaces. I wondered what the hell was going on because Arnason had nothing to do with operations or sonarmen. It was a legal order, however, so I pulled on my dungarees and laid up to Sonar. When I got up there no one knew why Arnason had rousted me out. I found a corner of deck in the Main Battery Gun Director room, just outside sonar, and tried to nap.

A little later the word was passed that we were going to escort the collision-damaged Lind back into Norfolk. That seemed reasonable, and given that we were so shorthanded, we were glad to get out of the exercises. During the day as we proceeded toward Hampton Roads there was quite a bit of strange activity. Mr. Arnason, the new Paymaster, Ensign Sam Massey, and other officers were asking different people a lot of questions about their activities during that mornings' General Quarters. It was all very secret and no one would let on as to what the problem was. Of course rumors were rampant but none of them were even close to the truth. As we passed Cape Henry and

259

entered Thimble Shoals Channel a Harbor Tug (YTB) came alongside and a couple of civilians came aboard. We were told that they were engineers from Portsmouth Navy Yard that wanted to inspect the Linds' external damage. In fact they were R.L. Bonner and B.J. Dempsey, agents of the 5th Naval District Office of Naval Intelligence (ONI), investigating the theft of $2,000 from the paymasters safe! We proceeded to the Hampton Roads Explosive Anchorage and anchored. The word was passed that, because of damage to their bows, neither Lind nor English could anchor and so they would moor to either side of Wren. Before they came alongside, a group of Deck Force sailors were assigned to stand every six feet along both the port and starboard sides of Wren. They were ordered, in no uncertain terms, to insure that nothing was tossed or passed over to Lind or English while they were alongside Wren. Officers were on the 01 level scanning activity on both sides. Now the crew was really getting excited. "What the hell was going on?"

The Paymasters General Quarter's station was as cryptographic (code) officer in the closet-sized Crypto Compartment in a corner of the Radio Room. Evidently when GQ was sounded that morning he dashed out of his stateroom, down the passageway, through the wardroom and aft to the ladder up to the Radio Room on the 01 level. Shortly after he got into Crypto, he realized that he had left his safe open so he dashed below to close and lock it. The paymaster's safe was about 3 feet square with a thick, round door with a combination lock. It was located right next to his stateroom door, which was only closed over by a curtain. When he arrived back at his stateroom, the safe was indeed open and the cash drawer was pulled out. A quick check showed that $2,000 was missing. It was that discovery that triggered Arnasons frantic search through the berthing compartments. Although "Officers Country" was generally off-limits to enlisted personnel, some "white hats" used the passageway as the shortest path to their GQ stations. It appeared that someone on his way to battle stations saw the open safe and helped himself.

The NIS agents continued their investigation throughout the night. At about three in the morning they woke up the mailman to open the post office. He was terrified that he was being investigated for some breach of federal postal law. Although the agents couldn't search the mail, they did examine all the outgoing letters. They held them up to the light and flexed them to try and determine if they contained cash. At that point they were pretty sure that the cash was still on the ship and Wren was still anchored out in the harbor. Eventually the ONI agents decided that McCarthy was their primary suspect. McCarthy and I lived in the same compartment. His bunk was on the port side and mine was on the starboard side. The Masters-At–Arms (MA) cleared us all out of the berthing compartment and into the adjacent mess deck. Then they and the ONI agents brought in McCarthy and had him open his locker. They immediately found the cash and McCarthy fainted. McCarthy was taken into custody and charged with Theft of Public Funds. Shortly thereafter Wren got underway for CE piers.

By the time we were tied up it was late in the afternoon. Wren did not have a brig, and McCarthy was considered likely to flee, so it was decided to take McCarthy to the USS Everglades (AD-24), a Destroyer Tender that had a brig. McCarthy, in the custody of two MA's accompanied by an officer, was walking down the pier toward Everglades when he tried to make a break for it. He was quickly recaptured and delivered to the brig to await disciplinary action. He would have to go to Captains' Mast and would undoubtedly be awarded a court-martial. Two days later, Captain Johnson ordered McCarthy transferred to the Naval Retraining Facility (brig), Camp Allen, Norfolk. The next morning, the officer and MA's who were going to transport McCarthy from Grand Canyon to the Norfolk Brig were warned to keep him restrained and make sure he was safely delivered. They did and we all thought that we had heard the last of McCarthy. Not exactly!

Luter's Terrace was a restaurant and bar just across the street from the gate of the Convoy Escort (CE) Piers on Hampton Boulevard. Because of its proximity to the base it was a favorite hangout for tin can sailors including those from Wren. A couple of nights after

McCarthy had been delivered into the arms of the military justice system; he turned up at Luters. As usual there were a number of Wrens there. They couldn't believe their eyes and started asking questions. McCarthy said it was all a big mistake and that he had been let out of the brig. The Wrens, who all knew the paymaster safe story, were pretty skeptical of McCarthy's tale. They knew it was really bogus when McCarthy asked one of the Wrens to go through the gate and get his car for him out of the CE Piers parking lot. When no one would do it, and started asking McCarthy more questions he bolted out of Luters. When the Wrens got back to the ship, they notified the OD that they had seen McCarthy and thought that he had escaped and was on the run. At 9:08 that night Wren had received notification that McCarthy had escaped from Camp Allen at 2:45 that afternoon and had been declared a deserter.

Evidently while McCarthy was being processed into the brig, he was in the sick bay waiting to get a physical exam. He spotted a corpsman getting ready to go back to the main base. He convinced the corpsman that he was part of a detail that brought a prisoner to the brig and that they had gone back to the ship without him. He asked the corpsman to give him a lift back to the base so he could catch the Navy Bus back to his ship. The corpsman took him in his jeep right out through the brig gate. I would imagine that there were a number of red faces (and chewed asses) among the brig's U.S. Marine Security Detachment.

McCarthy next turned up in Charleston, South Carolina. Wren had been taken out of mothballs and put back in commission in Charleston Navy Yard and many of the Wrens had spent some time in and liked Charleston. Evidently McCarthy was among them. He was stopped by the Charleston Police for some minor traffic violation and couldn't produce the registration for the car. He contended that his wife had the registration and the police took him to the station while they got it all sorted out. The story that I heard was that while sitting in the station, he looked out the window and exclaimed "There's my wife – I'll get the registration" and dashed out the door.

He next turned up in Boca Raton, Florida. His family had often vacationed there and he checked into their usual hotel. He sent a telegram to his father, the Buffalo neurosurgeon, asking him to wire him some money. By this time his father had gotten a Deserters Notice from the Navy and knew that his son was a fugitive. He contacted the FBI and they picked up McCarthy in Boca Raton.

We never did hear what happened to McCarthy. Most of the crew figured that after robbing a paymasters safe and then several escapes, the military justice system probably had McCarthy hanging by his thumbs from some yardarm.

Back To The Future

Throughout most of history guns have been the primary surface attack weapons on naval vessels. For a time in the late 19th and through the mid-20th Century torpedoes[24] were the primary battery on destroyers, however, ships were still defined by their gun size. When I was in boot camp, we learned that destroyers carried 5-inch, light cruisers 6-inch, heavy cruisers 8-inch and battleships, 16-inch guns. The Navy was always looking for new weapons that could extend the range or destructive power of shipboard weapons. During World War-II rockets were used for shore bombardment from converted landing ships but they were not very accurate and were used mainly as a barrage weapon. When I was in the navy, a lot of work was going on in the new field of guided missiles to find a weapon with longer range and greater lethality than guns.

When Wren was in the Norfolk Naval Shipyard in early 1955, the heavy cruiser U.S.S. Macon (CA-132) was tied up with its stern directly behind us. We watched as its after 8-inch gun turret was being removed to make room for a Regulus Missile launcher. The SSM-N8 Regulus Missile was basically an air breathing, jet engine powered unmanned airplane with about a 500 mile range and capable of carrying a 3000 pound conventional or nuclear warhead. Unfortunately it was quite big and unwieldy and difficult to handle but it provided a nuclear bombardment capability for a few years until the Polaris submarines became operational.

Four heavy cruisers (Los Angeles, Helena, Toledo and Macon) and four converted fleet submarines (Barbero, Grayback, Growler and Tunny) were outfitted with Regulus. One new nuclear powered submarine the Halibut (SSGN-587) was built by Mare Island Naval Shipyard from the keel up to carry Regulus. The Regulus submarines patrolled the Western Pacific near the Kamchatka Peninsula with their missiles targeted on cities in the Soviet Union. As the Fleet Ballistic Missile (FBM) Polaris nuclear powered submarines

---

[24] Actually, torpedoes were the first guided missiles. They contained a compressed air-driven gyroscope that provided steering instructions to the torpedo. Mk-16 torpedoes had a pattern running gyro that increased their lethality (see "Hot, Straight and Normal"). Today the Pentagon spin-doctors would probably call them a "fire and forget missile".

came on station the Regulus subs were decommissioned. These subs provided an important interim strategic capability in maintaining equal nuclear deterrent to the Soviet Union. Historically Regulus was also important as the forerunner of today's Tomahawk Cruise Missile that has become such a formidable naval weapon.

The U.S.S. Tunny (SSG-287) is wreathed in smoke from a Regulus-I's Jet Assisted Takeoff (JATO) rockets as it is launched in the Pacific (U.S. Navy Photo)

The most promising Navy guided missile work in the 1950's, however, was focused on surface-to-air weapons. I was fortunate to have an opportunity to witness one of the early successful tests of these missiles. During the Lantflex exercises in the fall of 1954 there was a break in the exercises for a firepower demonstration for Washington bigwigs. They (and we) were to witness the firing of a brand new weapon, the surface-to-air missile (SAM). The Navy had contracted with the Johns Hopkins Applied Physics Laboratory (APL) under Project Bumblebee to develop a family of SAM's. The result had been the short range Tartar, the medium range Terrier and the long range Talos missiles. They were generally referred to as the "3T System". The Tartar was relatively small and homed on radar signals transmitted by the ship and reflected off the plane. Terrier was guided to the target by riding inside the cone of the ships fire control radar beam. Terrier was later modified to be either a "beam rider" or to use the Tartar homing guidance. The continuing evolution of the Terrier resulted in the present day Standard Missile. Talos was a large, long range, ramjet powered missile using controlled beam-rider and homing guidance requiring a separate beam transmitter in addition to the fire control radar. It was also the only one of the 3T's capable of carrying a nuclear weapon.

The Terrier was the first to approach operational status.   The old New Mexico class battleship U.S.S. Mississippi (BB-41) was converted to an Experimental Weapons Test Ship (EAG-128) to test the Terrier system.   The aft 14-inch gun turret was removed and replaced with a twin-rail Terrier Launcher.   Mississippi rendezvoused with the Lantflex task force off the East Coast for a firepower demonstration.

The USS Mississippi (EAG-128) firing a Terrier missile at a radio controlled F-80 fighter during 1954 LantFlex exercises. (US Navy Photo)

The battleship USS Iowa (BB-61) was about 1000 yards off Mississippi's quarter and was carrying congressmen and government officials including President Eisenhowers' Secretary of Defense "Engine Charlie" Wilson formerly of General Motors.   Wren was about 500 yards off Iowa's quarter.   The purpose of the demo was to prove that Terrier worked so that the Navy would get their Congressional Appropriation for Terrier production.   An old Lockheed F-80 Starfighter was flown under radio control toward the task force.   Fortunately it was a beautiful clear day because the F-80 was so high that I could barely see it.   It was flying in a meandering sinuous course as the Terrier was launched from the Mississippi in a great cloud of smoke.   The missile roared skyward until we could barely see its smoky trail.   All of a sudden there was an explosion and the F-80 came spinning down into the sea with one wing missing.   I was very impressed. Fire one missile -- scratch one airplane.   The first fleet ships converted for operational Terrier use were the heavy cruisers Boston (CA-69) and Canberra (CA-70) which became respectively CAG-1 and CAG-2.   As Talos became operational, three light cruisers, Galveston (CLG-3), Little Rock (CLG-4) and Oklahoma City (CLG-5) had their aft 6-inch gun turrets replaced with Talos Launchers.   The aft superstructure was enlarged to include an equipment room and a platform for new long-range, 3-dimensional, radar the AN/SPS-2.   The navy had been testing this radar at the Naval Research Lab facility at Randall Cliffs, Maryland for a number of years.   The cliffs were about the height of a ship mast above Chesapeake Bay and there were plenty of aircraft targets from the nearby Patuxent River NAS.   Unfortunately, the SPS-2 didn't live up to expectations and never went into production.   The prototype from Randall Cliffs was installed on the Little Rock and the Galveston and OK City got an old AN/SPS-8 Height Finding Radar.   The SPS-8, which I always thought was rather large, looked lonely sitting on the huge structure built for the SPS-2

The Navy had so many relatively new (about 10-year-old) ships[25] that the approach to providing platforms for the new missile systems was by conversion of existing hulls (such as Boston and Canberra, etc.).   Being a tin can sailor, I have to tell you about the one conversion that didn't work.   I got involved with this project when I first worked for RCA Service Company at the Systems Engineering Facility in Alexandria, Virginia.   It was probably about 1960.   RCA was under contract to the Navy's Bureau of Ordnance (BuOrd) to support the conversion of a Gearing class 2250-ton destroyer to carry a surface-to-air missile system.   The navy wanted rather badly to have some guided missile destroyers.   The USS Gyatt (DD-712) was to be converted to carry a Terrier Guided Missile System.   Gyatt's designation was changed first to DDG-712 and later to DDG-1.   I was impressed with how they used the existing Gun Fire Control System as the basis for the Missile Fire Control System.   The Mk-25 Radar on the Mk-37 Main Battery Director was modified so that the Terrier could ride in its conical scan.   The most ingenious thing was how the old mechanical analog Sperry Mk-1 Gun Fire Control Computer was coupled to the missile system.   A new analog Mk-107 Computer took

---

[25] Some of the ships available had never been completed when their construction was halted at the end of World War-II. This was the case for CLG-3, 4 and 5. These ships had never been to sea until they were completed and commissioned as guided missile cruisers.

azimuth and elevation and level and crosslevel outputs from the Mk-1 and converted them into the missile systems rectangular (X, Y and Z) coordinate system.

The USS Gyatt (DDG-712) with Terriers mounted aft. The missile magazine is the large structure just forward of the launcher. The launcher rails were placed in the horizontal position to load missiles from the magazine. (US Navy Photo)

The major problem was that the Terrier missile and its launcher were too big for the ship. The dual 5-inch Gun Mount 53 was removed from the fantail to make space for the Terrier Launcher. The launcher had been designed to load in a vertical position with the Terrier round coming straight up through the deck. Unfortunately the Gearing class hull wasn't deep enough to accommodate that configuration. The solution was to build the missile magazine just forward of the launcher on the main deck. The Terrier rounds were stored horizontally and slid aft onto the launcher rails when it was horizontal. The big problem was that the Gyatt's hull twisted and flexed (as did all destroyers of that class) in moderate to heavy seas. Because of this, the horizontal loading rails would sometimes become misalined with the launcher rails making it impossible to load missiles. While the Navy and RCA were trying to work out the problems, Gyatt was moved up to Annapolis, Maryland. Berthed less than an hour from Washington, it was more convenient to the BuOrd and RCA people trying to solve the problems. The ship did become operational as DDG-1 and made a deployment with the 6th Fleet in the Mediterranean. Ultimately, however, it was decided that a 2250 ton Gearing class destroyer was not a viable platform for a Terrier system. The Terrier system was removed from Gyatt and it went back to being DD-712.   There would be no more conversions of existing destroyers to missile firing ships.   Eventually the Charles F. Adams (DDG-2) Class destroyers were built from the keel up as Tartar missile ships and were quite successful.

Another area that the Navy was working very hard to improve in the 1950's was both prosubmarine and antisubmarine warfare.   Destroyer sonarmen were always interested in anything that might change the odds in antisubmarine warfare.   The main advantage that surface ships had over submarines when I was in the Navy was that the subs were very slow when submerged.   The World War-II fleet boats were generally in the 4 to 6 knot class.   In the 1950's, the navy was doing a Greater Underwater Propulsive Power (GUPPY) conversion to the fleet boats based on their study of the captured German Type XXI submarines.   All of the guns and other drag-producing protuberances were removed and the sail was streamlined.   An air-breathing snorkel was installed that allowed the sub to run diesels and charge batteries submerged.   More batteries were added and some subs were given new more efficient electric motors.   The conversion generally increased the sub speed, but they still couldn't run away from surface ships.   It was obvious that some more radical approach had to be taken with the new classes of submarines then under development.

In the spring of 1954 as Wren arrived in Key West, on our way to Guatemala, we saw this very strange looking submarine in the harbor.   All the sonarmen were gawking at it and wondering what the hell it was, how fast it could go and could we track it.   It was an experimental hull design sub, the USS Albacore (AGSS-569).   Up until that time all submarines, including the first two nuclear subs Nautilus and Seawolf, that were under construction, were designed as surface ships that could be submerged. Their hulls were designed to plunge through the waves to achieve maximum speed on the surface; Albacore was the first submarine designed for optimum performance submerged.

It was a relatively small ship (203 feet long) with conventional diesel/electric drive. It could only do 15 knots on the surface, but it could go 30 knots submerged! Albacore was in Key West so that the Surface Anti-Submarine Development Detachment (SURASDEVDET) could test its submerged performance and measure its sonar echo and noise signatures. It looked more like a blimp than a sub and had a V-tail like a Beechcraft Bonanza. The design was judged to be very effective and became the basis for all new submarine hull configurations. Coupling the Albacore hull with the long range and high speed provided by nuclear propulsion made a new and potent adversary for we surface antisubmarine folks. The shape of things to come – indeed! The prospect of nuclear powered Albacore type submarines forced a major change in antisubmarine warfare and started a frantic scramble for longer-range sonars and ASW weapons.

The USS Albacore (AGSS-569) at sea. What appeared so strange to us in 1954 became the common shape of U.S. Navy submarines. (US Navy Photo)

90 Days And A Wakeup

As 1954 wound down to a close, I started counting the days until my discharge. I had joined the Navy on March 5, 1951 and my four years of service were coming to an end. Wren was due to go into the Norfolk Naval Shipyard in Portsmouth, Virginia for a major overhaul in January 1955. I figured with the crew moved off the ship while it was in dry-dock, I might even get out a little early. I still wasn't sure what I was going to do as a civilian. I definitely wasn't going to continue my musical studies. I had finally figured out that with my talent I would probably starve. I was trying to figure out how to get into an electronics field and yet salvage as many credits as possible from my 2-1/2 years and an Associates in Arts Degree from Brevard College. I went up to Charlottesville and talked to the University of Virginia about studying Electrical Engineering. It was pretty discouraging. Very few credits would be transferable and I would just about have to start college over. At 25 years old, I wasn't prepared to do that. I didn't know whether to try to get a job in electronics with just the technical education I had gotten in the Navy or get more technical training under the GI Bill. I went home over Christmas and talked to my parents about it and still didn't know what to do. I returned to Wren after Christmas and continued to look at other educational possibilities including electronic technical institutes. Wrens' activities at that time were directed at getting ready to go into the yard – with one exception.

Remember back in the good old days when the military service academies had national class football teams? I remember it quite well because of the contrariness of the Wrens' Captain Johnson. In 1954, the U.S. Naval Academy had a very good football team that was invited to play in the Sugar Bowl in New Orleans against the University of Mississippi. The Navy, wanting to wring the maximum public relations benefit from the event, wanted to send some ships to New Orleans for the New Years holiday. That way there would be hundreds of sailors mingling with the football crowd on the streets of New Orleans. When the invitation message came from Commander, Destroyer Flotilla Four for Wren to go to New Orleans, the word spread through the ship like wildfire. I was willing to bet the crew knew about it before the paper message arrived on the captains' desk.   DesFlot-4 said that it was an invitation and the choice to go or not was the skipper's.   In a rare show of democratic process, Captain Johnson said that he would leave the decision up to the officers and crew.   When polled at morning quarters, the crew was hot to go.   There were a few grumpers of course who said, "it's a lot of steaming for a few days liberty in New Orleans".   They were booed down.   The Executive Officer polled the wardroom.   Out of 14 officers only two didn't want to go.   The XO was "go".   No contest – right? Wrong! The captain's message to DesFlot-4 was "Crew Yes, Officers split, Captain cold".   Wren spent the New Years weekend alongside CE Pier 21 in Norfolk.   So much for democracy!   Oh yeah……Navy 21, Ole Miss 0.

On New Years Eve my old buddy Gene Staunton and I both had the duty.   Neither of us had a watch that night but we couldn't leave the ship.   Just about everybody that had liberty were ashore celebrating.   All except Sonarman Seamen Roberson.   He was married, his wife was back in Cullman, Alabama and he didn't have any money.   Gene and I decided that inasmuch as we didn't have watches, we ought to have a little New Years Eve party in Sonar.   We gave Roberson some money told him that if he would go ashore and bring back a fifth of bourbon and some snacks we could have our own little celebration.   Not wanting to get into trouble for bringing booze aboard, he was a little reluctant but finally agreed.   When he got back, the bottle he pulled out from under his pea coat was Southern Comfort!   Gene and I called him a dumbass rebel who didn't know the difference between licorice flavored booze and real bourbon sipping whiskey.   We managed to drink it though.   Roberson didn't last too long and went to bed before midnight.   Gene had found a couple of candles somewhere.   He put one on top of the Sonar Console and one on the Attack Plotter and turned out the lights.   We sat there in the flickering light boozily reminiscing about our experiences in the Navy and wondering what the future held for each of us.   Gene, who was a devout Catholic, was in love with a divorced woman back in Minnesota.   Gene's family was upset about it and of course the church at that time made such a marriage very difficult.   Our discussion of a solution

272

for that was years ahead of the pope and most of the church. We mulled over my plans and what was the best way at 25 years old to prepare for a career in electronics. The candles were dripping wax down on the equipment but, by that time, neither of us thought it was a big problem. As midnight approached we went out on the wing of the bridge to see how Norfolk welcomed in the New Year 1955. At 12 o'clock, a few whistles were blown and a few firecrackers went off. Gene and I took the final swigs of Southern Comfort and then dropped the incriminating bottle over the side and went to bed. Sonar was Ed McDonald's cleaning station. He was a little upset the next morning when he found all the wax on the equipment but, being the good guy that he is, he made it all shipshape. However, later in the day, he did remind Gene and I of our transgression in case it had slipped our minds.

Early in January, we started to prepare Wren to go into the shipyard. We spent several backbreaking days off-loading all of the ammunition and other explosives. Because this is a dangerous business we were moored in the explosives anchorage in an isolated part of the harbor with a covered barge tied alongside to receive the ammunition. We had off-loaded all of the five-inch projectiles and they were lined up at the far end of the barge. Now we were transferring the five-inch powder cases in their long round cans with twist-lock tops. We had set up a human chain and were passing the cans one to another and the work was going pretty fast. I was near the end of the chain on the barge. A guy two down from me swung a can to hand it to the next man when the end of the can came off. The 2-1/2 foot brass powder case sailed out of the can and went bouncing end over end down the barge. Everyone just froze in place. If the powder case landed on the primer end, we and the barge full of ammunition would just be a big hole in the bottom of Hampton Roads. The case finally lay at rest on the deck and you could have heard a pin drop. I think if anyone had said "Bang" at that point we would have all crapped our pants. Finally someone went over, picked up the round and returned it to its can. We decided then that we would carry the powder cases to the barge one-by-one.

In mid-January Wren went over to the Craney Island Fuel Depot and they pumped out all of our black oil.   The next day, completely powerless, Wren was towed into the Navy Yard.   Life was actually pretty easy in the yard.   The "yard birds" did most of the work and we had plenty of sailors available to stand the few watches required.

The enlisted mens club in the Navy Yard was a marine facility called The Little Tun Tavern in honor of the birthplace of the United States Marine Corps in Philadelphia.   It was actually a pretty good EM Club.   The only complaint we had was that they didn't have pitchers of draft beer.   To make up for that, however, they had one-quart bottles of Schlitz.   Close enough!   One January Saturday afternoon a bunch of us Wrens and some Noas were sitting around, watching basketball on the telly and lowering the levels of Schlitz quarts.   There were about an equal number of marines in the club.   Around 6PM the Marine Officer of the Deck (OD) made his rounds through the club accompanied by the Sergeant-Of-The-Guard.   Two tables away from us were some Noas.   One of the guys, a short muscular redheaded Second Class Gunners Mate, was face down on the table.   The OD awakened him and told him to either straighten up or go back to the ship.   The gunny acknowledged the OD and had another drink of beer.   The OD left to check the kitchen.   When the OD came back, the Noa gunny was again face down.   The OD awakened him again and said "OK – you've had enough, go on back to the ship".   The gunny rose slowly to his feet, looked at the OD drew back his fist and hit him with a terrific punch.   It was like a scene out of a western movie.   The Marine OD went sliding across an adjacent table on his back scattering beer bottles in every direction.   All the sailors and marines in the place jumped to their feet – the sides were drawn – a sailor had hit a marine!   At that point the bartender jumped on top of the bar with a large baseball bat in his hand.   "Siddown – Siddown everybody sit down" he screamed over and over.   Not wanting to tangle with a rather large, angry marine with a baseball bat, we all sat down.   The Sergeant-Of-The-Guard had wrestled the Noa gunny to the deck.   The OD, a little groggy, picked himself up, straightened his uniform and started taking names of witnesses.   Then he and the sergeant took the redheaded gunners mate away.   I always wondered what happened to him.   I figured that an enlisted sailor punching out a marine officer – no less the Officer Of The Deck – would get the whole book thrown at him including the cover!   We ordered another round of Schlitzes.

As work on the ship progressed it was moved into drydock to repair, sandblast and paint the hull. It would not be habitable while in drydock so the crew had to move ashore. We packed all of our gear into our sea bags and moved into the Navy Yard Transient Barracks.   As I saluted the quarterdeck and the colors for the last time, I was little sad leaving Wren.   As anxious as I was to get out of the Navy, I couldn't forget the camaraderie and the spirit of the crew and all of the interesting, scary and fun times that we had shared.   It was a time of my life that I have always remembered.   It was four years of my life that changed my life.   When I left Brevard College and joined the Navy I was at a turning point.   I realized that music could not be my life work and yet I had no idea what I wanted to do.   The Navy gave me valuable training but it also allowed me to see the world and broaden my horizons.   At least now I knew what I wanted to do if not exactly sure how to get it done.

A couple of weeks later, I got orders to proceed to the Norfolk Naval Receiving Station to be discharged.   I went home to Arlington, VA and within a few weeks, at my fathers urging, started studies at the Capitol Radio Engineering Institute (CREI) in Washington, DC.   It was an excellent two-year program leading to an Associate Degree in Electronic Engineering Technology.   I basically got the electronics and math of an electrical engineering degree and it served me well through a long career in various technical, engineering and management jobs.

During the two-week summer break from CREI in 1955, I was vacationing at my family's summer place in Highland Lakes, New Jersey.   A friend of mine from the Navy invited me to a party in New York on a Saturday evening.   Phil Canfield was a Yeoman in the Base Office when I was stationed at Piney Point.   We used to talk politics over Gunthers beers in the Piney Point gedunk. He set me up with a blind date with Catherine Curley, whom Phil had known when they both worked at Metropolitan Life in

Manhattan. It was love at first sight. Catherine and I were married in 1956 while I was still going to school. It was undoubtedly the smartest thing I have ever done. While I was going to school, Catherine worked for MIT at the Operations Research Group in the office of the Chief of Naval Operations at the Pentagon. She was abstracting technical papers and reports. We used to talk about naval tactics and operations over dinner.

When I finished school, I got a job as a Technical Writer with RCA Service Company in Alexandria, Virginia. I worked on many Navy projects. On one of these jobs, a BuShips Maintenance Standards Project, I visited Wren in Norfolk in 1957 to check out test procedures. Ed McDonald and Jim O'Connell were still on board. It was nice to see them and reminisce a little but I was embarked on a new career and the navy was behind me.

In 1965, I transferred to an RCA group at NASA's Goddard Space Flight Center (GSFC) that was supporting the Scientific Satellite Programs. As Operations Support Manager, I was responsible for technical, engineering and orbital analysis groups providing support to NASA's 15 worldwide satellite tracking stations. Over nine years, I gained valuable experience in spacecraft operations.[26] In 1975, when RCA was starting up a commercial satellite communications business, I became their first Spacecraft Operations Manager. That was the best job I ever had! RCA was building technologically advanced communications spacecraft and I was getting to fly them. As cable television and digital communications grew, the business flourished and my responsibilities grew. GE bought RCA in 1986 and I retired from GE in 1992 as Manager, Network and Spacecraft Operations.

Being one of a very small group of people experienced in Communications Spacecraft Operations, I did consulting for seven years after I retired. I did work for GE, AT&T, Martin Marietta and Lockheed Martin besides some other smaller less well known

---

[26] I was working at GSFC during the Apollo Program and the first moon landings. Goddard provided the worldwide tracking facilities and communications for Apollo. Exciting times!

companies.   Catherine and I lived in Hong Kong during 1995 and 1996 when I was providing support for a new Series 7000 Communications Spacecraft for Asia Satellite Telecommunications (AsiaSat).   In 1998 we lived in Beijing while I was supporting launch and early orbit operations of an advanced A2100 Communications Spacecraft for ChinaStar Telecommunications Satellite Co., Ltd.

In 1998 I retired-retired and Catherine and I enjoyed living in a retirement community in central New Jersey.   When Catherine died on December 26, 2004, we had been married for 48 years had six children and at last count eight grandchildren.

In July 2008 I married Judy Prince and we continue to live in New Jersey.   Judy and I have done a lot of cruising and I still love going to sea.   It is certainly a helluva lot more comfortable going to sea in a 90,000 ton cruise ship than in a 2100 ton tin can but I would still not trade that experience for anything.

And I am still known to tell a sea story occasionally.

Made in the USA
Lexington, KY
25 August 2012